CBMR Monographs, No. 4

Jazz Standards on Record, 1900–1942:
A Core Repertory

by Richard Crawford
and Jeffrey Magee

Center for Black Music Research
Columbia College Chicago

Copyright © 1992 Columbia College Chicago

ISBN 0-929911-03-2

Library of Congress Cataloging-in-Publication Data

Crawford, Richard, 1935–
Jazz standards on record, 1900–1942 : a core repertory / by Richard Crawford and Jeffrey Magee
    p.   cm. — (CBMR monographs, ISSN 1042-8836 ; no. 4)
    Includes bibliographical references.
    ISBN 0-929911-03-2 : $10.00
    1. Jazz—Discography. 2. Jazz—Statistics. I. Magee, Jeffrey, 1961– . II. Title. III. Series.
ML156.4.J3C7 1992
016.78165'0266—dc29   91-47517

Center for Black Music Research
Columbia College Chicago
600 South Michigan Avenue
Chicago, IL 60605-1996
(312) 663-1600

Contents

Introduction

Musicology's traditional approach to canon making has been to identify a central group of works on the basis of their artistic excellence, their interrelationships, and, perhaps, their representation of the possibilities of a genre, a style, or an era as understood by the performers, scholars, and critics who define "the canon." The canon's authority reflects the belief that artistically informed choices, tested over time in traditions of performance, scholarship, and criticism will lead to the works that embody the essence of a musical repertory or genre.

The idea of a Core Repertory is that, however powerful the authority of canon makers, something can also be learned about a musical genre by discovering and studying the preferences of its own heyday. Thus, the Core Repertory notion complements the traditional approach to canon making. It seeks out contemporaneous opinion—the views of an earlier time—as a counterpoise to present-day opinion. Writings about the musical past inevitably reflect the perceptions of the writer's own day. But when today's perceptions are compared with those of people who actually produced, performed, and distributed a particular kind of music in its own time, differences as well as similarities appear. By providing an objectively derived roster with which it can be compared, a repertory can illuminate a canon.

The Core Repertory idea may be applied to any genre—any group of musical compositions of a given class or type in a particular time period: for example, renaissance motet, French *air de cour,* classical symphony, Broadway show song. **The Core Repertory of any genre is the group of pieces that may be shown empirically to have been favorites in a given period of time.** The list produced by the Core Repertory approach results from numerical score keeping: from counting within a field where numbers are meaningful. The Core Repertory approach depends upon bibliography. The better the bibliographic control, the more authoritative the Core Repertory.

Identifying a Core Repertory requires three steps, followed by a fourth in which the results are examined:

1. Index the music of an entire genre during a given period, or start with a reliable index someone else has made.

2. By counting, identify the pieces that appear most often.

3. Choose a suitable number of those pieces—say, the Top 40 or the Golden 100—and call them the Core Repertory.

4. Study the Core Repertory pieces, both individually and as a group, for the patterns and trends they reveal.

The Core Repertory idea first occurred to me more than two decades ago as I was working on a bibliography of the early American sacred tunebooks (Britton, Lowens, and Crawford, 1990). Eventually, as certain compositions showed up again and again in my sources, I identified a Core Repertory of early American psalmody even though no such entity was acknowledged or so described in its own day.

In the jazz tradition, the idea of a Core Repertory is explicit and fundamental. Every jazz style exists within a particular set of melodic, harmonic, and rhythmic conventions. And the expressive and inventive possibilities of each style are bound up with that style's standard repertory: the pieces its musicians most often play and sing. So-called "jazz standards"—the term is used by musicians and fans alike—are tunes accepted and shared so widely that jazz musicians who have never played together can be expected, on the spot and without notation, to be able to perform them.[1] Collectively, the standards of any jazz style seem to catch its spirit and character. Standards map out the territory within which jazz musicians explore the style's prevailing ethos. They also provide continuity and coherence. For players and listeners alike, the standards represent benchmarks against which craft and imagination can be measured. Moreover, each jazz standard carries its own tradition of performance, its own conventions of tempo, mood, and musical content, and its own array of customs, accumulated through continuous use over time. Musicians who sing or play a jazz standard are free to deal with its performance tradition in any way they choose. But because jazz is a strongly traditional art, steeped in a knowledge of what has already been done, jazz musicians who perform a standard can hardly manage to do so in ignorance of *its* traditions.

Everybody agrees, then, that there is such a thing as a repertory of jazz standards. But nobody has systematically defined one. Our attempt follows, first inspired by curiosity about George and Ira Gershwin's "I Got Rhythm" as a jazz standard.[2]

The selection process first used on psalmody has proved equal to the task at hand.

1. *Index the music of an entire genre during a given period, or start with an index someone else has made.*—The source here is the fifth edition of Brian Rust's (1982) discography, *Jazz Records 1897–1942.* In fact, the present study is mostly a selection and rearrangement of data from Rust's indispensable work.

Why count recordings rather than performances? Because recordings can be counted, and we do not know of any way that performances can. Why use Rust's book, which stops at 1942 and lists some recordings—especially recordings by English musicians—whose link to the heart of the jazz tradition may seem tenuous? We use it because Rust's is a standard scholarly work, corrected and updated through five editions and historical in its point of view.[3] In addition, Rust's cutoff date marks a break in the history of American commercial recording that lasted almost two years and that also coincides with the advent of bebop, a new jazz style that introduced a new repertory (DeVeaux 1988), and Rust's inclusion of all records made "in the name of jazz" offers a broad view of the music as it was understood during its early development.[4] And, not least of all, the fifth edition of Rust's work contains an index of tune titles that greatly simplifies counting.

2. *By counting, identify the pieces that appear most often.*— Thanks to Rust's title index, that part was straightforward once we decided what to count.[5]

3. *Choose a suitable number—say the Top 40 or the Golden 100—and call them the Core Repertory.*—Here, rather than first determining the size of the Core Repertory, we decided to list tunes recorded twenty times or more, which, upon reflection and some trial and error, seemed an apt number. Jazz evolved within the realm of popular music. Because the popular music business supported jazz in its early days, it seemed appropriate for the Core Repertory to contain not just pieces whose popularity persisted after 1942 and are known to many performers today, but also a certain number of hits: pieces recorded often by jazz artists for a short time but then dropped from the repertory.[6] A floor of twenty recordings admits standards without eliminating all hits, thus allowing preferences of the period to be recognized.[7] Table 1 arranges the ninety-seven Core Repertory tunes in alphabetical order by title. For those who know the jazz tradition, the list is sure to conjure up associations and powerful memories.

4. *Study the Core Repertory pieces, both individually and as a group, for the patterns or trends they reveal.*—This step, which involves collecting as many of the recordings as possible and listening to them, is still going on. Although our final result lies in the future, there are certain things that the list itself, and a familiarity with the tunes on it, reveal.

Which tunes were most often recorded during the period covered by our survey? Table 2 answers that question. "The St. Louis Blues" and "Tiger Rag" stand at the top of the popularity ratings, while "I Got Rhythm" comes in twelfth—a good showing for a tune composed as late as 1930. Noting that every piece in this Core Repertory of jazz standards was also published as sheet music, it's also worth observing which are the oldest pieces on the list ("Maple Leaf Rag" and "High Society") and which the newest ("Stompin' at the Savoy").[8] Table 3 gives a year-by-year chronicle of the repertory's publication in sheet-music form.

The variety of pieces listed in Table 3 raises the question of musical genres. Jazz performers have played and sung compositions of many different kinds: instrumental rags, songs from the Broadway musical theater, songs from the popular music business of Tin Pan Alley, the blues, and numbers originating in folk tradition or in the jazz tradition itself.[9] Table 4 interprets Table 3 by dividing its contents into time periods and classifying the genres of jazz standard favored in those years.

As Table 4 suggests, the Core Repertory list invites readers to consider the notion that the four periods marked off here represent different phases in the evolution of the jazz repertory. In the two decades that followed the publication of "Maple Leaf Rag" (1899), the dominant musical forms (as revealed by this study, at any rate) were rags, blues, and popular songs, many of them composed by black musicians.[10] Between 1920 and 1924, Tin Pan Alley made a stronger impact on the jazz tradition, with "blues" songs becoming especially fashionable. In the next five years (1925–29), Broadway gained somewhat on Tin Pan Alley in producing new jazz standards, while rags and new blues songs virtually dropped out of the picture. After 1930, the rags and blues being recorded were almost exclusively older ones. Jazz musicians took up some new Tin Pan Alley and show tunes (including "I Got Rhythm"); but almost half of the new favorites originated inside the folk or jazz traditions—the latter especially in the form of pieces by leaders of the popular swing bands.

Each Core Repertory tune's list of jazz recordings suggests its own story or poses its own questions. Some were hits in both popular and jazz traditions at the same time.[11] Some were accepted into the jazz tradition well after being introduced as popular songs.[12] The commercial maneuvering that surrounded the recording history of some is obvious.[13] Some kept their identity as songs, generally being performed with a vocalist, and others did not.[14] Some were favored by white musicians, others by black performers.[15] Some were recorded extensively overseas, while others were not.[16] And many offer mysteries that need further study. How, for example, in the second half of the 1920s, did "The St. Louis Blues," already a widely performed jazz standard, manage to log an unprecedentedly large number of recordings (forty-eight in the years 1926–29), and what happened in 1935 to bring twenty more new ones into being? And if "Dinah," interpolated into Florenz Ziegfeld's revue *Kid Boots* on December 31, 1923, was responsible for much of that show's success, then why was it not published until August 1925?[17]

It is the nature of any list to provide raw materials for more lists, for each item, in effect, is a moveable part. Indeed, like a child (or an adult) with blocks or an erector set, one could go on building list-like structures almost indefinitely from these ninety-seven titles. But, as a census of acceptability within a particular genre, a Core Repertory list carries the promise of uncovering patterns and trends that might not otherwise come to light. The songs with the word "blues" in the title are a case in point.[18]

First we should note that the standard idea of the blues, a vocal lament in twelve-bar form, covers only about half the pieces in our sample. Of the sixteen songs with "blues" in their title, six lack the twelve-bar progression entirely.[19] In fact, half of the blues songs, rather than dwelling upon pain, homesickness, and loss, celebrate in their lyrics good times or slow, sexy dancing.[20] Those matters aside, Table 5 complements Table 4 by tracing how this core of "blues" favorites was introduced into the recorded repertory of jazz.[21]

During the first period of the chronology, the four blues pieces together were recorded only a total of eleven times. Beginning in 1920, however, this African-American song genre gave rise to a popular music fad. So-called blues hits began to appear and to be recorded again and again, with peak figures reached in 1921 and 1923. By 1925 the fad had run its course, and the day of the new blues hit was over. Yet, during the third period (1925–29), the number of jazz recordings of this core of blues tunes declined very little. In the fourth period (1930–36), it topped even that of the second—and this in a time of economic hardship and radical retrenchment for the record industry.[22]

Beginning in the mid-1920s, the number of older blues tunes performed by jazz musicians increased. In Table 6 see, for example, how the recording of blues tunes in 1921 compares with that in 1927. In 1921, brand-new tunes dominated the recorded repertory of blues; in 1927, of the four most-recorded blues tunes, the only one not at least a decade old was "Wabash Blues," published in 1921. Table 7 shows that this trend was not peculiar to blues tunes.

The trend of relying on older tunes applies across the recorded Core Repertory as a whole. When we list the standards most frequently recorded in each year, using six recordings as a minimum, the pattern comes clearly into focus. We can see that, after running, in the early 1920s, almost parallel to popular music, the jazz repertory gradually diverged from it, as performers, while still recording a few of the latest hits, reached into the past for more and more of the music they played. In Table 7 the asterisks stand for newly published tunes. Note that they become less frequent as the list goes on. The earliest clear evidence of this trend in Table 7 can be seen in 1927, when older tunes like "Beale Street," "The Memphis Blues," and "Some of These Days" first came to be recorded favorites. And 1939 confirms that jazz performers were riding the wave of their future on an increasingly traditional repertory. "Star Dust," the newest tune on that year's list, was already a decade old.

Since this excursion began with Gershwin's "I Got Rhythm," let us return to it for a moment. The tables help to measure the song's place in the jazz tradition: Table 2 shows it near the top in sheer numbers of recordings; Table 3 reveals it as the most frequently recorded jazz standard from 1930 on; Table 4 pegs it as one of several show tunes from the early 1930s that jazz performers took up; Tables 5 and 6 omit it, since its title does not contain the word "blues"; and it reappears in Table 7 as a perennial that received six or more recordings in 1930, 1932 (when the first film version of *Girl Crazy* was made; see Mordden 1981, 55), and 1937. The considerable success of "I Got Rhythm" as a popular song occurred outside the jazz tradition and thus is a matter separate from the subject of this work. But Table 8, to which we invite additions, documents another stream of the song's history in the jazz tradition: "I Got Rhythm" as a basis for "contrafacts"—tunes with different melodies, under different titles, but based on its harmonic progressions. Through 1942, twelve such contrafacts have been found, beginning with Sidney Bechet's "Shag" in 1932, and including at least one from each of the most prominent black swing bands of the 1930s: that is, those led by Fletcher Henderson, Jimmy Lunceford, Chick Webb, Earl Hines, Erskine Hawkins, Count Basie, Johnny Hodges, and Duke Ellington. Doubtless there were many more. Other standards known to have fathered substantial families of contrafacts are "Tiger Rag," "Oh, Lady Be Good," and "Honeysuckle Rose." Perhaps the Core Repertory lists will help to uncover more such families in the future.[23]

The persistent reuse of certain chord progressions dramatizes that, in the jazz tradition, a piece of music as written by its composer is, in many cases, simply a starting point: a formal shape, a melody (or group of melodies), a harmonic structure, an expressive framework that performers are free to adopt, transform, or comment upon as the spirit moves them. Given that fact, it seems remarkable that certain jazz standards have proved such durable starting points. It is hard to imagine what jazz might be like without a standard repertory. The presence of a standard repertory, used in this way, must surely reveal something essential about jazz as an art that has not yet been fully described.

* * *

By focusing on repertory rather than style, the idea of a Core Repertory serves as a counterweight to the strong stylistic orientation of musicological study. Knowing which pieces have been preferred by musicians in any tradition, and studying the performance history of these pieces, provides a perspective that complements the usual emphasis on talented, creative, innovative composers and performers. In addition, as noted earlier, by defining a contemporaneous repertory rather than a canon, a Core Repertory also provides historical background for judgments of musical significance made in the here and now.

The idea of a Core Repertory may be applied to any musical genre that can be indexed reliably.[24] Perhaps authors working with other large repertories will find the notion useful and will turn it to their own ends.

Richard Crawford
The University of Michigan
June 1991

A Note on Procedure

The names of performing groups in the entries below appear as they do in Rust. Rounded parentheses and question marks are also reproduced from Rust, but information in square brackets is editorial. The authors have included some bracketed information to help users find Rust's citations. (For example, the Rhythm Makers Orchestra was Benny Goodman's Orchestra under another name, and Rust lists its recordings under Goodman. Similarly, the Dixie Stompers was an ensemble of players from Fletcher Henderson's band, recording for the Harmony label; their recordings can be found in Rust under Henderson.) Other bracketed information adds data deemed important by the authors (e.g., that Fats Waller plays on Anna Jones's 1923 recording of "I Wish I Could Shimmy Like My Sister Kate," or that Billie Holiday sings on the recording of "Dinah" that Count Basie's Orchestra made in 1937). In addition, if a tune is recorded in a medley with other songs, or if the recording of a tune fills more than one record side, that information is reported in brackets.

Many recordings were issued on more than one label. Our entries report only the first label listed by Rust.

From the beginning of this project, the authors have had questions about what to count. We made an early decision to count rejected recordings—that is, those withheld from commercial release—on the premise that a performer's or record company's or publisher's desire to record a piece, and even to rerecord it if the first attempt fails, testifies to the attractiveness of that piece, for whatever reason, and hence strengthens its claim to be considered a standard. We have been less sure how to deal with multiple recordings made the same day by the same performer. To take one example, on March 12, 1923, the New Orleans Rhythm Kings made three different recordings of "That's a Plenty" in Richmond, Indiana, and all were released on the Gennett label. Should these recordings be counted separately? Or, since all involve the same group, the same label, and the same tune, should they be counted as just one? What about the three recordings of "Rockin' Chair" made January 10, 1931, by Duke Ellington's Whoopee Makers, two released on the Banner label and one on Oriole? Should the difference in the label be registered in the count? Or what about cases where, of two recordings made the same day, one was released and the other rejected: for example, the Sizzlers' two performances of "Somebody Stole My Gal" for Edison Diamond Disc on November 27, 1928? Or what about Mills' Merry Makers' two recordings of "Farewell Blues" made on January 31, 1930, one of which was released immediately and the other, much later, on an LP recording? Should it matter in the count that the second performance circulated only after 1942? Finally, we found eight tunes for which two recordings were made the same day, one with a singer and the other without: for example, Red Nichols and His Five Pennies made two such recordings of "Dear Old Southland" for Brunswick on May 31, 1928.[25] Should this difference receive more or less consideration in the count than other kinds of duplication?

Ultimately, having already relied so heavily on Rust, we decided to follow him in the count as well. Therefore, our counts tally every recording of every Core Repertory tune listed in Rust—released or rejected, duplicated or not.

Table 1. Jazz Standards in the Core Repertory

After You've Gone
Ain't Misbehavin'
Ain't She Sweet?
Alexander's Ragtime Band
Arkansas Blues
Aunt Hagar's Children Blues
Avalon

Baby Won't You Please Come Home
Basin Street Blues
Beale Street
Blue Skies
Body and Soul
Bugle Call Rag
China Boy
Chinatown, My Chinatown
Clarinet Marmalade
Copenhagen
Coquette

The Darktown Strutters' Ball
Dear Old Southland
Diga Diga Doo
Dinah
Down Hearted Blues

Eccentric
Everybody Loves My Baby
Exactly Like You
Farewell Blues

Georgia on My Mind
A Good Man Is Hard to Find

Hallelujah!
High Society
Honeysuckle Rose
Hot Lips
How Come You Do Me Like You Do

I Ain't Got Nobody
I Can't Believe That You're in Love with Me
I Can't Give You Anything but Love
I Got Rhythm
I Never Knew
I Wish I Could Shimmy Like My Sister Kate
(I Would Do) Anything for You
If I Could Be with You
I'm Coming Virginia
Indiana
I've Found a New Baby

The Jazz Me Blues

King Porter Stomp

Limehouse Blues
Liza

Loveless Love (Careless Love)

Maple Leaf Rag
Margie
The Memphis Blues
Milenberg Joys
Mood Indigo
Moonglow
My Blue Heaven
My Melancholy Baby

Nagasaki
Nobody's Sweetheart

Oh, Lady Be Good
Ol' Man River
Old Fashioned Love
On the Sunny Side of the Street

Panama

Rockin' Chair
Rosetta
Royal Garden Blues
Runnin' Wild

St. James Infirmary
The St. Louis Blues
San
The Sheik of Araby
Shine
Solitude
Some of These Days
Somebody Stole My Gal
Someday Sweetheart
Star Dust
Stompin' at the Savoy
Sugar
Sugar Blues
Sugar Foot Stomp (Dipper Mouth Blues)
Sweet Georgia Brown
Sweet Sue

Tea for Two
That's a Plenty
There'll Be Some Changes Made
Three Little Words
Tiger Rag
Tin Roof Blues
12th Street Rag

Wabash Blues
The Wang Wang Blues
'Way down Yonder in New Orleans
The Weary Blues

You Rascal You

Titles are given as they appear in the published sheet music.

Table 2. Jazz Standards by Number of Recordings

Number of Recordings	Title of Tune	Date of Tune's Publication
165	The St. Louis Blues	1914
136	Tiger Rag	1917
76	Dinah	1925
66	I Ain't Got Nobody	1916
60	After You've Gone	1918
59	Farewell Blues	1923
59	Some of These Days	1910
57	Bugle Call Rag	1923
55	Star Dust	1929
53	Sweet Sue	1928
52	Honeysuckle Rose	1929
52	I Got Rhythm	1930
50	Nobody's Sweetheart	1924
48	I Can't Give You Anything but Love	1928
47	The Darktown Strutters' Ball	1917
47	I've Found a New Baby	1926
46	Milenberg Joys	1925
45	Ain't Misbehavin'	1929
45	Beale Street	1917
45	China Boy	1922
43	Limehouse Blues	1922
43	Someday Sweetheart	1919
42	The Sheik of Araby	1921
41	I Wish I Could Shimmy Like My Sister Kate	1919
41	Sweet Georgia Brown	1925
39	Oh, Lady Be Good	1924
39	That's a Plenty	1914
38	Clarinet Marmalade	1918
36	Everybody Loves My Baby	1924
36	Loveless Love (Careless Love)	1921
36	My Melancholy Baby	1912
36	San	1920
35	The Memphis Blues	1912
35	Rockin' Chair	1930
34	Basin Street Blues	1933
34	Royal Garden Blues	1919
34	Sugar Foot Stomp (Dipper Mouth Blues)	1926
34	Tea for Two	1924
34	12th Street Rag	1914
34	Wabash Blues	1921
33	King Porter Stomp	1924
32	Copenhagen	1924
32	The Jazz Me Blues	1921
31	High Society	1901
31	I Never Knew	1925
31	Maple Leaf Rag	1899
31	Nagasaki	1928
31	Somebody Stole My Gal	1922
31	'Way down Yonder in New Orleans	1922
29	Baby Won't You Please Come Home	1919
29	St. James Infirmary	1930
29	Shine	1924
29	Tin Roof Blues	1923
28	Body and Soul	1930
28	Margie	1920

Number of Recordings	Title of Tune	Date of Tune's Publication
28	Solitude	1934
27	How Come You Do Me Like You Do	1924
27	Mood Indigo	1931
27	Rosetta	1935
27	Runnin' Wild	1922
27	The Weary Blues	1915
27	You Rascal You	1931
26	A Good Man Is Hard to Find	1918
26	Three Little Words	1930
25	Avalon	1920
25	Chinatown, My Chinatown	1910
25	Diga Diga Doo	1928
25	Down Hearted Blues	1923
25	Exactly Like You	1930
25	Georgia on My Mind	1930
25	Hot Lips	1922
25	I Would Do Anything for You	1932
25	I'm Coming Virginia	1927
25	Sugar	1926
25	Sugar Blues	1919
25	There'll Be Some Changes Made	1923
23	Alexander's Ragtime Band	1911
23	Aunt Hagar's Children Blues	1920
23	Eccentric	1912
23	I Can't Believe That You're in Love with Me	1926
23	If I Could Be with You	1926
23	Indiana	1917
23	Moonglow	1934
23	On the Sunny Side of the Street	1930
23	The Wang Wang Blues	1921
22	Arkansas Blues	1921
22	Blue Skies	1927
22	Dear Old Southland	1921
22	Hallelujah!	1927
22	Panama	1912
21	Coquette	1928
21	Liza	1929
21	My Blue Heaven	1927
21	Ol' Man River	1927
21	Old Fashioned Love	1923
21	Stompin' at the Savoy	1936
20	Ain't She Sweet?	1927

Table 3. Jazz Standards in Order of Publication

Year	Month/Day	Title of Tune	Composer/Lyricist	Number of Recordings
1899	09/18	Maple Leaf Rag	Joplin	31
1901	10/18	High Society	Steel	31
1910	07/06	Chinatown, My Chinatown	Schwartz & Jerome	25
1910	07/06	Some of These Days	Brooks	59
1911	03/18	Alexander's Ragtime Band	Berlin	23
1911	03/27	Panama	Tyers	22
1912	01/22	Eccentric*	Robinson	23
1912	09/28	The Memphis Blues	Handy & Norton	35
1912	10/31	My Melancholy Baby	Burnett & Norton	36
1914	01/30	12th Street Rag	Bowman	34
1914	02/25	That's a Plenty	Pollack	39
1914	09/11	The St. Louis Blues	Handy	165
1915	10/25	The Weary Blues	Matthews	27
1916	02/07	I Ain't Got Nobody	S. Williams, Graham, & Peyton	66
1917	01/18	The Darktown Strutters' Ball	Brooks	47
1917	02/17	Indiana	Hanley & MacDonald	23
1917	03/23	Beale Street	Handy	45
1917	09/08	Tiger Rag	Original Dixieland Jazz Band	136
1918	05/25	After You've Gone	Layton & Creamer	60
1918	07/16	A Good Man Is Hard to Find	Eddie Green	26
1918	09/04	Clarinet Marmalade	Shields & Ragas	38
1919	07/16	Royal Garden Blues	C. Williams & S. Williams	34
1919	11/15	Baby Won't You Please Come Home	Warfield & C. Williams	29
1919	12/05	I Wish I Could Shimmy Like My Sister Kate	Piron	41
1919	12/09	Sugar Blues	C. Williams & Fletcher	25
1919	12/15	Someday Sweetheart	J. Spikes & B. Spikes	43
1920	04/10	San	McPhail & Michels	36
1920	09/04	Avalon	V. Rose, Jolson, & B. Rose	25
1920	11/02	Aunt Hagar's Children Blues	Handy & Brymn	23
1920	11/05	Margie	Conrad, Robinson, & David	28
1921	01/01	Loveless Love (Careless Love)	Handy	36
1921	01/03	The Wang Wang Blues	Mueller, Johnson, & Busse	23
1921	03/05	The Jazz Me Blues	Delaney	32
1921	09/17	Arkansas Blues	S. Williams & Lada	22
1921	09/26	Wabash Blues	Meinken & Ringle	34
1921	11/17	The Sheik of Araby	Snyder, Smith, & Wheeler	42
1921	12/06	Dear Old Southland	Creamer & Layton	22
1922	03/23	Somebody Stole My Gal	Wood	31
1922	05/10	Limehouse Blues	Braham & Furber	43
1922	05/18	Hot Lips	Busse, Lange, & Davis	25
1922	07/06	'Way down Yonder in New Orleans	Layton & Creamer	31
1922	11/17	China Boy	Winfree, Boutelje	45
1922	12/11	Runnin' Wild	Biggs, Grey, & Wood	27
1923	02/24	Down Hearted Blues	Austin & Hunter	25
1923	05/03	Farewell Blues	Schoebel, Mares, & Roppollo	59
1923	06/13	Bugle Call Rag	Pettis, Schoebel, & Meyers	57
1923	08/15	Tin Roof Blues	New Orleans Rhythm Kings	29
1923	09/05	Old Fashioned Love	Johnson & Mack	21
1923	09/15	There'll Be Some Changes Made	Overstreet & Higgins	25
1924	02/04	Nobody's Sweetheart	Schoebel, Erdman, Kahn, & Meyers	50
1924	03/31	How Come You Do Me Like You Do	Austin & Bergere	27
1924	05/07	Shine	Dabney, Mack, & Brown	29

*Copyright lists "That Eccentric Rag"; published as "Eccentric," in revised form, in 1923.

Year	Month/Day	Title of Tune	Composer/Lyricist	Number of Recordings
1924	06/10	Tea for Two	Youmans & Caesar	34
1924	09/18	Everybody Loves My Baby	Palmer & S. Williams	36
1924	10/01	Copenhagen	Davis & Melrose	32
1924	12/01	Oh, Lady Be Good	G. Gershwin & I. Gershwin	39
1924	12/06	King Porter Stomp	Morton	33
1925	03/18	Sweet Georgia Brown	Bernie, Pinkard, & Casey	41
1925	06/20	Milenberg Joys	Roppollo, Morton, & Mares	46
1925	08/12	Dinah	Akst, Lewis, & Young	76
1925	10/05	I Never Knew	Fio Rito & Kahn	31
1926	02/04	I've Found a New Baby	Palmer & S. Williams	47
1926	04/30	Sugar	Pinkard, Alexander, & Mitchell	25
1926	08/15	Sugar Foot Stomp (Dipper Mouth Blues)	Oliver & Armstrong	34
1926	12/15	If I Could Be with You	Johnson & Creamer	23
1926	12/31	I Can't Believe That You're in Love with Me	McHugh & Gaskill	23
1927	01/03	I'm Coming Virginia	Heywood & Cook	25
1927	01/14	Blue Skies	Berlin	22
1927	01/17	Ain't She Sweet?	Ager & Yellen	20
1927	04/22	Hallelujah!	Youmans, Robin, & Grey	22
1927	10/10	My Blue Heaven*	Donaldson & Whiting	21
1927	11/30	Ol' Man River	Kern & Hammerstein	21
1928	02/10	Coquette	C. Lombardo, Green, & Kahn	21
1928	03/06	I Can't Give You Anything but Love	McHugh & Fields	48
1928	04/10	Sweet Sue	Young & Harris	53
1928	06/09	Diga Diga Doo	McHugh & Fields	25
1928	07/13	Nagasaki	Warren & Dixon	31
1929	01/29	Star Dust	Carmichael & Parish	55
1929	07/08	Ain't Misbehavin'	Waller & Razaf	45
1929	07/10	Liza	G. Gershwin & I. Gershwin	21
1929	11/20	Honeysuckle Rose	Waller & Razaf	52
1930	02/03	Exactly Like You	McHugh & Fields	25
1930	02/03	On the Sunny Side of the Street	McHugh & Fields	23
1930	02/11	St. James Infirmary	Primrose	29
1930	02/18	Body and Soul	Green, Heyman, Sour, & Eyton	28
1930	07/14	Rockin' Chair	Carmichael	35
1930	10/14	I Got Rhythm	G. Gershwin & I. Gershwin	52
1930	10/20	Three Little Words	Ruby & Kalmer	26
1930	12/22	Georgia on My Mind	Carmichael & Gorrell	25
1931	02/21	Mood Indigo	Ellington, Bigard, & Mills	27
1931	10/10	You Rascal You	Theard	27
1932	01/25	I Would Do Anything for You	Hopkins, Hill, & B. Williams	25
1933	02/18	Basin Street Blues	S. Williams	34
1934	01/16	Moonglow	Hudson, DeLange, & Mills	23
1934	09/21	Solitude	Ellington, DeLange, & Mills	28
1935	04/01	Rosetta	Hines & Woode	27
1936	02/26	Stompin' at the Savoy	Sampson, Goodman, Webb, & Razaf	21

*This copyright, granted on October 10, 1927, is for an orchestration. I found no copyright for the song form.

Table 4. Jazz Standards by Genre

Number of Tunes/ Black Authorship	Rags	Show	TPA & Pop	Blues	Other
Period 1, 1899–1919: 26/17	8[1]	1[2]	11[3]	6[4]	0
Period 2, 1920–1924: 31/12	2[5]	3[6]	14[7]	9[8]	3[9]
Period 3, 1925–1929: 24/9	1[10]	7[11]	14[12]	0	2[13]
Period 4, 1930–1936: 16/7	0	3[14]	5[15]	1[16]	7[17]

1. Maple Leaf Rag, High Society, Panama, Eccentric (That Eccentric Rag), 12th Street Rag, That's a Plenty, Tiger Rag, Clarinet Marmalade.

2. Chinatown, My Chinatown (*Up and Down Broadway,* 1910).

3. Some of These Days, Alexander's Ragtime Band, My Melancholy Baby, I Ain't Got Nobody, The Darktown Strutters' Ball, Indiana, After You've Gone, A Good Man Is Hard to Find, Baby Won't You Please Come Home, I Wish I Could Shimmy Like My Sister Kate, Someday Sweetheart.

4. The Memphis Blues, The St. Louis Blues, The Weary Blues, Beale Street, Royal Garden Blues, Sugar Blues.

5. Bugle Call Rag, King Porter Stomp.

6. Old Fashioned Love (*Runnin' Wild,* 1923), Tea for Two (*No No Nanette,* 1924), Oh, Lady Be Good (*Lady Be Good,* 1924).

7. San, Avalon, Margie, The Sheik of Araby, Somebody Stole My Gal, Hot Lips, 'Way down Yonder in New Orleans, China Boy, There'll Be Some Changes Made, Nobody's Sweetheart, How Come You Do Me Like You Do, Shine, Everybody Loves My Baby, Runnin' Wild.

8. Aunt Hagar's Children Blues, The Wang Wang Blues, The Jazz Me Blues, Arkansas Blues, Wabash Blues, Limehouse Blues, Down Hearted Blues, Farewell Blues, Tin Roof Blues.

9. Loveless Love (Careless Love), Dear Old Southland, Copenhagen.

10. Milenberg Joys.

11. Blue Skies (*Betsy,* 1926), Hallelujah! (*Hit the Deck,* 1927), Ol' Man River (*Show Boat,* 1927), I Can't Give You Anything but Love (*Blackbirds of 1928*), Diga Diga Doo (*Blackbirds of 1928*), Ain't Misbehavin' (*Hot Chocolates,* 1929), Liza (*Show Girl,* 1929).

12. Sweet Georgia Brown, Dinah, I Never Knew, I've Found a New Baby, Sugar, If I Could Be with You, I Can't Believe That You're in Love with Me, I'm Coming Virginia, Ain't She Sweet?, My Blue Heaven, Coquette, Sweet Sue, Nagasaki, Star Dust.

13. Sugar Foot Stomp (Dipper Mouth Blues), Honeysuckle Rose (featured in *Load of Coal,* 1929, review at Connie's Inn, Harlem).

14. Exactly Like You (*The International Revue,* 1930), On the Sunny Side of the Street (*The International Revue,* 1930), I Got Rhythm (*Girl Crazy,* 1930).

15. Body and Soul, Rockin' Chair, Three Little Words, Georgia on My Mind, Moonglow.

16. Basin Street Blues.

17. St. James Infirmary, Mood Indigo, You Rascal You, I Would Do Anything for You, Solitude, Rosetta, Stompin' at the Savoy.

Table 5. Jazz Standards with "Blues" in the Title

Year	Recordings	Number of Pieces	Newly Published Titles
1914	2	1	The Memphis Blues
1915	1	1	The St. Louis Blues
1916	0	0	
1917	2	2	Beale Street
1918	0	0	
1919	6	4	The Weary Blues
1920	9	6	The Jazz Me Blues, Royal Garden Blues, The Wang Wang Blues
1921	45	10	Arkansas Blues, Aunt Hagar's Children Blues, Wabash Blues
1922	11	7	Down Hearted Blues, Farewell Blues, Sugar Blues
1923	70	11	Tin Roof Blues
1924	19	8	Limehouse Blues
1925	12	6	
1926	24	7	
1927	55	13	
1928	38	10	Basin Street Blues
1929	31	10	
1930	18	11	
1931	23	10	
1932	11	4	
1933	11	6	
1934	24	11	
1935	57	12	
1936	35	11	
1937	27	11	
1938	29	13	
1939	29	12	
1940	28	11	
1941	19	9	
1942	15	9	

Note: Total recordings by period: Period 1, 11; Period 2, 158; Period 3, 160; Period 4, 179; Period 5, 147.

Table 6. "Blues" Standards with Six or More Recordings per Year

Year	Tune	Number of Recordings
1921	Arkansas Blues	8*
	Royal Garden Blues	7
	The Wang Wang Blues	11*
1923	Aunt Hagar's Children Blues	7
	Down Hearted Blues	16*
	Farewell Blues	16*
	Sugar Blues	11
	Tin Roof Blues	9*
1926	The St. Louis Blues	14
1927	Beale Street	10
	The Memphis Blues	6
	The St. Louis Blues	10
	Wabash Blues	6
1928	The St. Louis Blues	14
1929	The St. Louis Blues	10
1933	The St. Louis Blues	6
1934	The St. Louis Blues	6
1935	Farewell Blues	8
	Limehouse Blues	6
	The St. Louis Blues	20
1936	Basin Street Blues	7
	The St. Louis Blues	6
1937	The St. Louis Blues	7
1938	The St. Louis Blues	7
1940	The St. Louis Blues	11
1942	The St. Louis Blues	6

*Recordings made in the year of the tune's publication.

Table 7. Jazz Standards with Six or More Recordings per Year

Year	Title	Year of Publication	Records
1921	Arkansas Blues	1921*	8
	Royal Garden Blues	1919	7
	The Wang Wang Blues	1921*	11
1922	Hot Lips	1922*	13
	I Wish I Could Shimmy Like My Sister Kate	1919	14
	Runnin' Wild	1922*	7
1923	Aunt Hagar's Children Blues	1921	7
	Down Hearted Blues	1923*	16
	Farewell Blues	1923*	16
	Sugar Blues	1919	11
	Tin Roof Blues	1923*	9
1924	Copenhagen	1924*	15
	Everybody Loves My Baby	1924*	9
	How Come You Do Me Like You Do	1924*	12
	San	1920	9
1925	Everybody Loves My Baby	1924	10
	I Ain't Got Nobody	1916	6
	Milenberg Joys	1925*	12
	Sweet Georgia Brown	1925*	12
1926	Dinah	1925	8
	Everybody Loves My Baby	1924	10
	I've Found a New Baby	1926*	8
	The St. Louis Blues	1914	14
	Tiger Rag	1917	8
1927	After You've Gone	1918	8
	Ain't She Sweet?	1927*	13
	Beale Street	1917	10
	Clarinet Marmalade	1918	7
	A Good Man Is Hard to Find	1918	6
	I Ain't Got Nobody	1916	11
	I'm Coming Virginia	1927*	7
	The Memphis Blues	1912	6
	The St. Louis Blues	1914	10
	Some of These Days	1910	7
	Someday Sweetheart	1919	10
	Sugar	1926	9
	Tiger Rag	1917	10
	Wabash Blues	1921	6
1928	Diga Diga Doo	1928*	6
	I Ain't Got Nobody	1916	10
	I Can't Give You Anything but Love	1928*	18
	I Wish I Could Shimmy Like My Sister Kate	1919	7
	Nobody's Sweetheart	1924	6
	Ol' Man River	1927	8
	The St. Louis Blues	1914	14
	Somebody Stole My Gal	1922	7
	Sweet Sue	1928*	11
	Tiger Rag	1917	7
1929	After You've Gone	1918	8
	Ain't Misbehavin'	1929*	13
	The St. Louis Blues	1914	10
	Some of These Days	1910	6

* Recordings made in the year of the tune's publication.

Year	Title	Year of Publication	Records
1929	That's a Plenty	1914	9
	Tiger Rag	1917	10
1930	After You've Gone	1918	6
	Body and Soul	1930*	8
	Exactly Like You	1930*	6
	I Got Rhythm	1930*	7
	If I Could Be with You	1926	10
	Mood Indigo	1931**	6
	St. James Infirmary	1930*	16
	Three Little Words	1930*	10
	Tiger Rag	1917	8
1931	Georgia on My Mind	1930	7
	Loveless Love (Careless Love)	1926	9
	Rockin' Chair	1930	15
	Star Dust	1929	7
	Sugar Foot Stomp	1926	6
	Tiger Rag	1917	6
	You Rascal You	1931*	10
1932	Dinah	1925	9
	I Got Rhythm	1930	6
	I Would Do Anything for You	1932*	6
	Tiger Rag	1917	6
	You Rascal You	1931	6
1933	High Society	1901	6
	I Got Rhythm	1930	6
	Nobody's Sweetheart	1924	6
	The St. Louis Blues	1914	6
	Tiger Rag	1917	6
1934	Dinah	1925	8
	Moonglow	1934*	8
	The St. Louis Blues	1914	6
	Solitude	1934*	7
	Tiger Rag	1917	9
1935	After You've Gone	1918	6
	Avalon	1920	6
	Bugle Call Rag	1923	8
	Chinatown, My Chinatown	1910	7
	Dinah	1925	8
	Farewell Blues	1923	8
	I Never Knew	1925	7
	Limehouse Blues	1922	6
	Moonglow	1934	6
	Nagasaki	1928	9
	Rosetta	1935*	9
	The St. Louis Blues	1917	20
	Solitude	1934	10
	Some of These Days	1910	6
	Sweet Sue	1928	6
	Tiger Rag	1917	10
1936	After You've Gone	1918	6
	Basin Street Blues	1933	7
	Bugle Call Rag	1923	7
	Dinah	1925	7
	I Ain't Got Nobody	1915	6
	I Can't Give You Anything	1928	7

* Recordings made in the year of the tune's publication.
** Recordings made before the year of the tune's publication.

Year	Title	Year of Publication	Records
1936	Nobody's Sweetheart	1924	6
	Oh, Lady Be Good	1924	6
	The St. Louis Blues	1914	6
	Some of These Days	1910	7
	Stompin' at the Savoy	1936*	13
	Sweet Sue	1928	6
	Tiger Rag	1917	16
1937	Ain't Misbehavin'	1929	9
	Blue Skies	1927	7
	China Boy	1922	6
	Dinah	1925	6
	Exactly Like You	1930	8
	Honeysuckle Rose	1929	14
	I Ain't Got Nobody	1916	8
	I Got Rhythm	1930	10
	I've Found a New Baby	1926	7
	Oh, Lady Be Good	1924	8
	The St. Louis Blues	1914	7
	The Sheik of Araby	1921	7
	Star Dust	1929	7
	Tea for Two	1924	6
1938	Honeysuckle Rose	1929	6
	My Melancholy Baby	1912	6
	The St. Louis Blues	1914	7
	The Sheik of Araby	1921	6
	Star Dust	1929	6
	Sweet Sue	1928	6
	Tiger Rag	1917	8
1939	I've Found a New Baby	1926	6
	Someday Sweetheart	1919	6
	Star Dust	1929	6
	Tea for Two	1924	9
1940	My Melancholy Baby	1912	7
	The St. Louis Blues	1914	11
1941	Georgia on My Mind	1930	6
1942	The St. Louis Blues	1914	6

* Recordings made in the year of the tune's publication.

Table 8. "I Got Rhythm" and Its Contrafacts to 1942

Performers	Location	Date	Recording Company
Fred Rich & Orch (v)	New York	October 20, 1930	Columbia
Red Nichols & Five Pennies (v)	New York	October 23, 1930	Brunswick
Luis Russell & Orch (v)	New York	October 24, 1930	Melotone
Fred Rich & Orch (v)	New York	October 30, 1929	Harmony and OKeh
Ethel Waters (v)	New York	November 18, 1930	Columbia
Cab Calloway & Orch (v)	New York	December 17, 1930	ARC (rejected)
Adelaide Hall with piano (v)	London	October 1931	Oriole
Louis Armstrong & Orch (v)	Chicago	November 6, 1931	OKeh
Billy Banks (v; medley)	New York	April 13, 1932	Victor (test)
Bobby Howes (v)	London	May 10, 1932	Columbia
Roy Fox & Band (v)	London	May 19, 1932	Decca
Blue Mountaineers (v)	London	June 18, 1932	Broadcast
Don Redman & Orch	New York	June 30, 1932	Brunswick
Ray Starita & Ambassadors (v)	London	August 12, 1932	Sterno
New Orleans Feetwarmers (v) ("Shag")	New York	September 15, 1932	Victor
Joel Shaw & Orch (v) ("Yeah Man")	New York	October 1932	Crown
Arthur Briggs & Boys (v)	Paris	circa June 1933	Brunswick
The King's Jesters ("Yeah Man")	Chicago	July 29, 1933	Bluebird
Fletcher Henderson & Orch ("Yeah Man")	New York	August 18, 1933	Vocalion and Brunswick
Spirits of Rhythm (v)	New York	September 29, 1933	ARC (rejected)
Five Spirits of Rhythm (v)	New York	October 24, 1933	Brunswick
Freddy Johnson & Harlemites	Paris	circa October 1933	Brunswick
Freddy Johnson & Harlemites	Paris	December 7, 1933	Brunswick
Casa Loma Orch	New York	December 30, 1933	Brunswick
Jimmy Lunceford & Orch ("Stomp It Off")	New York	October 29, 1934	Decca
Chick Webb's Savoy Orch ("Don't Be That Way")	New York	November 19, 1934	Decca
Joe Venuti & Orch	New York	December 26, 1934	London (LP)
Stephane Grappelli & Hot Four	Paris	October 1935	Decca
Nat Gonella & the Georgians (v) ("Yeah Man")	London	November 20, 1935	Parlophone
Garnet Clark (piano)	Paris	November 25, 1935	HMV
Fats Waller & Rhythm (v)	New York	December 4, 1935	HMV
Chick Webb & Orch ("Don't Be That Way")	New York	February 1936	Polydor (LP)
Red Norvo & Swing Sextette	New York	March 16, 1936	Decca
The Ballyhooligans (v)	London	April 2, 1936	HMV
Joe Daniels & the Hot Shots	London	July 15, 1936	Parlophone
Count Basie & Orch ("Don't Be That Way")	New York	circa February 1937	Vanguard
Jimmy Dorsey & Orch	Los Angeles	March 3, 1937	Decca
Lionel Hampton & Orch*	New York	April 26, 1937	Victor
Benny Goodman Quartet	New York	April 29, 1937	MGM
Glenn Miller & Orch	New York	June 9, 1937	Brunswick
Count Basie & Orch	New York	June 30, 1937	Collector's Corner (LP)
Dicky Wells & Orch	Paris	July 7, 1937	Swing
Valaida [Snow] (v)	London	July 9, 1937	Parlophone
Chick Webb & the Little Chicks	New York	September 21, 1937	Decca
Emilio Caceres Trio	New York	November 5, 1937	Victor
Scott Wood & Six Swingers (medley)	London	November 12, 1937	Columbia
Benny Goodman Quartet	New York	January 16, 1938	Columbia
Benny Goodman & Orch ("Don't Be That Way")	New York	January 16, 1938	Columbia
Bud Freeman Trio	New York	January 17, 1938	Commodore
Lionel Hampton & Orch ("Don't Be That Way")	New York	January 18, 1938	Victor
Benny Goodman & Orch ("Don't Be That Way")	New York	February 16, 1938	Victor

Note: (v) indicates that there is a vocal in the recording. Contrafacts are those entries accompanied by tune titles in parentheses.

Performers	Location	Date	Recording Company
Ozzie Nelson & Orch ("Don't Be That Way")	Hollywood	March 5, 1938	Bluebird
Mildred Bailey & Orch (v) ("Don't Be That Way")	New York	March 14, 1938	Vocalion
Jimmy Dorsey & Orch ("Don't Be That Way")	New York	March 16, 1938	Decca
Teddy Wilson & Orch ("Don't Be That Way")	New York	March 23, 1938	Brunswick
Larry Adler with the Quintette of the Hot Club of France	Paris	May 31, 1938	Columbia (2 recordings)
Johnny Hodges & Orch ("The Jeep Is Jumpin'")	New York	August 24, 1938	Vocalion/OKeh
Louis Armstrong & Fats Waller (v)	New York	October 19, 1938	Palm Club
Clarence Profit Trio	New York	February 15, 1939	Epic
Erskine Hawkins & Orch ("Raid the Joint")	New York	April 8, 1939	Bluebird
Earl Hines & Orch ("Father Steps In")	New York	July 12, 1939	Bluebird
Tommy Dorsey & Orch ("Stomp It Off")	New York	July 20, 1939	Victor
Count Basie's Kansas City Seven ("Lester Leaps In")	New York	September 5, 1939	Vocalion (2 recordings)
Earl Hines & Orch ("XYZ")	Chicago	October 6, 1939	Bluebird
Benny Goodman Sextet (medley)	New York	December 24, 1939	Vanguard
Casper Reardon (v)	New York	February 5, 1940	Schirmer
Count Basie & Orch	Boston	February 20, 1940	Collector's Corner
Fletcher Henderson & Horace Henderson's Orch (v)	Chicago	Feburary 27, 1940	Vocalion
Duke Ellington & Orch ("Cotton Tail/Shuckin' and Stiffin'")	Hollywood	May 4, 1940	Victor
Sid Phillips Trio	London	May 6, 1940	Parlophone
Count Basie & Orch ("Blow Top")	New York	May 31, 1940	Epic
Max Geldray Quartet	London	July 26, 1940	Decca
Felix Mendelssohn & Hawaiian Serenaders	London	October 28, 1940	Columbia
Johnny Hodges & Orch ("Good Queen Bess")	Chicago	November 2, 1940	Bluebird
Duke Ellington & Orch ("Cotton Tail")	Fargo, N.D.	November 7, 1940	Palm
Johnny Hodges & Orch ("Squatty Roo")	Hollywood	July 3, 1941	Bluebird
Metronome All-Star Leaders	New York	January 16, 1942	Columbia (2 recordings)

Notes

Some of the information in this Introduction was presented in "The Idea of a Core Repertory," a paper delivered by Richard Crawford at the annual meeting of the Sonneck Society in Boulder, Colorado, April 1986, and, in revised form, at the annual meeting of the American Musicological Society in New Orleans, October 1987. Thanks are due to John Hasse, Frank Gillis, and especially Michael Montgomery for help in gathering materials, and to James Dapogny and Lawrence Gushee for advice and information. Jeffrey Magee's collaboration was made possible by the University of Michigan's Horace H. Rackham School of Graduate Studies. Samuel A. Floyd, Jr., had the idea of publishing these lists, which were made as part of another project.

1. Robert S. Gold (1964, 264) defines a standard as "a number which has stood the test of time and found a permanent place in the repertory of jazz performers." When the list was first shown to jazz pianist James Dapogny, he recognized every tune on it except "Arkansas Blues."

2. While writing about Gershwin's "I Got Rhythm," I recognized the need to know more about the song's place in the jazz tradition. How did its performance history compare with that of other jazz standards? Without a list of other standards, that question was unanswerable. Jeffrey Magee and I intend this monograph to serve as the answer. "I Got Rhythm" will be mentioned from time to time as the tables accompanying this Introduction are surveyed. Gershwin's song is the subject of the last chapter of *The American Musical Landscape* (Crawford, in press, a).

3. Rust (1982, ii) describes his book as "aimed at the documentation of history."

4. In his introduction, Rust (1982, ii) defines his purview more precisely as "discs made in the name of jazz, or of dance music with close affiliation to jazz, as well as vocal records with jazz groups used as accompaniment, made between 1917 and 1942." He continues, "Also included are important and interesting records made of ragtime, reaching back to 1897 and the earliest known recordings of the then new, exciting, even daringly syncopated rhythm that preceded jazz by two decades." Rust goes on to say that "microgroove issues are not included" except for "the LPs and EPs that offer music coming within the scope of the work that is not and never has been available on a 78 rpm disc. There are many such: airshots, . . . soundtracks of films . . . featuring prominent jazz personalities, and transfers from hitherto unissued test pressings that . . . have survived the years in good enough condition to make pleasant listening possible."

5. See "A Note on Procedure," p. viii.

6. We considered titling this work "Jazz Standards and Hits," but no dictionary supports the definition of "hit" as a work or song whose impact is strong but temporary. For example, the supplement to *The Oxford English Dictionary*, (Oxford 1987) calls a hit "any popular success (a person, a play, a song, etc.) in public entertainment." In the *American Heritage Dictionary* (Boston 1969), a hit is "a successful popular venture: *a Broadway hit.*" And Arnold Shaw, in the *Dictionary of American Pop/Rock* (1982, 173), reports that "a hit is a hit—a song, record, or artist that garners widespread acceptance or popularity as reflected in sales."

7. Some experts and players who have seen the list have decried certain omissions and inclusions. An interesting aspect of the list is the absence of tunes one might expect to see, such as "When the Saints Go Marching In," and the presence of some unexpected ones, such as "Hot Lips" and "My Blue Heaven." Such divergence between expectation and evidence helps to reveal the distance between present-day perspectives and past practice.

8. The publication dates were found in the Copyright Division of the Library of Congress in Washington, D.C.

9. Rags are classified here as pieces made up of strains rather than verses and choruses. Most are published without words, though "Bugle Call Rag" and "Milenberg Joys" are exceptions. ("Milenberg Joys" is called "song" on the sheet music and is printed with a verse and chorus. The chorus, however, is based on the chord progression of "Tiger Rag." In addition, performers of the period invariably played it as either a two-strain or a three-strain piece, and only five of the forty-six recorded performances include a vocal.) Show songs are those composed for a particular Broadway show or closely identified with and popularized by one. Tin Pan Alley and pop songs are those written independently of shows by composers and lyricists in the professional New York City world of songwriting. Blues are defined here simply as songs with the word "blues" in the title. (Even though, e.g., the English "Limehouse Blues" lacks the musical earmarks of the blues, the song was obviously inspired by the fad for "blues" songs—i.e., songs about melancholy moods—in the early 1920s.) "Other" numbers are compositions originating in oral tradition or with jazz musicians and not belonging to any of the first four categories.

10. See Crawford (in press, b) for an article based on the forty-five compositions in Table 1 to which black authors and composers contributed.

11. To choose just two of many examples, "Body and Soul," published in February 1930, was interpolated into *Three's a Crowd*, a revue by Arthur Schwartz and Howard Dietz, which opened on Broadway October 15 of that year. According to Joel Whitburn (1986, 216), a recording by Libby Holman, a member of the revue cast, was already one of the top-selling records by the week of October 18, 1930, and reached a peak position of no. 3 (Whitburn 1986, 216). In the meantime, a recording by Paul Whiteman and his orchestra had reached the charts Octo-

ber 11 and was no. 1 for six weeks (Whitburn 1986, 452). "Body and Soul" also received eight recordings in the jazz tradition in that year. "Ain't She Sweet?," published on January 17, 1927, received thirteen jazz recordings before the year was out, eight of them within two months of publication. Whitburn (1986, 53) shows that Ben Bernie's band also had a no. 1 popular hit with "Ain't She Sweet?" which reached the chart of top recordings in April and stayed no. 1 for four weeks. Unlike "Body and Soul," however, "Ain't She Sweet?" never won a place in the center of the jazz repertory, logging only seven more recordings in the years 1928–42.

12. "China Boy," published in 1922, was never a no. 1 popular hit song on record, according to Whitburn (1986, 485); in 1936 a jazz recording by Benny Goodman reached no. 9 in sales, the song's high point of popularity. The first jazz recording of "China Boy" was not made until 1926. However, between 1934 and 1937 "China Boy" was one of the songs most often recorded by jazz musicians. "Margie," published in November 1920, was a no. 1 hit in Eddie Cantor's performance by early 1921 (Whitburn 1986, 75), and the Original Dixieland Jazz Band (ODJB) immediately recorded it. However, between the ODJB's December 1920 recording and Red Nichols's of June 1928, no jazz musicians recorded "Margie"; as a jazz standard, it was a tune of the 1930s. "Tea for Two" is another example. Taken from the show *No No Nanette* (1924), it was a no. 1 hit in 1925 in Marion Harris's recording (Whitburn 1986, 197). But of the thirty-four jazz recordings of "Tea for Two" from our period, only one was made before 1930.

13. Dorothy Fields and Jimmy McHugh's "Diga Diga Doo," e.g., written for a Broadway revue, was published by Jack Mills, Inc., in June 1928. In July, Duke Ellington's Orchestra (performing for OKeh Records) and the Hotsy Totsy Gang both recorded it, the latter in two performances for Brunswick, one with and one without a vocal. Ellington "and his Cotton Club Orchestra" recorded the song again in November. Beginning in 1926, Ellington's manager was Irving Mills, the brother of Jack Mills; the Hotsy Totsy Gang was a group organized and recorded by Irving Mills. Thus, the first four jazz recordings of the Mills-owned "Diga Diga Doo" were all made by Mills-directed ensembles.

14. Virtually all jazz performances of "Down Hearted Blues," "Rockin' Chair," and "You Rascal You" are recorded with a singer. In contrast, "Limehouse Blues" and "Tea for Two" have shed their vocals almost entirely.

15. Except for one by Lizzie Miles, all twenty-five recordings of "Hot Lips" were made by white groups; except for Buster Bailey and his sextet, all recordings of "Eccentric" were made by white musicians; and except for performances by Bessie Smith, the Georgia Washboard Stompers, and Louis Armstrong, "Alexander's Ragtime Band" was the property of white musicians on record. "Loveless Love," on the other hand, and "Down Hearted Blues" were recorded mostly, though by no means exclusively, by black performers.

16. "Avalon" was the only Core Repertory tune recorded more often in Europe than in the United States (thirteen of twenty-five recordings, or 52 percent). Forty percent of the recordings of "Ain't She Sweet" and "Nobody's Sweetheart" were made in Europe. Other tunes with at least 35 percent of their recordings made there are "After You've Gone," "Ain't Misbehavin'," "Dinah," "I Got Rhythm," "I Never Knew," "Limehouse Blues," "Margie," "Moonglow," "Nagasaki," "Oh Lady Be Good," "The Sheik of Araby," "Some of These Days," "Sweet Sue," and "Tiger Rag." On the other hand, all recordings of "Sugar Blues" and "Tin Roof Blues" were made in the United States, and so were all but one recording of "Down Hearted Blues," "A Good Man Is Hard to Find," "High Society," "I Would Do Anything for You," "King Porter Stomp," "Old Fashioned Love," "Panama," "The Wang Wang Blues," and "The Weary Blues."

17. On the song's popularity and the success of the show, see Bordman (1978). According to Whitburn, recordings by Ethel Waters, the Revelers, and Cliff Edwards made "Dinah" a popular hit in 1926 (Whitburn 1986, 439, 367, 146). In 1932, in a recording by Bing Crosby and the Mills Brothers, "Dinah" returned to no. 1 status for two weeks (Whitburn 1986, 103).

18. Included are two pieces by W. C. Handy originally published under non-blues titles. "Beale Street," a piano piece copyrighted March 23, 1917, was called "Beale Street Blues" in an instrumental arrangement (copyright February 7, 1928). "Aunt Hagar's Children," originally published as a piano piece (November 2, 1920), gained lyrics in a publication of June 23, 1921, called "Aunt Hagar's Children Blues."

19. See "Basin Street Blues," "Farewell Blues," "The Jazz Me Blues," "Limehouse Blues," "Wabash Blues," and "The Wang Wang Blues." The verse of "Sugar Blues" is twelve bars long and follows the standard blues harmonic progression up to the last two bars. Many recordings of "Basin Street Blues"— including those made by Louis Armstrong in 1929—introduce a blues strain, however, that does not appear in the sheet music.

20. See "Aunt Hagar's Children Blues," "Beale Street," "The Jazz Me Blues," "Limehouse Blues," "The Memphis Blues," "Royal Garden Blues," "Sugar Blues," and "Tin Roof Blues." Albert Murray confirms the fun-loving side of the blues tradition and devotes an entire chapter to a critique of standard definitions of the blues in dictionaries and reference works. They "leave the impression," Murray writes, that the blues represents "the expression of sadness. Not one characterizes it as good-time music. Nor is there any reference whatsoever to its use as dance music" (Murray [1976] 1987, 57).

21. Rust (1982, ii) notes that records of "blues singers" are excluded "unless accompanied by jazz musicians."

22. Russell Sanjek (1988, 117) reports that record sales stood at $106 million in 1921, half that in 1925, $16.9 million in 1931, and $11 million in 1932. The advent of jukeboxes helped an upward turn by the middle of the decade.

23. Martin Williams (1989, 29) writes: "By 1929 almost every big band had two or three pieces based on the *Tiger Rag* changes, one or two from, say, *I Ain't Got Nobody* or *After You've Gone*. And by 1932 *You're Driving Me Crazy,* a comparatively complex piece, had lost its melody and acquired the more jazzlike theme called *Moten Swing*. Almost every big band soon had one piece based on *King Porter Stomp*'s chord changes, and some had more than one." He goes on to call "Shag" by Sidney Bechet "the first of hundreds (thousands?) of new *I Got Rhythm* themes to come." And he goes on to mention more examples, of which all but "Rose Room" are Core Repertory tunes. "Try to imagine the Count Basie book of 1938 without changes borrowed from *Tea for Two, Honeysuckle Rose,* and *Diga Diga Doo*. Or Ellington without *Rose Room, Exactly Like You,* or the ubiquitous *Tiger Rag*."

24. The index of psalmody was made by hand in the early 1970s, when computers were not yet part of the standard scholarly tool kit. It has since been superseded by Nicholas Temperley's census of settings of sacred, metrical poetry printed before 1821 in England and North America (in press). In the bibliography, I identified the 101 compositions most frequently printed in America from 1698 to 1810 as the Core Repertory. As a separate project, I chose a representative version of each Core Repertory tune and published them in a critical edition (Crawford 1984) which includes "biographies" of each composition.

25. Conventional wisdom holds that such instrumental versions were made for release in non-English-speaking countries. And the release number of this example, in fact, is that of the Brunswick series distributed in France and Germany (see Rust 1982, viii).

References

Bordman, Gerald. 1978. *American musical theater: A chronicle*. New York: Oxford University Press.

Britton, Allen Perdue, Irving Lowens, and completed by Richard Crawford. 1990. *American sacred music imprints, 1698–1810: A bibliography*. Worcester, Mass.: American Antiquarian Society.

Crawford, Richard. In press, a (1992). *The American musical landscape*. Berkeley and Los Angeles: University of California Press.

———. In press, b (1992). Notes on jazz standards by black authors and composers, 1899–1942. In *New perspectives on music: Essays in honor of Eileen Southern*, edited by Josephine R. B. Wright with Samuel A. Floyd, Jr. Detroit Monographs in Musicology/Studies in Music, no. 11. Warren, Mich.: Harmonie Park Press.

———. 1984. *The core repertory of early American psalmody*. Recent Researches in American Music, vols. 11 and 12. Madison, Wis.: A-R Editions.

DeVeaux, Scott. 1988. Bebop and the recording industry: The 1942 AFM recording ban reconsidered. *Journal of the American Musicological Society* 41:126–165.

Gold, Robert S. 1964. *A jazz lexicon*. New York: Knopf.

Mordden, Ethan. 1981. *The Hollywood musical*. New York: St. Martin's Press.

Murray, Albert. [1976] 1987. *Stomping the blues*. New York: Da Capo.

Rust, Brian. [1961] 1982. *Jazz records, 1897–1942*, 2 vols. Chigwell: Storyville.

Sanjek, Russell. 1988. *American popular music and its business: The first four hundred years*. Vol. 3: From 1900 to 1984. New York: Oxford University Press.

Temperley, Nicholas, with the assistance of Charles G. Manns and Joseph Herl. Forthcoming (1993). *The hymn tune index*. London: Oxford University Press.

Whitburn, Joel. 1986. *Joel Whitburn's Pop Memories, 1890–1954*. Menomonee Falls, Wis.: Record Research, Inc.

Williams, Martin. 1989. *Jazz in its time*. New York: Oxford University Press.

Jazz Standards on Record, 1900–1942
A Core Repertory

Jazz Standards on Record, 1900–1942

After You've Gone

Date	Performer	Vocal	Place	Label	Issue	Matrix
05/29/19	Savoy Quartet	–	Hayes, Middlesex	His Master's Voice	B-1088	HO-4928ae
c 09/19	The Versatile Four	V	London	Edison Bell Winner	3379	6399
01/04/27	Charleston Chasers	–	New York City	Columbia	rejected	143259-1-2-3
01/27/27	Charleston Chasers	–	New York City	Columbia	861-D	143259-5
c 01/31/27	Evelyn Thompson	V	New York City	Vocalion	1083	E-4499
03/02/27	Bessie Smith and her Band	V	New York City	Columbia	14197-D	143567-2
04/11/27	Sophie Tucker	V	New York City	OKeh	40837	80716-B
06/24/27	California Ramblers	–	New York City	Pathe Actuelle	36653	107644-1-2
10/08/27	Johnny Dodds' Black Bottom Stompers	V	Chicago	Brunswick	3568	C-1239; E-6746
10/08/27	Johnny Dodds' Black Bottom Stompers	–	Chicago	Brunswick	80074	C-1241; E-6748
04/16/29	Julie Wintz and his Orchestra	–	New York City	Harmony	1169-H	150470-3
05/17/29	Mills' Musical Clowns	–	New York City	American Record Corp.	rejected	8761-(1-2-3?)
06/06/29	Mills' Merry Makers	V	New York City	Banner	6441	8761-5-6
09/24/29	Miff Mole's Molers	–	New York City	OKeh	41445	402987-C
10/18/29	Paul Whiteman and his Orchestra	V	New York City	Columbia	2098-D	149159-3
10/21/29	Jimmy Noone's Apex Club Orchestra	V	Chicago	Brunswick	7124	C-4688
11/26/29	Louis Armstrong and his Orchestra	V	New York City	OKeh	41350	403454-B
12/06/29	Coon-Sanders Orchestra	V	Chicago	Victor	22342	57234-3
01/28/30	Gene Austin	V	New York City	Victor	22299	58529-2
02/03/30	Red Nichols and his Five Pennies	V	New York City	Brunswick	4839	E-31924-A
03/05/30	Alphonse Trent and his Orchestra	V	Richmond, IN	Gennett	7161	16349-A
03/21/30	Fats Waller	–	New York City	Victor	22371	59721-1
07/15/30	Jimmy Dorsey	–	London	Decca	F-1876	MB-1619-2
07/21/30	Henny Hendrickson's Louisville Serenaders	–	Camden, NJ	Victor	Special	62682-2
03/31	Fletcher Henderson and his Orchestra	V	New York City	Crown	3093	1230-2
03/03/31	Blue Lyres	–	London	Decca	F-3068	GB-2706-2
10/22/31	Joe Venuti-Eddie Lang and their All-Star Orchestra	V	New York City	Vocalion	15834	E-37270-A
07/29/33	The King's Jesters	–	Chicago	Bluebird	B-5149	75979-1
07/23/34	Pat Hyde	V	London	Parlophone	R-1898	CE-6584-1
08/17/34	Georgia Washboard Serenaders	V	New York City	Decca	7006	38345-B
08/24/34	Art Tatum	–	New York City	Decca	306	38426-A
10/09/34	Art Tatum	–	New York City	Decca	468	38426-C
12/18/34	Six Swingers [medley]	–	London	Regal Zonophone	MR-1567	CAR-3122-1

Date	Performer	Vocal	Place	Label	Issue	Matrix
02/04/35	Coleman Hawkins	–	The Hague	Decca	F-42052	AM-149-1
02/04/35	Coleman Hawkins	–	The Hague	Ace of Clubs	1247 (LP)	AM-149-2
07/05/35	Clyde McCoy and his Orchestra	–	Chicago	Champion	40108	C-90076-A
07/13/35	Benny Goodman Trio	–	New York City	Victor	25115	92704-2
09/35	Art Tatum	–	Hollywood	Jazz Panorama	LP-15	–
09/26/35	Mario "Harp" Lorenzi and his Rhythmics	–	London	Columbia	FB-1168	CA-15285-1
01/18/36	Billy Cotton's Cotton Pickers	V	London	Regal Zonophone	MR-2028	CAR-3877-1
01/31/36	Bill Coleman	V	Paris	His Master's Voice	K-7764	OLA-850-1-2
03/13/36	Stuff Smith	V	New York City	Vocalion	3201	18819-1
05/25/36	Max Abrams and his Rhythm Makers	–	London	Parlophone	F-512	CE-7650-1
07/21/36	Joe Daniels and his Hot Shots	–	London	Parlophone	F-629	CE-7769-1
10/18/36	Tommy Dorsey and his Orchestra	–	New York City	Victor	25467	02163-1
01/07/37	Nat Gonella and his Georgians	V	London	Parlophone	F-646	CE-8002-1
01/28/37	Roy Eldridge and his Orchestra	V	Chicago	Vocalion	3458	C-1798-2
09/05/37	Lionel Hampton and his Orchestra	V	Hollywood	Victor	25674	09684-1
10/37	Adelaide Hall [medley]	V	Copenhagen	Tono	K-6001	D-599
11/12/37	Bill Coleman	V	Paris	Swing	22	OLA-1977-1
03/29/38	Ray Ventura and his Orchestra	V	Paris	Pathe Actuelle	1582	CM-185-1
04/18/38	Ben Pollack and his Orchestra	–	Los Angeles	Decca	2057	DLA-1232-A
c 08/38	Jelly Roll Morton	–	Baltimore	Swaggie	JCS-116 (LP)	–
04/07/39	Paul Whiteman's Sax Soctette	–	New York City	Decca	2467	65365-A
08/07/39	Fats Waller and his Rhythm	V	New York City	Victor	RD-7553	–
02/07/40	Billy Cotton and his Band	V	London	Rex	9789	R-4316-1
07/30/40	Stephane Grappelly and his Musicians	–	London	Decca	F-7570	DR-4903-2
06/05/41	Gene Krupa and his Orchestra	–	New York City	OKeh	6278	30605-1
06/27/41	Willie Lewis and his Negro Band	V	Zurich	Elite Special	4080	1924
07/27/42	Benny Goodman and his Orchestra	–	New York City	Columbia	36699	CO-33049-1

Ain't Misbehavin'

Date	Performer	Vocal	Place	Label	Issue	Matrix
06/28/29	Charleston Chasers	V	New York City	Columbia	1891-D	148762-2
07/06/29	Ben Selvin and his Orchestra	V	New York City	Harmony	965-H	148791-3
07/16/29	Sammy Fain	V	New York City	Harmony	993-H	148817-3
07/18/29	Jimmy Noone's Apex Club Orchestra	V	Chicago	Vocalion	15819	C-3898
07/19/29	Louis Armstrong and his Orchestra	V	New York City	OKeh	8714	402534-B
08/02/29	Fats Waller	–	Camden, NJ	Victor	22092	49492-3
08/22/29	California Ramblers	–	New York City	Edison Diamond Disc	14064	N-1084
08/23/29	Seger Ellis	V	New York City	OKeh	41291	402881-B
08/26/29	Seger Ellis	V	New York City	OKeh	rejected	402881-D-E-F
09/04/29	Mills and his Hotsy Totsy Gang	–	New York City	Brunswick	4535	E-30526
09/20/29	Fess Williams and his Royal Flush Orchestra	V	Camden, NJ	Victor	V-38085	55929-3
10/22/29	Arcadians Dance Orchestra	–	London	Zonophone	5479	Yy-17822-3

Date	Performer	Vocal	Place	Label	Issue	Matrix
11/01/29	Cecil and Leslie Norman	V	London	Worldecho	A-1017 (SPB)	142
03/03/33	Claude Hopkins and his Orchestra	V	New York City	Jazz Archives (LP)	4	B-13134-A
07/13/33	Duke Ellington and his Orchestra	–	London	Decca	M-439	GB-6040-1
11/09/34	Pat Hyde [medley]	V	London	Parlophone	R-1973	CE-6714-1
03/11/35	Fats Waller and his Rhythm [medley]	–	New York City	Victor	LPT-6001	–
07/09/35	Paul Whiteman and his Orchestra	V	New York City	Victor	25086	92580-1
11/02/35	Mario "Harp" Lorenzi and Rhythmics	–	London	Columbia	FB-1230	CA-15419-1
11/19/35	Arthur Young	–	London	Paramount	R-2153	CE-7286-1
01/18/36	Billy Cotton's Cotton Pickers	V	London	Regal Zonophone	MR-2161	CAR-3876-1
04/27/36	Frankie Trumbauer and his Orchestra	V	New York City	Brunswick	7665	B-19115-2
09/19/36	The Four Stars	V	London	His Master's Voice	BD-5112	OEA-3865-2
10/07/36	Nat Gonella and his Georgians	V	London	Parlophone	F-593	CE-7865-1
03/03/37	Jimmy Mundy and his Swing Club Seven	V	New York City	Vri	598	M-160-1
04/22/37	Quintette of the Hot Club of France	–	Paris	His Master's Voice	B-8690	OLA-1708-1
05/18/37	Casper Reardon and his Orchestra	–	New York City	Mas	133	M-476
07/20/37	Teddy Weatherford	–	Paris	Swing	38	OLA-1919-1
08/29/37	Teddy Wilson Quartet	–	Los Angeles	Brunswick	rejected	LA-1408-A-B
09/05/37	Teddy Wilson Quartet	–	Los Angeles	Brunswick	7964	LA-1408-C
09/17/37	Boots and his Buddies	V	San Antonio	Bluebird	B-7241	014296-1
09/28/37	Joe Daniels and his Hotshots	–	London	Parlophone	F-951	CE-8612-1
11/30/37	Max Abrams and his Rhythm Makers	–	London	Parlophone	R-2474	CE-8766-1
05–07/38	Jelly Roll Morton	V	Washington, DC	Circle (LP)	26-44	1685
06/28/38	Louis Armstrong and his Orchestra	V	New York City	Decca	2042	64230-B
08/21/38	Fats Waller and his Continental Rhythm	V	London	World Record Club (LP)	SHB-29	OEA-6384-1
08/21/38	Fats Waller and his Continental Rhythm	V	London	His Master's Voice	BD-5415	OEA 6384-2
04/13/39	Bobby Hackett and his Orchestra	–	New York City	Vocalion/OKeh	4877	WM-1018-A
06/28/39	Freddie Johnson and his Orchestra	V	Paris	Swing	210	OSW-84-1
08/07/39	Fats Waller and his Rhythm	V	New York City	Jazz Society	AA-535	–
09/06/40	Sidney Bechet and his New Orleans Feetwarmers	–	Chicago	Victor	PM-42409 (LP)	053433-1
09/06/40	Sidney Bechet and his New Orleans Feetwarmers	–	Chicago	Victor	26746	053433-2
10/23/40	Horace Henderson and his Orchestra	–	New York City	OKeh	5900	23960-1
11/07/40	Fats Waller and his Rhythm	V	New York City	RFW	1	–
05/07/41	Cootie Williams and his Orchestra	–	New York City	OKeh	6224	30424-1

Ain't She Sweet?

Date	Performer	Vocal	Place	Label	Issue	Matrix
01/20/27	[Fletcher Henderson] Dixie Stompers	–	New York City	Harmony	353-H	143333-2
01/21/27	Ted Wallace and his Orchestra	V	New York City	OKeh	40760	80319-B
01/28/27	Annette Hanshaw	V	New York City	Pathe Actuelle	32244	E-2668
02/03/27	Varsity Eight	V	New York City	Cameo	1114	2325-C

Date	Performer	Vocal	Place	Label	Issue	Matrix
c 02/11/27	Jack Pettis and his Band	V	New York City	Banner	1942	7107-2
03/10/27	California Ramblers	V	New York City	Edison Diamond Disc	rejected	11567
03/10/27	Nat Shilkret and Victor Orchestra	V	New York City	Victor	20508	38153-2
c 03/28/27	Fred Elizalde and his Varsity Band	–	London	Brunswick	1001	–
05/06/27	Lillie Delk Christian	V	Chicago	OKeh	8475	80842-A-B
05/24/27	Bobbie Leecan	V	Camden, NJ	Victor	20958	38929-2
06/28/27	Charles Remue and his New Stompers Orchestra	–	London	Edison Bell Electron	0153	10929-2
c 07/27	Orchestre The Playboys	V	Paris	Pathe	6996	8257
c 11/27	Arthur Briggs' Savoy Syncop's Orchestra	–	Berlin	Deutsche Grammophone/Polydor	21095	648bd
06/16/33	Fred Elizalde	–	London	Decca	M-450	GB-5986-1
03/28/35	Brian Lawrence and the Quagliano Quartet	V	London	Decca	rejected	GB-7026-1-2
04/04/35	Brian Lawrence and the Quagliano Quartet	V	London	Panophone	25723	GB-7026-3
11/02/35	Mario "Harp" Lorenzi and his Rhythmics	V	London	Columbia	FB-1230	CA-15417-1
06/18/38	Sammy Williams and his Three Naturals	V	New York City	Vocalion	4259	23129-1
04/07/39	Jimmie Lunceford and his Orchestra	V	New York City	Vocalion/OKeh	4875	24352-A
11/28/39	Bunny Berigan and his Orchestra	–	New York City	Victor	26753	043927-1

Alexander's Ragtime Band

Date	Performer	Vocal	Place	Label	Issue	Matrix
01/26/27	Miff Mole's (Little) Molers	–	New York City	OKeh	40758	80338-A
03/02/27	Bessie Smith and her Band	V	New York City	Columbia	14219-D	143568-1
c 03/13/27	Jimmy Lytell	–	New York City	Pathe Actuelle	36607	107420-C
06/02/27	Ted Lewis Band	V	New York City	Columbia	1084-D	144247-4
12/13/27	All Star Orchestra	V	New York City	Victor	rejected	41168-1-2
12/06/30	Casa Loma Orchestra	V	New York City	OKeh	41476	404568-B
03/23/31	Casa Loma Orchestra	V	New York City	Brunswick	6100	E-36498-A
01/25/32	Gene Kardos and his Orchestra	V	New York City	Victor	22920	71274-1
02-03/32	Joel Shaw and his Orchestra	–	New York City	Crown	3285	1671-2
09/13/33	Billy Cotton and his Band	–	London	Regal Zonophone	MR-1062	CAR-2192-1
05/23/34	Boswell Sisters	V	New York City	Brunswick	7412	B-15254-A
05/25/34	Monia Liter	–	London	Brunswick	01814	TB-1272-2
08/17/34	Georgia Washboard Stompers	V	New York City	Decca	7006	38347-A
08/06/35	Arthur Young and his Youngsters [medley]	–	London	Decca	F-5645	TB-1856-1
05/15/36	Brian Lawrence and his Lansdowne House Sextet	V	London	Decca	F-5981	TB-2176-1
10/07/36	Benny Goodman and his Orchestra	–	New York City	Victor	25445	02104-1
10/21/36	Joe Daniels and his Hotshots	–	London	Parlophone	F-656	CE-7899-1
02/27/37	The Three Peppers	–	New York City	Vri	523	M-140
06/29/37	Benny Goodman and his Orchestra	–	Los Angeles	MGM	E/X-3790	–

Date	Performer	Vocal	Place	Label	Issue	Matrix
07/07/37	Louis Armstrong and his Orchestra	V	New York City	Decca	1408	62336-A
10/04/37	Alix Combelle et son Orchestre	–	Paris	Swing	11	OLA-1956-1
03/20/38	Ray Noble and his Orchestra	–	Los Angeles	Brunswick	8180	LA-1601-A
09/26/38	The Ballyhooligans [2 parts]	–	London	His Master's Voice	rejected	OEA-6582-1-2; -6583-1-2

Arkansas Blues

Date	Performer	Vocal	Place	Label	Issue	Matrix
c 02/21	Lucille Hegamin	V	New York City	Arto	9053	18016-1-2
04–05/21	Tim Brymn and his Black Devil Orchestra	–	New York City	OKeh	8002	7866-A
c 07/27/21	Noble Sissle and his Orchestra	–	New York City	Emerson	10443	41922-2
c 09/05/21	Mamie Smith and her Jazz Band	V	New York City	OKeh	4446	70141-A
09/28/21	Mary Stafford	V	New York City	Columbia	A-3493	80001-3
10/21	Eliza Christmas Lee	V	New York City	Gennett	4801	7678
11/21	Yerkes' S.S. Flotilla Orchestra	–	New York City	Vocalion	14272	8243
c 12/07/21	Lanin's Southern Serenaders	–	New York City	Emerson	10496	42095-2-4
02/23/24	Mound City Blue Blowers	–	New York City	Brunswick	2581	77-CH
07/03/24	The Little Ramblers	–	New York City	Columbia	175-D	81860-2
07/24/24	Five Birmingham Babies	–	New York City	Pathe Actuelle	036142	105483
10/17/24	Eva Taylor	V	New York City	OKeh	8183	72913-B
04/14/27	Goofus Five	–	New York City	OKeh	40817	80733-B
06/24/27	Varsity Eight	–	New York City	Cameo	1209	2521-A
03/11/28	Fred Elizalde	–	London	Brunswick	164	517
04/02/28	Bessie Brown	V	Chicago	Vocalion	1182	C-1859
02/23/29	The Mystery Orchestra	V	Chicago	Victor	rejected	50517-1-2
10/30/30	McKenzie's Mound City Blue Blowers	V	New York City	CBS (LP)	D-77	10195-1
03/09/37	Bram Martin's Borderliners	V	London	Columbia	rejected	CA-16280-1-2
05/06/38	Joe Daniels and his Hotshots	–	London	Parlophone	F-1148	CE-9098-1
03/16/39	Mildred Bailey and her Oxford Greys	V	New York City	Vocalion	4801	24230-1
05/09/39	Teddy Grace	V	New York City	Decca	2602	65558-A

Aunt Hagar's Children Blues

Date	Performer	Vocal	Place	Label	Issue	Matrix
08/21	Ladd's Black Aces	–	New York City	Gennett	4762	7577-A
c 08/01/21	Lanin's Southern Serenaders	–	New York City	Emerson	10439	41925-2-3
c 08/30/21	Lanin's Southern Serenaders	–	New York City	Paramount/Bluebird	20068	837-1-2
c 09/21	Alice Leslie Carter	V	New York City	Arto	9103	–
09/21	Brown and Terry's Jazzola Boys	–	New York City	OKeh	8018	70190-A
11/22	Isham Jones and his Orchestra	–	New York City	Brunswick	5178	9132
01/23	Abe Small and his Melody Boys	–	New York City	Strong	10002	001-1
c 01/05/23	Handy's Orchestra	–	New York City	OKeh	4789	71150-A-B
01/11/23	Original Memphis Five	–	New York City	Pathe Actuelle	020900	69997

Date	Performer	Vocal	Place	Label	Issue	Matrix
02/01/23	Virginians	–	New York City	Victor	19021	27446-3
03/23	Gene Fosdick's Hoosiers	–	New York City	Vocalion	14535	11030
03/29/23	Frank Westphal and his Orchestra	–	Chicago	Columbia	rejected	80916-1-2-3
04/16/23	Ted Lewis and his Band	–	New York City	Columbia	A-3879	80970-3
10/14/27	King Oliver and his Dixie Syncopators	–	New York City	Vocalion	rejected	E-6667/8
02/25/28	King Oliver and his Dixie Syncopators	–	New York City	Vocalion	rejected	E-7174/5
09/10/28	King Oliver and his Dixie Syncopators	–	New York City	Vocalion	1225	E-28186-A(or -B)
01/20/30	Ted Lewis and his Band	–	New York City	Columbia	2113-D	149784-3
11/12/37	Scott Wood and his Six Swingers [medley]	–	London	Columbia	FB-1832	CA-16699-1
09/09/38	Paul Whiteman and his Swing Wing	V	New York City	Decca	2145	64618-A
07/19/39	Jack Teagarden and his Orchestra	V	Chicago	Columbia	35206	WC-2657-A
10/12/39	Bob Chester and his Orchestra	–	Chicago	Bluebird	B-10513	040957-1
05/22/41	Lew Stone and his Band	–	London	Decca	F-7916	DR-5787-1
06/25/41	[Henry Levine] Dixieland Jazz Group of NBC . . .	V	New York City	Victor	27544	066144-1

Avalon

Date	Performer	Vocal	Place	Label	Issue	Matrix
02/27/28	Red Nichols and his Five Pennies	–	New York	Brunswick	3854	E-26693
03/12/30	George Monkhouse and his Cambridge University Quinquaginta Ramblers	–	London	Parlophone	R-656	E-3140-1
05/23/30	Spike Hughes and his Dance Orchestra	–	London	Decca	rejected	MB-1393-1-2
08/32	Joel Shaw and his Orchestra	V	New York	Crown	3382	1850-1
07/21/33	Billy Cotton and his Band	–	London	Regal Zonophone	MR-1035	CAR-2133-1
08/16/34	Casa Loma Orchestra	–	New York	Brunswick	7532	B-15655-A
09/04/34	Cab Calloway and his Orchestra	V	Chicago	Brunswick	7411	CP-1106-A
12/18/34	Scott Wood and his Six Swingers [medley]	–	London	Regal Zonophone	MR-1675	CAR-3124-1
12/26/34	Joe Venuti and his Orchestra	–	New York	London	HMG-5023(LP)	–
01/29/35	KXYZ Novelty Band	–	San Antonio	Bluebird	B-5831	87765-1
03/02/35	Coleman Hawkins	–	Paris	His Master's Voice	K-7527	OLA-347-1
07/35	Quintette of the Hot Club of France	–	Paris	Ultraphon	AP-1512	P-77434
09/30/35	Jimmie Lunceford and his Orchestra	–	New York	Decca	668	60014-A
11/08/35	Harry Roy and his Orchestra	V	London	Parlophone	F-483	CE-7269-1
11/18/35	Val Rosing and his Swing Stars	V	London	Columbia	FB-1719	CA-15456-1
07/07/36	Ballyhooligans	–	London	His Master's Voice	BD-5086	OEA-3827-1
09/01/36	Scott Wood and his Six Swingers [medley]	V	London	Columbia	FB-1504	CA-15896-1
06/29/37	Benny Goodman Quartet	–	Los Angeles	MGM	E/X-3789	–
07/30/37	Benny Goodman Quartet	–	Hollywood	Victor	25644	09627-2
09/28/37	Joe Daniels and his Hotshots	–	London	Parlophone	F-951	CE-8611-1
10/04/37	Alix Combelle et son Orchestre	–	Paris	Swing	24	OLA-1959-1
01/16/38	Benny Goodman Quartet	–	New York	Columbia	A-1049	–
07/13/39	Harry James and his Orchestra	–	New York	Brunswick	rejected	B-25060-1-2

Date	Performer	Vocal	Place	Label	Issue	Matrix
11/08/39	Harry James and his Orchestra	–	Los Angeles	Columbia	35316	LA-2048-A
06/27/41	Willie Lewis and his Negro Band	–	Zurich	Elite Special	4083	1930

Baby Won't You Please Come Home

Date	Performer	Vocal	Place	Label	Issue	Matrix
c 11/25/22	Eva Taylor	V	New York City	OKeh	4740	71057-B
04/23	Lillian Harris	–	New York City	Banner	1212	5152-3
04/11/23	Bessie Smith	V	New York City	Columbia	A-3888	80952-3
01/19/27	Fletcher Henderson and his Orchestra	V	New York City	Vocalion	1079	E-4394/5
09/23/27	Clarence Williams' Blue Seven	–	New York City	OKeh	8510	81472-A
03/27/28	Chicago Rhythm Kings	V	Chicago	Vocalion	rejected	C-1804
04/28/28	Louisiana Rhythm Kings	V	Chicago	Vocalion	15692	C-1907-B
04/28/28	Louisiana Rhythm Kings	V	Chicago	Vocalion	rejected	C-1908-A-B
12/12/28	Earl Hines	V	Chicago	OKeh	rejected	402217-A
c 03/29	Clarence Williams' Jazz Kings	–	New York City	Grey Gull/Radiex	1724	3396-B
04/17/29	Frankie Trumbauer and his Orchestra	V	New York City	OKeh	41286	410811-C
c 01/30	Bill Carlsen Orchestra	V	Grafton, WI	Broadway	1365	L-127-1
07/28/30	McKinney's Cotton Pickers	V	Camden, NJ	Victor	22511	64003-3
10/31/30	Clarence Williams and his Orchestra	V	New York City	Banner	32021	10201-2-3
02/02/35	Mack Rogers and the Gunter Hotel Orchestra	V	San Antonio	Bluebird	B-5835	87865-1
07/02/35	Cab Calloway and his Orchestra	–	Chicago	Brunswick	7530	C-1057-A
08/01/35	Bill Staffon and his Orchestra	–	New York City	Bluebird	B-6175	92905-1
03/07/36	Freddy Gardner and his Orchestra	–	London	Parlophone	R-2191	CE-7492-1
09/05/37	Lionel Hampton and his Orchestra	V	Hollywood	Victor	25674	09682-2
11/19/37	Bill Coleman et son Orchestre	–	Paris	Swing	14	OLA-1980-1
05/15/38	Spencer Trio	V	New York City	Decca	1941	63782-A
08/31/38	Pee Wee Russell's Rhythmakers	–	New York City	Hot Record Society	1000	23391-1
08/31/38	Pee Wee Russell's Rhythmakers	–	New York City	Hot Record Society	17	23391-2
10/05/38	Vic Lewis and his American Jazz men	V	New York City	Esquire	10-246	M-7-296
01/31/39	Jimmie Lunceford and his Orchestra	V	New York City	Vocalion/OKeh	4667	24051-2
05/18/39	Don Redman and his Orchestra	V	New York City	Victor	26266	036964-1
06/15/39	Louis Armstrong and his Orchestra	V	New York City	Decca	2729	65824-A
02/15/40	Ella Fitzgerald and her Orchestra	V	New York City	Decca	3186	67195-A
01/08/41	Sidney Bechet and his New Orleans Feetwarmers	–	New York City	Victor	27386	058778-1

Basin Street Blues

Date	Performer	Vocal	Place	Label	Issue	Matrix
12/04/28	Louis Armstrong and his Orchestra	V	Chicago	OKeh	8690	402154-A
03/13/29	Fletcher Henderson and his Orchestra	V	New York City	Columbia	rejected	148065-1-2-3
06/11/29	Louisiana Rhythm Kings	V	New York City	Vocalion	15815	E-30030
02/09/31	Charleston Chasers	V	New York City	Columbia	2415-D	151292-2

Date	Performer	Vocal	Place	Label	Issue	Matrix
07/09/31	Cab Calloway and his Orchestra	V	New York City	Banner	32237	10728-2
07/32	Joel Shaw and his Orchestra	–	New York City	Crown	3362	1778-1
08/09/32	Paul Whiteman's Rhythm Boys	–	New York City	Victor	rejected	73180-1
09/21/32	The Three Keys	–	New York City	Brunswick	6423	B-12341-A
01/27/33	Louis Armstrong and his Orchestra	V	Chicago	Victor	24351	75103-1
08/23/34	Dorsey Brothers Orchestra	V	New York City	Decca	118	38412-A
08/23/34	Dorsey Brothers Orchestra	V	New York City	Decca	118	38412-B
01/22/35	Nat Gonella and his Georgians	V	London	Parlophone	F-117	CE-6809-1
01/29/35	KXYZ Novelty Band	–	San Antonio	Bluebird	B-5832	87766-1
03/15/35	Al Bowlly	V	New York City	Victor	25007	89330-1
05/17/35	Louis Prima and his New Orleans Gang	V	New York City	Brunswick	7456	B-17615-1
11/22/35	Benny Goodman and his Orchestra	V	Chicago	Victor	25258	96503-1
04/21/36	Milt Herth	–	Chicago	Decca	rejected	90695
05/08/36	Wingy Manone and his Orchestra	V	New York City	Bluebird	B-6411	101573-1
05/16/36	Billy Cotton's Cotton Pickers	–	London	Regal Zonophone	MR-2119	CAR-4069-1
06/11/36	Milt Herth	–	Chicago	Decca	1344	90767-A
07/03/36	"T" Toll's Swingtown Five	V	London	Parlophone	R-2280	CE-7721-1
07/07/36	The Ballyhooligans	–	London	His Master's Voice	BB-5089	OEA-3829-1
09/28/36	Scott Wood and his Six Swingers	V	London	Columbia	FB-1520	CA-15944-1
03/05/37	Joe Daniels and his Hotshots	–	London	Parlophone	F-760	CE-8213-1
06/11/37	Fats Waller	–	New York City	Victor	25631	010654-1
09/25/37	Bing Crosby	V	Los Angeles	Decca	1483	DLA-971-A
10/18/37	Willie Lewis and his Orchestra	–	Paris	Pathe Actuelle	PA-1297	CPT-3479-1
10/19/38	Vic Lewis and his American Jazz Men	–	New York City	Esquire	10-241	M-7-301
39	Andy Anderson's Pelican State Jazz Band	–	New Orleans	Mono	MNLP-12-B	–
01/20/39	Hickory House Jam Session	V	New York City	Jazz Panorama	LP-9	–
06/08/39	J. C. Higginbotham Quintet	–	New York City	Blue Note	7	GM-532-B
11/11/40	Henry Levine's Barefoot Dixieland Philharmonic	–	New York City	Victor	27304	057617-1
11/15/40	Lew Stone and his Stone-Crackers	V	London	Decca	F-7685	DR-5112-1
c 08/42	Teddy Weatherford	V	Calcutta	Columbia	FB-40225	CEI-22183-1

Beale Street

Date	Performer	Vocal	Place	Label	Issue	Matrix
08/13/17	Earl Fuller's Jazz Band	–	New York City	Victor	18369	20505-2
03/19	Synco Jazz Band	–	New York City	Arrow	504	–
c 09/19	Handy's Memphis Blues Band	–	New York City	Lyratone	4211	–
05/24/20	Herb Wiedoeft's Cinderella Roof Orchestra	–	Los Angeles	Brunswick	2795	A-109
10/14/20	Billy Arnold's Novelty Band	–	Hayes, Middlesex	His Master's Voice	rejected	HO-5922ae
11/20	Al Bernard	V	New York City	Brunswick	2062	4605
01–02/21	Ray Miller's Black and White Melody Boys	–	New York City	OKeh	4274	7751-B
03/23	Esther Bigeou	V	New York City	OKeh	8058	71374-B

Date	Performer	Vocal	Place	Label	Issue	Matrix
04/19/23	Ted Lewis and his Band	–	New York City	Columbia	A-3972	80979-3
06/26/24	George Olsen and his Music	–	New York City	Victor	rejected	30326-1-2-3
10/14/25	Eddie Peabody	–	New York City	Banner	1646	6239-2
12/27/26	University Six	–	New York City	Harmony	414-H	143222-3
03/16/27	Jack Linx and his (Birmingham) Society Serenaders	–	Atlanta	OKeh	40803	80544-A
c 04/25/27	Al Bernard	V	New York City	Brunswick	3547	E-22634
05/20/27	Fats Waller	–	Camden, NJ	Victor	20890	38047-1
05/20/27	Alberta Hunter [w/Fats Waller]	V	Camden, NJ	Victor	20771	38046-2
06/07/27	Boyd Senter	–	New York City	OKeh	40836	80987-A
06/08/27	Ted Lewis and his Band	–	New York City	Columbia	1050-D	144262-2-3
06/10/27	Jelly Roll Morton's Red Hot Peppers	–	Chicago	Victor	20948	38661-1
06/10/27	Jelly Roll Morton's Red Hot Peppers	–	Chicago	Victor	XLVA-3028	38662-2
07/26/27	California Ramblers	–	New York City	Banner	6048	7406-2
c 09/27	[Novelty Blue Boys] Wabash Trio	V	New York City	Grey Gull/Radiex	1479	2646-B
04/05/29	Original Memphis Five	V	New York City	Vocalion	15805	E-29580
c 06/29	[Grey Gull studio band] Atlanta Syncopators	–	New York City	Madison	50015	–
10/03/29	Mal Hallett and his Orchestra	–	New York City	Edison Diamond Disc	rejected	N-1178
10/29/29	Boyd Senter and his Senterpedes	–	New York City	Victor	22303	57034-3
c 11/29?	Atlanta Syncopators	–	New York City	Madison	50015	125-A-B
05/30	Paul Estabrook	–	Chicago	Brunswick	4801	C-5739-A
c 09/30	Gil Rodin and his Orchestra	V	New York City	Crown	3017	1010-2
02/09/31	Charleston Chasers	V	New York City	Columbia	2415-D	151293-3
02/12/31	Ben Pollack and his Orchestra	V	New York City	Banner	rejected?	10422-1-2-3
03/02/31	Ben Pollack and his Orchestra	V	New York City	Banner	32463	10422-4-5
10/22/31	Joe Venuti-Eddie Lang and their All Star Orchestra	V	New York City	Vocalion	15864	E-37269-A
03/29/35	Nat Gonella and his Georgians [medley]	V	London	Parlophone	F-148	CE-6906-1
06/01/35	Bob Crosby and his Orchestra	V	New York City	Decca	479	39565-A
07/15/36	Joe Daniels and his Hotshots	–	London	Parlophone	F-576	CE-7767-1
03/18/37	Scott Wood and his Six Swingers	–	London	Columbia	FB-1666	CA-16296-1
05/26/37	Tommy Dorsey and his Orchestra	–	New York City	Victor	36207	010345-2
07/15/37	Jan Savitt and his Top Hatters	–	New York City	Vri	rejected	M-252-1-2
06/19/39	Wingy Manone and his Orchestra	V	New York City	Bluebird	B-10401	037730-1
11/01/39	Jack Teagarden and his Orchestra	V	New York City	Columbia	35323	26243-A
12/26/39	W. C. Handy's Orchestra	–	New York City	Varsity	8163	US-1225-1
10/15/40	Benny Carter and his Orchestra	V	New York City	OKeh	6001	28877-1
05/22/41	Lew Stone and his Stone-Crackers	–	London	Decca	rejected	DR-5788-1-2
06/25/41	[Henry Levine] Dixieland Jazz Group of NBC . . .	V	New York City	Victor	27543	066145-1

Blue Skies

Date	Performer	Vocal	Place	Label	Issue	Matrix
01/17/27	Don Voorhees and his Earl Carroll Vanities Orchestra	V	New York City	Edison Diamond Disc	51919	11444
06/25/35	Benny Goodman and his Orchestra	–	New York City	Victor	25136	92522-2
02/05/36	Roy Eldridge and his Orchestra	–	Chicago	Decca	rejected	90601-A
01/30/37	Mario "Harp" Lorenzi and his Rhythmics	V	London	Columbia	FB-1665	CA-16178-1
04/11/37	Bob Pope and his Orchestra	–	Birmingham, AL	American Record Corp.	7-06-16	B-118-2
05/18/37	Artie Shaw and his New Music	–	New York City	Brunswick	7907	B-21169-1
08/02/37	Dixieland Swingsters	–	Charlotte, NC	Bluebird	B-7258	011854-1
08/06/37	Maxine Sullivan	V	New York City	Vocalion/OKeh	3679	21475-2
08/10/37	Earl Hines and his Orchestra	V	Chicago	Jazz Archives	2	C-1979-1
09/07/37	Edgar Hayes Quintet	–	New York City	Decca	1684	62574-A
01/16/38	Benny Goodman and his Orchestra	–	New York City	Columbia	A-1049	–
01/09/39	Chick Webb and his Orchestra	–	New York City	Polydor	423248	–
04/07/39	Paul Whiteman's Sax Soctette	–	New York City	Decca	2698	65362-A
08/10/39	John Kirby and his Orchestra	–	New York City	Vocalion/OKeh	5187	24996-A
10/23/39	Royal Rhythm Boys	–	New York City	Decca	7759	66466
02/22/40	Philippe Brun and his Jam Band	–	Paris	Swing	190	OSW-112-1
03/40	Sonny Dunham	–	New York City	Varsity	8234	US-1426-1
06/27/41	Willie Lewis Presents	–	Zurich	Elite Special	4081	1928
07/15/41	Tommy Dorsey and his Orchestra	V	New York City	Victor	27566	066923-1
12/21/41	Cyril Blake and his Jig's Club Band	V	London	Regal Zonophone	MR-3623	CAR-6240-1
c 02/42	Mel Powell and his Orchestra	–	New York City	Commodore	543	76988-A
03/12/42	Jimmy Dorsey and his Orchestra	–	New York City	Decca	18385	70484-A

Body and Soul

Date	Performer	Vocal	Place	Label	Issue	Matrix
03/30	Elsie Carlisle	V	London	Dominion	C-307	1713-1-3
03/12/30	Spike Hughes and his Decca-Dents	V	London	Decca	F-1703	MB-1056-1
09/13/30	Leo Reisman and his Orchestra	V	New York City	Victor	rejected	62370-8-9-10-11
09/19/30	Leo Reisman and his Orchestra	V	New York City	Victor	22537	62370-13
10/07/30	Annette Hanshaw	V	New York City	Harmony	1224-H	150863-5
10/09/30	Louis Armstrong and his Orchestra	V	Los Angeles	OKeh	41468	404411-D
10/10/30	Leo Reisman and his Orchestra	V	New York City	Victor	22537	62370-17
10/30/30	Seger Ellis	V	New York City	OKeh	41467	404516-C
04/29/35	Henry Allen and his Orchestra	V	New York City	Vocalion	2965	17396-1
07/13/35	Benny Goodman Trio	–	New York City	Victor	25115	92705-1
12/05/35	Joe Paradise and his Music	V	London	Parlophone	F-427	CE-7343-1
02/26/37	Art Tatum and his Swingsters	–	Los Angeles	Decca	1197	DLA-724-A
04/22/37	Quintette of the Hot Club of France	–	Paris	His Master's Voice	B-8598	OLA-1710-1
01/16/38	Benny Goodman Trio	–	New York City	Columbia	A-1049	–
05/31/38	Larry Adler	–	Paris	Columbia	DF-2427	CL-6716

Date	Performer	Vocal	Place	Label	Issue	Matrix
11/11/38	Chu Berry and his "Little Jazz" Ensemble	–	New York City	Commodore	1502	23701-1
06/23/39	Jimmy Dorsey and his Orchestra	V	New York City	Decca	2735	65880-A
10/11/39	Coleman Hawkins	–	New York City	Bluebird	B-10253	042936-1
11/29/39	Clarence Profit Trio	–	New York City	Columbia	35378	26308-A
02/15/40	Raymond Scott and his Orchestra	–	New York City	Columbia	rejected	26520-A-B
02/26/40	Earl Hines	–	New York City	Bluebird	B-10642	047700-1
02/29/40	Billie Holiday	V	New York City	Vocalion/OKeh	5481	26573-A
10/01/40	Duke Ellington and Jimmy Blanton	–	Chicago	Victor	27406	153505-3
04/09/41	Stephane Grappelly and his Quartet	–	London	Decca	F-8128	DR-5581-1
04/11/41	Teddy Wilson	–	Chicago	Columbia	36634	CCO-3694-1
06/27/41	Willie Lewis and his Negro Band	–	Zurich	Elite Special	4080	1925
07/17/41	Jimmy Noone Quartet	–	Chicago	Swaggie	S-1226 (LP)	–
09/09/41	Henry Levine and his Dixieland Octet . . .	V	New York City	Victor	27623	067761-1

Bugle Call Rag

Date	Performer	Vocal	Place	Label	Issue	Matrix
03/22	Ford Dabney's Syncopated Orchestra	–	New York City	Paramount	20125	1018-3
08/29/22	New Orleans Rhythm Kings	–	Richmond, IN	Gennett	4967	11181-B
05/23	Albert E. Short and his Tivoli Syncopators	–	New York City	Vocalion	14658	11436
c 08/23	[Jimmy Joy] Jimmy's Joys	–	Los Angeles	Golden	B-1865	G-1863
03/30/23	Frank Westphal and his Orchestra	–	Chicago	Columbia	A-3872	80919-1
c 05/07/23	Joseph Samuels and his Orchestra	–	New York City	Banner	1229	5162-2
08/02/23	Abe Lyman Orchestra	–	New York City	Brunswick	2481	11116/9
10/23/24	Tar Heels Jazz Orchestra	–	Camden, NJ	Victor	rejected	21357-1-2
02/13/26	Bud Lincoln and his Orchestra	–	Camden, NJ	Victor	test	–
11/22/26	Ted Lewis and his Band	–	Chicago	Columbia	826-D	142950-4
03/03/27	Red Nichols and his Five Pennies	–	New York City	Brunswick	3490	E-21718; E-4643
03/16/27	Jack Linx and his (Birmingham) Society Serenaders	–	Atlanta	OKeh	rejected	80546-A-B-C
c 06/27	Arthur Briggs' Savoy Syncop's Orchestra	–	Berlin	Vox	8470	1537-BB
01/09/28	[Duke Ellington] The Washingtonians	–	New York City	Harmony	577-H	145490-3
c 11/23/28	Mills' Musical Clowns	–	New York City	Cameo	9035	3562
c 11/23/28	Mills' Musical Clowns	–	New York City	Pathe Actuelle	36945	108515-2
05/09/29	Jack Pettis and his Pets	–	New York City	Victor	V-38105	51694-2
05/22/29	Eddie Lang and his Orchestra	–	New York City	OKeh	41410	401958-C
06/25/29	Reuben "River" Reeves and his River Boys	V	Chicago	Vocalion	1297	C-3697
12/31/30	Chocolate Dandies	–	New York City	Columbia	2543-D	404598-B; 151823
09/23/31	Cab Calloway and his Orchestra	V	New York City	Brunswick	6196	E-37220-A
02/09/32	Duke Ellington and his Famous Orchestra	–	New York City	Victor	22938	71839-1

Date	Performer	Vocal	Place	Label	Issue	Matrix
04/18/32	Billy Banks and his Orchestra	–	New York City	Banner	32459	11716-1
04/18/33	Spike Hughes and his Negro Orchestra	–	New York City	Decca	F-3606	B-13260-A
05/06/33	Cambridge University Quinquaginta Ramblers	–	London	Parlophone	PO-20	CE-6055-1
05/17/33	Harry Roy and his Orchestra	–	London	Parlophone	R-1526	CE-6073-1
05/19/33	Billy Cotton and his Band	–	London	Regal Zonophone	MR-958	CAR-1981-1
11/18/33	Jack Hylton and his Orchestra	–	London	Decca	F-3764	GB-6351-2
06/34	Herman Chittison	–	Paris	Brunswick	A-500438	1249wpp
08/16/34	Benny Goodman and his Music Hall Orchestra	–	New York City	Columbia	2958-D	CO-15644-1
09/19/34	Candy and Coco	–	Los Angeles	Vocalion	2849	LA-211-A
01/29/35	KXYZ Novelty Band	–	San Antonio	Bluebird	B-5852	87767-1
03/27/35	Zutty [Singleton] and his Band	–	Chicago	Decca	465	C-9883-A
06/06/35	[Benny Goodman] Rhythm Makers Orchestra	–	New York City	NBC Thesaurus	165	92214-1
07/02/35	Jimmy Grier and his Orchestra	–	Los Angeles	Brunswick	7528	LA-1052-A
08/06/35	Arthur Young and his Youngsters [medley]	–	London	Decca	F-5645	TB-1856-1
10/09/35	Ray Noble and his Orchestra	–	New York City	Victor	25223	95190-1
11/19/35	Rhythm Rascals	–	London	Crown	89	H-319
12/30/35	Ballyhooligans	–	London	His Master's Voice	BD-5013	OEA-2661-1
06/04/36	Bob Howard [medley]	–	London	Brunswick	02230	TB-2212-1
06/10/36	Casa Loma Orchestra	–	New York City	Decca	869	61157-A
08/21/36	Benny Goodman and his Orchestra	–	Hollywood	Victor	LPM-10022 (LP)	97751-2
08/26/36	Benny Carter with Kai Ewans' Orchestra	–	Copenhagen	His Master's Voice	X-4698	OCS-436-2
09/30/36	Don Redman and his Orchestra	–	New York City	American Record Corp.	6-12-18	19982-1
10/07/36	Nat Gonella and his Georgians	–	London	Parlophone	F-569	CE-7867-1
11/05/36	Benny Goodman and his Orchestra	–	New York City	Victor	25467	02460-1
03/10/37	Hudson-DeLange Orchestra	–	New York City	Mas	125	M-213-1
03/17/37	Roly's Tap Room Gang [Adrian Rollini]	–	New York City	Vri	rejected	M-270-1-2
07/06/37	Benny Goodman and his Orchestra	–	Hollywood	Columbia	ML-4591	–
07/07/37	Dicky Wells and his Orchestra	–	Paris	Swing	6	OLA-1884-1
03/03/38	Joe Daniels and his Hotshots	–	London	Parlophone	F-1077	CE-8983-1
03/29/38	Ray Ventura and his Orchestra	–	Paris	Pathe Actuelle	PA-1582	CM-184-1
07/17/39	Bobby Hackett and his Orchestra	–	New York City	Vocalion/OKeh	5375	WM-1050-A
01/16/40	George Wettling's Chicago Rhythm Kings	–	New York City	Decca	18044	67060-A
07/23/40	Rex Stewart's Big Seven	–	New York City	Hot Record Society	2005	76398-A
01/16/41	Metronome All Stars	–	New York City	Victor	27314	060331-1
07/24/42	Count Basie and his All-American Rhythm Section	–	Hollywood	Columbia	36709	HCO-875-1

China Boy

Date	Performer	Vocal	Place	Label	Issue	Matrix
c 05/26	Purple Pirates Orchestra	–	New York City	Paramount	none	2528-2
12/08/27	McKenzie and Condon's Chicagoans	–	Chicago	OKeh	41011	82031-B
c 02/28	Charles Pierce and his Orchestra	–	Chicago	Paramount	12619	20400-3
03/31/28	Princeton Triangle Club Jazz Band	–	New York City	Columbia	115-P	170301-2
05/03/29	Paul Whiteman and his Orchestra	–	New York City	Columbia	1945-D	148404-4
07/02/29	Henry Lange and his Baker Hotel Orchestra	–	Chicago	Brunswick	rejected	C-3765-A-B
07/19/29	Henry Lange and his Baker Hotel Orchestra	–	Chicago	Brunswick	4478	C-3902
07/02/30	Red Nichols and his Five Pennies	–	New York City	Brunswick	4877	E-33306-A
08/27/31	Gene Kardos and his Orchestra	V	New York City	Victor	22790	70190-1
11/10/31	Jack Teagarden and his Orchestra	–	New York City	Meritt	6	10976-1
32	French Hot Boys	–	Paris	Salabert	3166	SS-872-B
07/26/32	Pickens Sisters	V	New York City	Victor	24355	73123-1
07/29/33	King's Jesters	–	Chicago	Bluebird	B-5184	75981-1
c 12/33	Garland Wilson	–	Paris	Brunswick	A-500358	5748bdp
02/23/34	Frankie Trumbauer and his Orchestra	–	New York City	Brunswick	6912	B-14848-A
05/10/34	Isham Jones and his Orchestra	–	New York City	Victor	24649	82515-1
08/31/34	Isham Jones and his Orchestra	–	New York City	Decca	443	38503-A
09/19/34	Candy and Coco	–	Los Angeles	Vocalion	2849	LA-209-A
10/21/35	Stephane Grappelly and his Hot Four	–	Paris	Decca	F-5824	2081hpp
10/24/35	Mike Riley, Eddie Farley and their Onyx Club Boys	–	New York City	Decca	rejected	60108
10/28/35	Brian Lawrance and his Lansdowne House Sextet	V	London	Decca	rejected	TB-2016-1-2
11/14/35	Brian Lawrance and his Lansdowne House Sextet	V	London	Decca	F-5762	TB-2016-3
12/16/35	Freddy Gardner	–	London	Parlophone	R-2153	CE-7302-1
02/15/36	Locke Brothers Rhythm Section	V	Charlotte, NC	Bluebird	B-6332	99150-1
04/24/36	Benny Goodman Trio	–	Chicago	Victor	25333	100395-1
07/07/36	Ballyhooligans	–	London	His Master's Voice	BD-5117	OEA-3826-1
07/21/36	Milt Herth	–	Chicago	Decca	rejected	90802
c 10/36	Bond Street Swingers	–	London	Octacros	1301	5966
03/26/37	Bogan's Birmingham Busters	V	Birmingham, AL	Vocalion	03540	B-40-1
04/23/37	Teddy Hill and his NBC Orchestra	–	New York City	Bluebird	B-6941	07930-1
07/02/37	Nat Gonella and his Georgians [medley]	V	London	Parlophone	F-832	CE-8457-1
07/06/37	Joe Daniels and his Hotshots	–	London	Parlophone	F-924	CE-8475-1
11/12/37	Scott Wood and his Six Swingers [medley]	V	London	Columbia	FB-1832	CA-16698-1
11/18/37	Gene Austin	V	Los Angeles	Decca	1656	DLA-1097-C
01/16/38	Benny Goodman Trio	–	New York City	Columbia	A-1049	–
11/05/38	Jam Session at St. Regis	–	New York City	Jazz Panorama	LP-9	–
01/27/39	Teddy Wilson	–	New York City	Teddy Wilson School	none	P-24025
01/30/39	Danny Polo and his Swing Stars	–	Paris	Decca	F-7126	4863hpp

Date	Performer	Vocal	Place	Label	Issue	Matrix
06/26/39	Glenn Hardman and his Hammond Five	–	Chicago	Columbia	35341	WC-2636-A
07/19/39	Bud Freeman and his Summa Cum Laude Orchestra	–	New York City	Bluebird	B-10386	038293-1
10/11/39	Jimmy McPartland and his Orchestra	–	Chicago	Decca	18042	91833-A
03/40	Frankie Trumbauer and his Orchestra	–	New York City	Varsity	8215	US-1402-1
03/28/40	Bechet-Spanier Big Four	–	New York City	Hot Record Society	2001	2776-1
03/28/40	Bechet-Spanier Big Four	–	New York City	Hot Record Society	Dividend	2776-2
04/11/41	Teddy Wilson	–	Chicago	Columbia	36634	CCO-3688-2

Chinatown, My Chinatown

Date	Performer	Vocal	Place	Label	Issue	Matrix
01/11/28	Art Gillham	V	New York City	Columbia	1619-D	145505-3
02/05/29	Red Nichols and his Five Pennies	–	New York City	Brunswick	4363	E-29222
10/03/30	Fletcher Henderson and his Orchestra	–	New York City	Columbia	2329-D	150857-1
11/03/31	Louis Armstrong and his Orchestra	V	Chicago	OKeh	41534	405059-4
01/28/32	Roane's Pennsylvanians	V	New York City	Victor	22919	71287-1
05/06/33	Cambridge University Quinquaginta Ramblers	–	London	Parlophone	PO-19	CE-6053-1
09/28/33	[Dave Rose] Hotcha Trio	V	Chicago	Bluebird	B-5296	77034-1
08/17/34	Georgia Washboard Stompers	V	New York City	Decca	7005	38346
09/17/34	Casa Loma Orchestra	–	New York City	Decca	199	38677-A
12/18/34	Six Swingers [medley]	–	London	Regal Zonophone	MR-1675	CAR-3124-1
05/10/35	Ray Noble and his Orchestra	–	New York City	Victor	LPV-536	88966-1
05/17/35	Louis Prima and his New Orleans Gang	V	New York City	Brunswick	7456	B-17613-1
06/10/35	Ray Noble and his Orchestra	–	New York City	Victor	25070	88966-4
08/14/35	Joe Kennedy and his Rhythm Orchestra	V	San Antonio	Bluebird	B-6233	94511-1
09/30/35	Stephane Grappelly and his Hot Four	–	Paris	Decca	rejected	2010hpp
10/35	Stephane Grappelly and his Hot Four	–	Paris	Decca	rejected	2037hpp
11/06/35	Joe Daniels and his Hotshots	–	London	Parlophone	F-322	CE-7241-1
06/04/36	Bob Howard [medley]	–	London	Brunswick	02239	TB-2215-2
04/26/37	Lionel Hampton	–	New York City	Victor	25586	07866-1
01/19/38	Slim [Gaillard] and Slam [Stewart]	V	New York City	Vocalion	rejected	22319-1-2
02/17/38	Slim [Gaillard] and Slam [Stewart]	V	New York City	Vocalion	4021	22319-5
07/11/38	Tommy Dorsey and his Orchestra	–	Hollywood	Victor	26023	019428-1
02/09/39	Scott Wood and his Six Swingers	–	London	Columbia	FB-2179	CA-17347-1
01/28/41	Kid Punch Miller Trio	–	Chicago	Paramount	CJS-102 (LP)	–
06/19/41	Willie Lewis Presents	V	Zurich	Elite Special	4072	1897

Clarinet Marmalade

Date	Performer	Vocal	Place	Label	Issue	Matrix
07/17/18	Original Dixieland Jazz Band	–	New York City	Victor	18513	22066-2
c 05/07/19	James Reese Europe's 369th Infantry Band	–	New York City	Pathe	22167	67668

Date	Performer	Vocal	Place	Label	Issue	Matrix
07/17/23	New Orleans Rhythm Kings	–	Richmond, IN	Gennett	5220	11540
07/17/23	New Orleans Rhythm Kings	–	Richmond, IN	Gennett	5220	11540-A
10/24	Jimmy Joy's St. Anthony Hotel Orchestra	–	Dallas	OKeh	40329	8755-A
06/25	Merritt Brunies and his Friars Inn Orchestra	–	Chicago	Autograph	624	817
12/08/26	Fletcher Henderson and his Orchestra	–	New York City	Vocalion	1065	E-4182/3; E-20988/0
01/21/27	The Emperors	–	New York City	Harmony	362-H	143336-2
02/04/27	Frankie Trumbauer and his Orchestra	–	New York City	OKeh	40772	80392-A
02/07/27	Phil Napoleon and his Orchestra	–	New York City	Victor	20647	37745-2
03/22/27	Phil Napoleon and his Orchestra	–	New York City	Edison	52021	11595
06/22/27	Fred Elizalde and his Cambridge Undergraduates	–	Hayes, Middlesex	His Master's Voice	B-5315	Bb-11051-2
09-08/27	Fred Elizalde and his Orchestra	–	London	Brunswick	120	–
11/27	New Yorkers Tanzorchester	–	Berlin	Tri-Ergon	TE-5136	MO-1167
c 04/20/28	Berlyn Baylor Orchestra	–	Richmond, IN	Gennett	6457	13651
c 04/20/28	Berlyn Baylor Orchestra	–	Richmond, IN	Champion	16422	13651-A
07/16/28	Ted Lewis and his Band	–	New York City	Columbia	1573-D	146643-4
11/15/28	Lud Gluskin Ambassadonians	–	Paris	Pathe	X-8584	N-8932
c 12/29	Bill Carlsen and his Orchestra	–	Grafton, WI	Paramount	20797	L-55-2
12/06/29	The Eight Heels [medley]	–	Chicago	Victor	test	321
03/19/31	Fletcher Henderson and his Orchestra	–	New York City	Columbia	2513-D	151441-2
12/18/31	Casa Loma Orchestra	–	New York City	Banner	32551	E-37473-A
02/18/32	Red Nichols and his Five Pennies	–	New York City	Brunswick	6266	B-11314-A
c 08/32	Joel Shaw and his Orchestra	–	New York City	Crown	3383	1854-3
03/27/35	Zutty [Singleton] and his Band	–	Chicago	Decca	432	C-9884-A
09/02/36	Nick LaRocca and the Original Dixieland Band	–	New York City	Victor	25411	0305-1
09/25/36	Original Dixieland Five	–	New York City	Victor	rejected	0495-1
11/10/36	Original Dixieland Five	–	New York City	Victor	25525	0495-2
04/21/37	Joe Marsala's Chicagoans	–	New York City	Vri	rejected	M-415-1-2
05/11/37	Harry Roy and his Orchestra	–	London	Parlophone	F-1133	CE-8356-1
11/23/37	Benny Goodman and his Orchestra	–	New York City	Columbia	48329	–
08/01/39	Drummer Man Johnny Williams and his Boys	–	New York City	Vocalion	5213	24954-A
01/25/40	Bobby Hackett and his Orchestra	–	Los Angeles	Vocalion/OKeh	5493	LA-2126-B
08/21/40	Henry "Kid" Rena's Jazz Band	–	New Orleans	Delta	805	805
01/13/41	Bud Jacobson's Jungle Kings	–	Chicago	Signature	rejected	–
03/09/41	Bud Jacobson's Jungle Kings	–	Chicago	Signature	903	1608
03/09/41	Bud Jacobson's Jungle Kings	–	Chicago	Signature	106	1612
10/01/41	Fats Waller and his Rhythm	–	New York City	Bluebird	B-11469	067951-1

Copenhagen

Date	Performer	Vocal	Place	Label	Issue	Matrix
05/06/24	Wolverine Orchestra	–	Richmond, IN	Gennett	5453	11853
09/24	Sammy Stewart and his Orchestra	–	Chicago	Paramount	20359	1891-1-2
09/08/24	Benson Orchestra of Chicago	–	Camden, NJ	Victor	19470	30781-3
09/15/24	Charlie Fry and his Million-Dollar Pier Orchestra	–	New York City	Edison Diamond Disc	51406	9709
c 10/24	International Dance Orchestra	–	New York City	Grey Gull/ Globe/Radiex	1251	3540-A
c 10/24	Al Turk's Princess Orchestra	–	New York City?	Olympic	1461	B-1641
10/24	Kitty Irvin	V	Chicago	Gennett	5592	616
10/18/24	Russo and Fiorito's Oriole Orchestra	–	Chicago	Brunswick	2752	14017
10/22/24	Varsity Eight	–	New York City	Cameo	622	1186-C
c 10/23/24	New Orleans Jazz Band	–	New York City	Banner	1445	5680-1
c 10/23/24	New Orleans Jazz Band	–	New York City	Apex	8272	5680-2
10/23/24	California Ramblers	–	New York City	Columbia	236-D	140115-1
10/30/24	Fletcher Henderson and his Orchestra	–	New York City	Vocalion	14926	13928/9
11/10/24	Five Birmingham Babies	–	New York City	Pathe Actuelle	036169	105655-B
11/19/24	The Arkansas Travelers	–	New York City	OKeh	40236	72980-C
01/21/25	Savoy Orpheans	–	Hayes, Middlesex	His Master's Voice	B-1954	Bb-5644-2
06/25	Alex Hyde m. sein New Yorker Original-Jazz Orchester	–	Berlin	Deutsche Grammo- phone/Polydor	20250	2012at
08/25	Julian Fuhs Follies Band	–	Berlin	Homochord	B-1877	M-17958
09/20/29	Elmer Schoebel and his Friars Society Orchestra	–	Chicago	Brunswick	rejected	C-4381-A-B
10/18/29	Elmer Schoebel and his Friars Society Orchestra	–	Chicago	Brunswick	4652	C-4559-D
10/29/29	Boyd Senter and his Senterpedes	–	New York City	Victor	rejected	57032-1-2-3
11/25/29	Boyd Senter and his Senterpedes	–	New York City	Victor	22303	57032-5
09/13/34	Earl Hines and his Orchestra	–	Chicago	Decca	337	C-9474-A
07/30/35	Ambrose and his Orchestra	–	London	Decca	F-5696	TB-1839-1
06/10/36	Casa Loma Orchestra	–	New York City	Decca	1048	61153-A
12/23/36	Artie Shaw and his Orchestra	–	New York City	Brunswick	7827	B-20449-1
02/19/37	Artie Shaw and his Orchestra	–	New York City	Thesaurus	377	06233-1
07/25/38	Tommy Dorsey and his Orchestra	–	Hollywood	Victor	26016	019443-2
10/18/38	Eddie DeLange and his Orchestra	–	New York City	Bluebird	B-10027	028118-1
11/17/38	Artie Shaw and his Orchestra	–	New York City	Bluebird	B-10054	028978-1
12/12/39	Al Donahue and his Orchestra	–	New York City	Vocalion	5314	26328-A
04/04/40	Bud Freeman and his Summa Cum Laude Orchestra	–	New York City	Decca	18064	67480-A
09/12/41	Sid Phillips Quintet	–	London	Decca	F-9446	DR-6232-1

Coquette

Date	Performer	Vocal	Place	Label	Issue	Matrix
03/02/28	Paul Whiteman and his Orchestra	–	New York City	Victor	21301	43125-1
03/02/28	Paul Whiteman and his Orchestra	–	New York City	Victor	25675	43125-3

Date	Performer	Vocal	Place	Label	Issue	Matrix
03/14/28	Dorsey Brothers' Orchestra	V	New York City	OKeh	41007	400144-B
04/11/28	Seger Ellis	V	New York City	OKeh	41024	400606-C
07/02–11/28	Fred Elizalde and his Music	–	London	Brunswick	188	–
01/31/36	Bill Coleman et son Orchestre	–	Paris	His Master's Voice	K-7705	OLA-852-1-2
02/25/36	Boots and his Buddies	–	San Antonio	Bluebird	B-6307	99361-1
09/08/36	Erskine Hawkins and his 'bama State Collegians	V	New York City	Vocalion	3318	19823-1
06/15/37	Jimmie Lunceford and his Orchestra	V	New York City	Decca	1340	62259-A
07/30/37	Teddy Wilson and his Orchestra	–	Los Angeles	Brunswick	7943	LA-1383-A
11/13/37	Bob Crosby's Bob Cats	–	Los Angeles	Decca	1756	DLA-1062-A
05/04/38	Willie Lewis and his Orchestra	–	Hilversum	Panachord	H-1038	AM-485-3
01/27/39	Teddy Wilson	–	New York City	Teddy Wilson School	none	P-24024-1-2
06/21/39	Red Nichols and his Orchestra	–	New York City	Bluebird	rejected	037669-1
04/29/40	Joe Sullivan and his Cafe Society Orchestra	–	New York City	OKeh	5647	26779-A
07/09/40	John Kirby and his Orchestra	–	New York City	Columbia	35999	28003-A
08/13/40	Horace Henderson and his Orchestra	–	Chicago	OKeh	5841	WC-3274-A
c 12/02/40	Jay McShann Combo	–	Wichita, KS	Spotlite	SJ-120	–
06–09/41	John Kirby and his Orchestra	–	New York City	Collector's	12-11 (LP)	–
04/17/42	Louis Armstrong and his Orchestra	V	Los Angeles	Decca	4327	DLA-2976-A
04/28/42	George Shearing	–	London	Ace of Clubs	1161 (LP)	DR-6801

The Darktown Strutters' Ball

Date	Performer	Vocal	Place	Label	Issue	Matrix
01/30/17	Original Dixieland Jazz Band	–	New York City	Columbia	A-2297	77086-3-4
05/09/17	Six Brown Brothers	–	Camden, NJ	Victor	18376	19847-2
c 08/17	[Ford] Dabney's Band	–	New York City	Aeolian Vocalion	1204	–
c 08/17	[Ford] Dabney's Band	–	New York City	Aeolian Vocalion	1219	–
09/28/18	Savoy Quartet	–	Hayes, Middlesex	His Master's Voice	B-991	HO-4425ae
09/28/18	Wilbur Sweatman's Jazz Orchestra	–	New York City	Columbia	A-2596	77856-3
03/03–07/19	Lt. Jim Europe's 369th Infantry Band	–	New York City	Pathe	22081	67475
06/21	Brown and Terry's Jazzola Boys	–	New York City	OKeh	8006	7980-A
03/07/27	Miff Mole's (Little) Molers	–	New York City	OKeh	40784	80502-A
03/23/27	Ted Lewis and his Band	V	New York City	Columbia	1084-D	143708-2
c 04/09/28	Jungle Kings	–	Chicago	Paramount	12654	20564-2
05/28	Fred Elizalde and his Hot Music	–	London	Brunswick	177	574-3
12/12/29	Coon-Sanders Orchestra	V	Chicago	Victor	22352	57254-2
06/30/31	Mound City Blue Blowers	V	New York City	OKeh	41526	404994-A
10/13/31	Spike Hughes and his Orchestra	–	London	Decca	rejected	GB-3435-1-2
10/21/31	Spike Hughes and his Orchestra	–	London	Decca	F-2611	GB-3435-4
c 03/10/32	Joel Shaw and his Orchestra	V	New York City	Crown	3319	1702-1
07/26/32	Pickens Sisters	V	New York City	Victor	24355	73122-1
12/20/33	Chick Webb's Savoy Orchestra	–	New York City	CBS	CL-2689 (LP)	152659-2
01/15/34	Chick Webb's Savoy Orchestra	–	New York City	Columbia	CB-754	152659-4

Date	Performer	Vocal	Place	Label	Issue	Matrix
05/23/34	Boswell Sisters	V	New York City	Columbia	DO-1255	B-15255-A
08/08/34	Luis Russell and his Orchestra	V	New York City	Banner	33179	15571-1
09/19/34	Tiny Bradshaw and his Orchestra	V	New York City	Decca	194	38695-A
06/06/35	[Benny Goodman] Rhythm Makers Orchestra	–	New York City	NBC Thesaurus	123	92213-1
07/01/35	Six Swingers	V	London	Regal Zonophone	MR-1784	CAR-3506-1
07/10/35	Paul Whiteman and his Orchestra	V	New York City	Victor	25192	92593-1
10/28/35	Brian Lawrence and his Lansdowne House Sextet	V	London	Decca	rejected	TB-2014-1-2
11/14/35	Brian Lawrence and his Lansdowne House Sextet	V	London	Decca	F-5852	TB-2014-3
01/24/36	Darktown Strutters	V	London	His Master's Voice	BD-5038	OEA-2680-1
02/36	Chick Webb and his Orchestra	V	New York City	Jazz Archives	33 (LP)	–
02/28/36	Louis Prima and his New Orleans Gang	V	Los Angeles	Brunswick	7657	LA-1102-A
11/19/36	Ella Fitzgerald and her Savoy Eight	V	New York City	Decca	1061	61422-B
02/27/37	Phil Harris and his Orchestra	V	Los Angeles	Vocalion	3565	LA-1259
11/03/37	Benny Goodman and his Orchestra	–	New York City	Columbia	ML-4591	–
04/29/38	Jimmy Dorsey and his Orchestra	V	New York City	Decca	1939	6369-A
05/24/39	Andre Ekyan et son Orchestre	–	Paris	His Master's Voice	FELP-1120	OSW-75
05/26/39	Jack Hylton and his Orchestra	–	London	His Master's Voice	BD-5550	OEA-7953-1
11/03/39	Fats Waller and his Rhythm	V	New York City	Bluebird	B-10573	043350-1
01/16/40	George Wettling's Chicago Rhythm Kings	–	New York City	Decca	Y-5615	67062-A
01/16/40	George Wettling's Chicago Rhythm Kings	–	New York City	Decca	18045	67062-B
04/04/40	Joe Daniels and his Hotshots	–	New York City	Parlophone	F-1721	CE-10434-1
08/02/41	Royal Air Force Dance Orchestra	–	London	Decca	rejected	DR-6087-1-2
09/13/41	Royal Air Force Dance Orchestra	–	London	Decca	F-7968	DR-6087-3
11/27/41	Sid Phillips Quintet	–	London	Decca	F-9446	DR-6498-1
01/15/42	Benny Goodman and his Orchestra	–	New York City	Columbia	36699	CO-32241-1
01/15/42	Benny Goodman and his Orchestra	–	New York City	V-Disc	205	CO-32241-2
c 05/42	Teddy Weatherford	–	Calcutta	Columbia	FB-40164	CEI-22064-1

Dear Old Southland

Date	Performer	Vocal	Place	Label	Issue	Matrix
12/05/21	James P. Johnson's Harmony Eight	–	New York City	OKeh/Apex	4504	70350-B
05/24/28	The Original Wolverines	V	Chicago	Vocalion	15708	C-1972- ; E-7354
05/31/28	Red Nichols and his Five Pennies	V	New York City	Brunswick	20070	XE-27621-
05/31/28	Red Nichols and his Five Pennies	–	New York City	Brunswick	A-5081	XE-27621-G
04/05/30	Louis Armstrong	–	New York City	OKeh	41454	403895-A
05/18/31	Garland Wilson	–	New York City	Columbia	Special	230205-1
12/04/33	Duke Ellington and his Orchestra	V	Chicago	Victor	24501	77199-1
12/22/33	Gene Austin	V	New York City	Banner	33172	14400-3
06/06/35	[Benny Goodman] Rhythm Makers Orchestra	–	New York City	NBC Thesaurus	126	92220-1

Date	Performer	Vocal	Place	Label	Issue	Matrix
06/25/35	Benny Goodman and his Orchestra	–	New York City	Victor	25136	92523-1
07/19/35	Washboard Serenaders	V	London	Parlophone	F-229	CE-7109-1
06/23/36	Dick McDonough and his Orchestra	V	New York City	American Record Corp.	6-09-08	19468-1
04/14/37	Noble Sissle and his Orchestra	–	New York City	CBS	CL-2102	M-400-2
04/19/37	Erskine Hawkins and his 'bama State Collegians	–	New York City	Vocalion	3567	21003-1
12/14/37	Benny Goodman and his Orchestra	–	New York City	MGM	E/X-3788	–
02/24/38	Casa Loma Orchestra	–	New York City	Decca	rejected	63340-A-B
06/14/38	Coleman Hawkins Trio	–	Hilversum	Panachord	H-1047	AM-489-2
04/05/39	Oscar Aleman Trio	V	Paris	Swing	213	OSW-70-1
03/20/40	Sidney Bechet's Blue Note Quartet	–	New York City	Blue Note	13	710-A
05/14/41	Duke Ellington	–	New York City	Victor	27564	065604-2
12/31/41	Metronome All-Stars	–	New York City	CBS	CL-2528	32080-1
07/17/42	Art Hodes	–	New York City	B & W	rejected	–

Diga Diga Doo

Date	Performer	Vocal	Place	Label	Issue	Matrix
07/10/28	Duke Ellington and his Orchestra	V	New York City	OKeh	8602	400859-B
07/27/28	[Irving Mills] Hotsy Totsy Gang	V	New York City	Brunswick	4014	E-27092-A
07/27/28	[Irving Mills] Hotsy Totsy Gang	–	New York City	Brunswick	A-7850	E-27092-G
11/15/28	Duke Ellington and his Cotton Club Orchestra	V	New York City	Victor	V-38008	48167-2
11/27/28	Sizzlers	–	New York City	Edison Diamond Disc	rejected	N-598
11/27/28	Sizzlers	–	New York City	Edison Diamond Disc	52463	18903
04/07/29	Jack Hylton and his Orchestra	V	London	His Master's Voice	B-5638	BR-2330-3
05/23/29	Three Blue Boys	–	New York City	Victor	rejected	53435-1-2
06/11/29	The Rhythmic Eight	–	Hayes, Middlesex	Zonophone	5383	Yy-16581-1
07/20/29	Philip Lewis and his Dance Orchestra	V	London	Decca	F-1512	DJ-2-1
12/22/32	Mills Brothers [w/Ellington Orchestra]	V	New York City	Brunswick	6519	B-12781-A
02/17/33	Duke Ellington and his Famous Orchestra [medley]	–	New York City	Brunswick	6516	B-13080-B
02/21/34	The Three Scamps	V	New York City	Victor	rejected	81730-1
06/06/35	[Benny Goodman] Rhythm Makers Orchestra	–	New York City	NBC Thesaurus	127	92219-1
06/15/36	Frankie Trumbauer and his Orchestra	–	New York City	Brunswick	7687	B-19443-1
03/08/37	Cootie Williams and his Rug Cutters	–	New York City	Vri	555	M-187-1
04/29/37	Benny Goodman Quartet	–	New York City	MGM	E/X-3788	–
10/19/38	Bob Crosby and his Orchestra [2 parts]	–	Chicago	Decca	2275	91538-A; 91539-A
12/28/38	Van Alexander and his Orchestra	–	New York City	Bluebird	B-10102	030768-1
09/28/39	Adrian Rollini Trio	–	Hollywood	Vocalion/OKeh	5376	WM-1086-A
11/11/39	Artie Shaw and his Orchestra	–	New York City	Victor	LPT-6000	–
c 03/40	Ella Fitzgerald and her Orchestra	V	New York City	Jazz Trip	5 (LP)	–
c 05/40	Art Hodes' Blue Three	–	New York City	Signature	102	1603

Date	Performer	Vocal	Place	Label	Issue	Matrix
07/23/40	Rex Stewart's Big Seven	–	New York City	Hot Record Society	2004	76399-A
c 03/14/41	George Hartman and his Orchestra	–	New Orleans	Keynote	K-601	GH-1-A

Dinah

Date	Performer	Vocal	Place	Label	Issue	Matrix
10/13/25	Al Handler and his Alamo Cafe Orchestra	V	Richmond, IN	Gennett	rejected	12367, -A
10/20/25	Ethel Waters	V	New York City	Columbia	487-D	141164-2
12/25	Cliff Edwards	–	New York City	Pathe Actuelle	025164	106434
01/04/26	Clarence Williams' Stompers	–	New York City	OKeh	40541	73894-B
01/06/26	Fletcher Henderson and his Orchestra	–	New York City	Vocalion	15204	E-2049
01/28/26	Jean Goldkette and his Orchestra	–	New York City	Victor	19947	34369-1
02/26	Louise Hegamin	V	New York City	Cameo	877	1812-C
c 02/01/26	Bailey's Lucky Seven	V	New York City	Gennett	3243	9954-B
c 02/05/26	Mike Speciale and his Orchestra	V	New York City	Pathe Actuelle	36388	106611
03/26	Noble Sissle-Eubie Blake	V	London	Edison Bell Winner	4402	9937
09/27/26	Bobby Leecan	–	New York City	Victor	test	–
03–04/27	Julian Fuhs und sein Orchester	–	Berlin	Electrola	EG-439	BW-805-2
03/28/28	Joe Venuti's Blue Four	–	New York City	OKeh	41025	400178-A
07/03/28	Peggy Hill	V	Chicago	Victor	V-40042	46045-1
04/18/29	Red Nichols and his Five Pennies	–	New York City	Brunswick	4373	E-29709-A
01/24/30	Ted Lewis and his Band	V	New York City	Columbia	2181-D	149911-4
05/04/30	Louis Armstrong and his Orchestra	V	New York City	OKeh	8800	404001-C
05/23/30	Spike Hughes and his Dance Orchestra	–	London	Decca	rejected	MB-1394-1
07/23/30	Fess Williams and his Royal Flush Orchestra	V	New York City	Victor	rejected	63302-1-2
07/31/30	Fess Williams and his Royal Flush Orchestra	V	Camden, NJ	Victor	23005	63302-4
01/02/31	Williams' Purple Knights	–	New York City	Victor	22625	67752-2
02/02/31	The Red Devils	–	New York City	Columbia	14586-D	151260-1
12/16/31	Bing Crosby	V	New York City	Brunswick	6240	E-37467-A
02/09/32	Duke Ellington and his Orchestra	V	New York City	Victor	22938	71838-1
c 03/10/32	Joel Shaw and his Orchestra	V	New York City	Crown	3319	1699-1
04/05/32	Frankie Trumbauer and his Orchestra [medley]	V	New York City	Columbia	18002-D	255004-1
04/13/32	Billy Banks	V	New York City	Victor	test	1129
05/03/32	Eddie Edinborough and his Washboard Band	V	New York City	Vocalion	1702	11768-A
06/07/32	Cab Calloway and his Orchestra	V	New York City	Banner	32483	11910-2
c 09/32	Lud Gluskin and his Orchestra	–	Paris	Pathe	none	301627
11/20/32	Spike Hughes and his Orchestra	–	London	Decca	F-3399	GB-5216-1
12/21/32	Louis Armstrong and his Orchestra [medley]	V	Camden, NJ	Victor	36084	74877-3
06/01/33	Washboard Rhythm Kings	V	Camden, NJ	Bluebird	B-5127	76240-1
06/01/33	Washboard Rhythm Kings	V	Camden, NJ	Victor	23403	76248-1

Date	Performer	Vocal	Place	Label	Issue	Matrix
09/28/33	[Dave Rose] Hotcha Trio	V	Chicago	Bluebird	B-5296	77036-1
11/18/33	Jack Hylton and his Orchestra	V	London	Decca	F-3764	GB-6355-2
05/25/34	Monia Liter	–	London	Brunswick	01814	TB-1273-1
08/20/34	Ethel Waters	V	New York City	Decca	234	38350-C
11/02/34	Nat Gonella and his Georgians [medley]	–	London	Parlophone	R-1982	CE-6704-1
12/34	Quintette of the Hot Club of France	–	Paris	Ultraphon	AP-1422	P-77161
12/07/34	Gladys Keep	V	London	Regal Zonophone	MR-1531	CAR-3098-1
12/08/34	Pat Hyde	V	London	Parlophone	R-2050	CE-6765-1
12/13/34	Boswell Sisters	V	Los Angeles	Brunswick	7412	LA-294-A
12/18/34	Six Swingers [medley]	–	London	Regal Zonophone	MR-1567	CAR-3123-1
01/11/35	Dorsey Brothers' Orchestra	V	New York City	Decca	376	39241-A
02/01/35	Brain Lawrance and the Quaglino Quartet	V	London	Panachord	25685	GB-6921-1
03/11/35	Fats Waller	V	New York City	Victor	LPT-6001	–
06/24/35	Fats Waller and his Rhythm	V	Camden, NJ	Victor	25471-1	88989-1
09/18/35	Billy Cotton and his Band	V	London	Regal Zonophone	MR-1946	CAR-3596-1
10/09/35	Ray Noble and his Orchestra	–	New York City	Victor	25223	95191-1
11/06/35	Joe Daniels and his Hotshots	–	London	Parlophone	rejected	CE-7243-1-2
11/26/35	Ike "Yowse Suh" Hatch and his Harlem Stompers	V	London	Regal Zonophone	MR-2050	CAR-3757-1
02/05/36	Joe Daniels and his Hotshots	–	London	Parlophone	F-405	CE-7243-3
02/27/36	Rhythm Rascals	V	London	Crown	160	H-440
02/28/36	Louis Prima and his New Orleans Gang	V	Los Angeles	Brunswick	7666	LA-1103-A
06/03/36	Ballyhooligans	–	London	His Master's Voice	BD-5074	OEA-2798-1
08/26/36	Benny Goodman Quartet	–	Hollywood	Victor	25398	97772-1
09/01/36	Scott Wood and his Six Swingers [medley]	V	London	Columbia	FB-1504	CA-15895-1
09/19/36	Billy Costello	V	London	Decca	F-6100	TB-2483-1
07/12/37	Dicky Wells and his Orchestra	–	Paris	Swing	39	OLA-1895-1
09/29/37	Eddie South and his International Orchestra	–	Paris	Swing	12	OLA-2148-1
11/37	Adelaide Hall [medley]	V	Copenhagen	Tono	K-6001	D-599
11/03/37	Count Basie and his Orchestra [w/Billie Holiday]	V	Cedar Grove, NJ	Collector's Corner	9	–
12/10/37	Eddie Carroll and his Swingphonic Orchestra	–	London	Parlophone	R-2473	CE-8795-1
12/17/37	Richard Himber and his Essex House Orchestra [medley]	–	New York City	Victor	25754	017732-1
06–09/38	Roy Peyton	–	Oslo	Rex	EB-385	RP-06
08/31/38	Pee Wee Russell's Rhythmakers	–	New York City	Hot Record Society	1000	23394-1
01/09/39	Chick Webb and his Orchestra	–	New York City	Polydor	423248	–
12/12/39	Muggsy Spanier and his Ragtime Band	V	New York City	Bluebird	B-10682	045746-1
12/21/39	Lionel Hampton and his Orchestra	–	New York City	Victor	26557	046024-1
12/21/39	Lionel Hampton and his Orchestra	–	New York City	Victor	LPV-501 (LP)	046024-2
02/28/40	Jimmie Lunceford and his Orchestra [2 parts]	V	Los Angeles	Columbia	36054	LA-2164-C; LA-2165-C

Date	Performer	Vocal	Place	Label	Issue	Matrix
08/22/40	Connie Boswell	V	New York City	Decca	3425	68003-A
10/04/40	Nat Gonella and his New Georgians	V	London	Columbia	FB-2564	CA-18164-1
04/09/41	Stephane Grappelly and his Quartet	–	London	Decca	F-7865	DR-5579-1
09/11/41	Quintette of the Hot Club of France	–	Paris	Swing	146	OSW-227-1

Down Hearted Blues

Date	Performer	Vocal	Place	Label	Issue	Matrix
07/22	Alberta Hunter	V	New York City	Paramount	12005	1105-1-2-3
01/23	Monette Moore	V	New York City	Paramount	12030	5053
c 01/10/23	Eva Taylor	V	New York City	OKeh	8047	71162-C
02/15/23	Bessie Smith	V	New York City	Columbia	rejected	80863-1-2-3-4
02/16/23	Bessie Smith	V	New York City	Columbia	A-3844	80863-5
03/23	Handy's Orchestra	–	New York City	OKeh	8059	71372-A
c 04/23	Mary Straine	V	Long Island City	Black Swan	14150	–
05/23	Fletcher Henderson and his Orchestra	–	New York City	Paramount	20235	1406-2-3
05–06/23	Lillian Harris	V	New York City	Banner	1224	5187-5
05/25/23	Noble Sissle-Eubie Blake	V	Camden, NJ	Victor	19086	27976-3
06/23	Lucille Hegamin	V	New York City	Cameo	381	554-A
06/07/23	Tennessee Ten	–	New York City	Victor	19094	28056-3
06/18/23	Edna Hicks	V	New York City	Brunswick	2463	10878
06/19/23	Emma Gover	V	New York City	Pathe Actuelle	021006	70232
06/28/23	Fletcher Henderson and his Orchestra	–	New York City	Vocalion	14636	11664/5
11/03/23	Savoy Havana Band	–	London	Columbia	954	AX-204
c 12/23	Hazel Meyers	V	New York City	Bell	P-255	–
08/19/26	Virginia Childs	V	New York City	Columbia	rejected	142540-1-2
11/03/26	Virginia Childs	V	Atlanta	Columbia	14175-D	143042-1
06/10/27	Boyd Senter	–	New York City	OKeh	4115	81001-B
11/18/31	Cab Calloway and his Orchestra	V	New York City	Banner	32340	11015-1
12/06/35	Mildred Bailey and her Alley Cats	V	New York City	Decca	18109	60204-A
09/01/38	Teddy Grace	V	New York City	Decca	2128	64494-A
02/28/39	Mildred Bailey and her Orchestra	V	New York City	Vocalion	4800	24181-1
08/15/39	Alberta Hunter	V	New York City	Decca	7727	66105-A

Eccentric

Date	Performer	Vocal	Place	Label	Issue	Matrix
08/29/22	Friars Society Orchestra [New Orleans Rhythm Kings]	–	Richmond, IN	Gennett	5009	11178-B
02/07/23	Original Memphis Five	–	New York City	Pathe Actuelle	020921	70048
05/31/23	Original Memphis Melody Boys	–	Chicago	Columbia	rejected	81049-1-2-3
02/23/24	Russo and Fiorito's Oriole Orchestra	–	Chicago	Brunswick	2616	70-CH
04/24	Savoy Orpheans	–	London	Columbia	3432	A-771
08/11/24	Ted Lewis and his Band	–	New York City	Columbia	195-D	81909-4
c 09/24	[Emlyn Thomas] The London Band	–	London	Vocalion	X-9500	03683

Date	Performer	Vocal	Place	Label	Issue	Matrix
10/29/24	Johnny DeDroit and his New Orleans Jazz Orchestra	–	New York City	OKeh	40240	72943-A
c 05/25	Richard Hitter's Cabineers	–	New York City	Everybody's	1062	SAH-6-2
c 05/25	Carlyle Stevenson's El Patio Orchestra	–	Los Angeles	Hollywood	1024	–
08/08/25	Benny Meroff and his Orchestra	–	Camden, NJ	Victor	rejected	33412-1-2
11/08/26	New Orleans Owls	–	Atlanta	Columbia	943-D	143115-2
08/15/27	Red Nichols and his Five Pennies	–	New York City	Brunswick	3698	E-24228
04/28	Alabama Red Peppers	–	New York City	Cameo	8205	3071-A
01/17/35	Dorsey Brothers' Orchestra	–	New York City	Design	DLP-20	–
02/06/35	Dorsey Brothers' Orchestra	–	New York City	Decca	1304	39343-C
04/24/36	Jimmy McPartland's Squirrels	–	Chicago	Hot Record Society	1004	90697-A
10/14/37	Henry Hall and his Orchestra	–	Liverpool	Columbia	FB-1818	CA-16627-1
07/07/39	Muggsy Spanier and his Ragtime Band	–	Chicago	Bluebird	B-10417	040262-1
01–03/40	Art Hodes	–	New York City	Jazz Records	1004	JR-104
06/40	Buster Bailey and his Sextet	–	New York City	Varsity	8365	US-1844-1
01/27/42	Bob Crosby and his Orchestra	–	Los Angeles	Odeon	286027	DLA-2854-A
07/42	Art Hodes	–	New York City	B & W	rejected	–

Everybody Loves My Baby

Date	Performer	Vocal	Place	Label	Issue	Matrix
09/24/24	Georgia Melodians	–	New York City	Edison Diamond Disc	51419	9734
11/06/24	Clarence Williams' Blue Five	V	New York City	OKeh	8181	72959-B
11/06/24	Alberta Hunter	V	New York City	Gennett	5594	9167
c 11/19/24	[Hal Kemp] Carolina Club Orchestra	–	New York City	Pathe Actuelle	036181	105672
11/24/24	Georgians	–	New York City	Columbia	252-D	140148-2
c 11/24/24	Clementine Smith	V	New York City	Regal	9760	5740-5
c 11/24/24	Fletcher Henderson and his Orchestra	V	New York City	Domino	3444	5748-1
c 11/24/24	Fletcher Henderson and his Orchestra	–	New York City	Banner	1471	5748-3
c 11/25/24	Goofus Five	–	New York City	OKeh	40244	72998-C
01/25	Gloria Geer	V	New York City	Emerson	10831	2-2540
01/25	Fletcher Henderson and his Orchestra	V	New York City	Paramount	rejected	1995-1-2
01/25	Original Memphis Five	V	New York City	Paramount	12249	1995-4-6
c 01/06/25	Lou Gold and his Orchestra	–	New York City	Cameo	678	1312-B
02/16/25	Tennessee Tooters	–	New York City	Vocalion	14985	373/5
02/17/25	Gene Rodemich and his Orchestra	–	Chicago	Brunswick	2843	14967
03/04/25	George Olsen and his Music	–	New York City	Victor	19610	32050-3
04/25	Leslie Jeffries and his Rialto Orchestra	V	London	Aco	G-15689	C-7014
04–05/25	Corona Dance Orchestra	–	London	Regal	G-8383	A-2056
c 07/25	The Stomp Six	–	Chicago	Autograph	626	829
02/13/29	Earl Hines and his Orchestra	V	Chicago	Victor	V-38042	48884-3
12/12/30	Spike Hughes and his Orchestra	–	London	Decca	F-2166	GB-2388-1
05/23/31	Taylor's Dixie Orchestra	V	Charlotte, NC	Victor	23277	69344-1
02/24/32	Boswell Sisters	V	New York City	Columbia	36520	B-11354-A-B
11/28/32	Red Nichols and his Orchestra	V	Chicago	Brunswick	6461	C-8826-1

Date	Performer	Vocal	Place	Label	Issue	Matrix
08/17/34	Georgia Washboard Stompers	V	New York City	Decca	7002	38338-A
09/13/35	Six Swingers [medley]	–	London	Regal Zonophone	MR-1909	CAR-3588-1
10/28/35	Brian Lawrance and his Lansdowne House Quartet	V	London	Decca	rejected	TB-2017-1-2
11/14/35	Brian Lawrance and his Lansdowne House Quartet	V	London	Decca	F-5852	TB-2017-3
03/21/36	Sharkey's [Bonano] New Orleans Boys	V	New Orleans	Decca	1014	60842-A
09/05/37	Lionel Hampton and his Orchestra	V	Hollywood	Victor	25682	09683-2
10/19/37	Benny Goodman Quartet	–	New York City	Philips	B-21208-H	–
08/31/38	Pee Wee Russell's Rhythmakers	–	New York City	Hot Record Society	1002	23396-1-2
12/19/38	Mezzrow-Ladnier Quintet	–	New York City	Bluebird	B-10090	030451-1
12/19/38	Mezzrow-Ladnier Quintet	–	New York City	Victor	X LVA-3027	030451-2
06/08/39	Milt Herth Trio	V	New York City	Decca	2632	65752-A
11/06/40	Fats Waller and his Rhythm	V	New York City	Bluebird	B-10989	05783-1

Exactly Like You

Date	Performer	Vocal	Place	Label	Issue	Matrix
03/28/30	Seger Ellis	V	New York City	OKeh	41424	403886-A
04/15/30	Casa Loma Orchestra	V	New York City	Parlophone	PNY-34070	403960-A
04/15/30	Casa Loma Orchestra	–	New York City	Odeon	ONY-36076	490062-A
04/23/30	Sam Lanin and his Orchestra	V	New York City	Banner	0688	9637-1-2-3
05/04/30	Louis Armstrong and his Orchestra	V	New York City	OKeh	41423	404000-B
06/27/30	Rhythmic Eight	–	Hayes, Middlesex	Zonophone	5649	Yy-19484-2
08/26/36	Benny Goodman Trio	–	Hollywood	Victor	25406	97773-1
03/26/37	Count Basie and his Orchestra	V	New York City	Decca	1252	62078-A
04/13/37	Kay Thompson and her Orchestra	V	New York	Victor	25582	07788-1
04/21/37	Quintette of the Hot Club of France	–	Paris	His Master's Voice	B-8629	OLA-1702-1
05/19/37	Gus Arnheim and his Orchestra	–	New York City	Brunswick	7904	21175-1
05/28/37	Don Redman and his Orchestra	V	New York City	Vri	580	M-506-1
06/09/37	Nat Gonella and his Georgians	V	London	Parlophone	F-809	CE-8415-2
c 09/13/37	Les Brown and his Orchestra	–	New York City	Thesaurus	444	013396-1
10/04/37	Alix Combelle et son Orchestre	–	Paris	Swing	52	OLA-1955-1
09/22/38	Ken "Snakehips" Johnson and his West Indian Dance Orchestra	V	London	Decca	F-6854	DR-2937-1
11/30/38	Bud Freeman Trio	–	New York City	Commodore	513	75960-A
12/12/38	Louis Prima and his New Orleans Gang	V	Los Angeles	Decca	2279	DLA-1638-A
06/26/39	Glenn Hardman and his Hammond Five	–	Chicago	Vocalion	4971	WC-2637-A
06/28/39	Teddy Wilson and his Orchestra	–	New York City	Columbia	35220	B-24827-A
c 07/40	Harry James and his Orchestra	–	New York City	Varsity	8411	US-1891-
10/04/40	Eddy Howard	V	New York City	Columbia	35915	28796-1
12/13/40	Quintette of the Hot Club of France	–	Paris	Swing	118	OSW-147-1
09/04/41	Ella Logan	V	Hollywood	Columbia	rejected	H-501-1
03/02/42	Lionel Hampton and his Orchestra	V	New York City	Brunswick	87526-LPBM (LP)	70419-A

Farewell Blues

Date	Performer	Vocal	Place	Label	Issue	Matrix
08/29/22	Friars Society Orchestra [New Orleans Rhythm Kings]	–	Richmond, IN	Gennett	4966	11179-C
12/22–01/23	Lada's Louisiana Orchestra	–	New York City	Emerson	10598	42327-1
01/23	Isham Jones and his Orchestra	–	New York City	Brunswick	2406	9768
02/07/23	Original Memphis Five	–	New York City	Pathe Actuelle	020920	70047
02/12/23	Joseph Samuels and his Orchestra	–	Montreal	Banner	1181	741
02/20/23	Virginians	–	New York City	Victor	19032	27609-2
02/28/23	Original Memphis Five	–	New York City	Arto	9210	–
03/23	Gene Fosdick's Hoosiers	–	New York City	Vocalion	14535	11025
03/23	Gene Fosdick's Hoosiers	–	New York City	Beltona	312	11026
03/07/23	Georgians	–	New York City	Columbia	A-3864	80887-1-4
04/23	Henderson's Dance Players	–	New York City	Black Swan	2125	574
05/23	Handy's Orchestra	–	New York City	OKeh	4880	71575-B
05/23	Hannah Sylvester	V	New York City	Paramount	12033	1408-1-2-3
c 05/04/23	Eva Taylor	V	New York City	OKeh	3055	71499-A
c 05/17–18/23	Eva Taylor	V	New York City	OKeh	3055	71499-F
07/20/23	Genevieve Stearns	V	Richmond, IN	Gennett	rejected	11558, -A
07/31/23	Nina Reeves	V	Richmond, IN	Gennett	none	11563-C
11/03/23	Savoy Havana Band	–	London	Columbia	953	AX-201
05/25	Alex Hyde m. sein New Yorker Original-Jazz Orchester	–	Berlin	Deutsche Grammophon/Polydor	20234	1946at
02/18/26	Gus Mulcay	–	New York City	Victor	test	–
06/18/26	Gus Mulcay	–	New York City	Harmony	408-H	142317-1
08/20/26	Virginia Childs	V	New York City	Columbia	rejected	142547-1-2-3
02/08/27	Goofus Five	–	New York City	OKeh	40767	80402-B
02/25/27	Charleston Chasers	–	New York City	Columbia	1539-D	143533-1
07/26/27	California Ramblers	–	New York City	Banner	6048	7408-3
10/14/27	King Oliver and his Dixie Syncopators	–	New York City	Vocalion	rejected	E-6669/70
11/18/27	King Oliver and his Dixie Syncopators	–	New York City	Vocalion	1152	E-6806; E-25352
02/03/28	Varsity Eight	–	New York City	Cameo	8141	2859-C
c 02/28	Devine's Wisconsin Roof Orchestra	–	Chicago	Paramount	20651	20392-1
03/28/28	Waring's Pennsylvanians	V	New York City	Victor	21508	43187-3
05/16/29	Campus Cut-Ups	–	New York City	Edison Diamond Disc	11049	N-898
05/16/29	Campus Cut-Ups	–	New York City	Edison Diamond Disc	21508	19194
08/21/29	Ted Lewis and his Band	–	New York City	Columbia	2029-D	148930-3
01/31/30	Mills' Merry Makers	–	New York City	Velvet	7121-V	149955-2
01/31/30	Mills' Merry Makers	–	New York City	IAJRC	2 (LP)	149955-3
03/09/31	Cab Calloway and his Orchestra	V	New York City	Banner	32152	10483-1-3
10/22/31	Joe Venuti-Eddie Lang and their All-Star Orchestra	–	New York City	Vocalion	15858	E-37271-A
05/02/32	Abe Lyman and his Orchestra	–	New York City	Brunswick	6314	B-11765-A
08/17/34	Georgia Washboard Stompers	V	New York City	Decca	7003	38339-B
01/09/35	Duke Ellington and his Famous Orchestra	–	Chicago	FDC	1003 (LP)	C-884-2

Date	Performer	Vocal	Place	Label	Issue	Matrix
06/06/35	[Benny Goodman] Rhythm Makers Orchestra	–	New York City	NBC Thesaurus	125	92212-1
07/05/35	Clyde McCoy and his Orchestra	–	Chicago	Rex	9933	C-90078-A
07/24/35	Nat Gonella and his Georgians	V	London	Parlophone	F-209	CE-7085-1
08/06/35	Arthur Young and his Youngsters [medley]	–	London	Decca	F-5709	TB-1859-1
09/07/35	Paul Whiteman and his Orchestra	–	New York City	Victor	25192	94192-1
c 11/35	Claude Hopkins and his Orchestra	–	New York City	Polydor	423269	–
12/20/35	Delta Four	–	New York City	Decca	737	60271-A
01/20/36	Duke Ellington and his Orchestra	–	Chicago	Columbia	rejected	C-1198-1
07/03/36	T. Toll's Swingtown Five	–	London	Parlophone	R-2267	CE-7720-1
12/17/36	Dude Skiles and his Vine Street Boys	–	Hollywood	Vri	584	L-0368
07/06/37	Joe Daniels and his Hotshots	–	London	Parlophone	F-294	CE-8476-1
03/07/38	Benny Carter and his Orchestra	–	Paris	Swing	36	OSW-5-1
11/23/38	Benny Goodman and his Orchestra	–	New York City	Victor	26095	030308-1
05/24/39	Woody Herman and his Orchestra	–	New York City	Decca	2582	65637-A
06/19/39	Wingy Manone and his Orchestra	–	New York City	Bluebird	B-10401	037732-1
11/15/40	Lew Stone and his Stone-Crackers	–	London	Decca	F-7698	DR-5115-2
12/40	Art Hodes' Columbia Quintet	–	New York City	Jazz Records	1003	HS-1205
08/11/41	Henry Levine and his Dixieland Octet . . .	–	New York City	Victor	27625	067549-1
07/24/42	Count Basie and his All-American Rhythm Section	–	Hollywood	Columbia	36712	HCO-877-1

Georgia on My Mind

Date	Performer	Vocal	Place	Label	Issue	Matrix
09/15/30	Hoagy Carmichael and his Orchestra	V	New York City	Victor	23013	63653-1
04/10/31	Frankie Trumbauer and his Orchestra	V	Chicago	Brunswick	rejected	C-7693-
06/10/31	Gene Kardos and his Orchestra	V	New York City	Timely Tunes	C-1581	69924-
06/24/31	Frankie Trumbauer and his Orchestra	V	Chicago	Brunswick	6159	C-7879-A
06/30/31	Mound City Blue Blowers	V	New York City	OKeh	41515	404966-C
09/23/31	Washboard Rhythm Kings	V	Camden, NJ	Victor	23301	70534-1
11/05/31	Louis Armstrong and his Orchestra	V	Chicago	OKeh	41541	405063-3
11/24/31	Mildred Bailey	V	Chicago	Victor	22891	70624-1
02/04/32	Roy Fox and his Band	V	London	Decca	F-2804	GB-3923-3
12/26/34	Joe Venuti and his Orchestra [medley]	–	New York City	London	HMG-5023 (LP)	–
10/06/35	Nat Gonella and his Georgians [medley]	V	London	Parlophone	F-356	CE-7194-1
01/24/36	Bill Coleman	V	Paris	Ultraphon	AP-1235	77625
02/25/36	Boots and his Buddies	–	San Antonio	Bluebird	B-6301	99363-1
07/16/36	Joe Paradise and his Music	V	London	Parlophone	F-580	CE-7735-1
10/15/36	Quintette of the Hot Club of France	V	Paris	His Master's Voice	K-7790	OLA-1292-1
07/19/37	Nat Gonella and his Georgians	V	London	Parlophone	F-853	CE-8507-1
03/15/39	Casa Loma Orchestra	–	New York City	Decca	2399	65183-A
08/15/39	Ethel Waters	V	New York City	Bluebird	B-11028	041554-2

Date	Performer	Vocal	Place	Label	Issue	Matrix
01/21/41	Nat Gonella and his New Georgians	V	London	Columbia	FB-2570	CA-18293-1
03/12/41	Gene Krupa and his Orchestra	V	New York City	OKeh	6118	29922-1
03/14/41	Mildred Bailey	V	New York City	Decca	3691	68819-A
03/20/41	Artie Shaw and his Orchestra	–	New York City	Victor	27499	062768-1
03/21/41	Billie Holiday	V	New York City	OKeh	6134	29988-1
05/13/41	Fats Waller	–	New York City	Victor	27765	063887-1
02/04/42	Henry Levine and his Strictly from Dixie Jazz Band	V	New York City	Victor	27830	071765-1

A Good Man Is Hard to Find

Date	Performer	Vocal	Place	Label	Issue	Matrix
c 12/18	Louisiana Five	–	New York City	Emerson	7481	–
c 12/18	Louisiana Five	–	New York City	Emerson	9158	3441-2
02/06/19	Wilbur Sweatman's Original Jazz Band	–	New York City	Little Wonder	1091	–
02/06/19	Wilbur Sweatman's Original Jazz Band	–	New York City	Columbia	A-2721	78292-2
09/16/19	Savoy Quartet	–	Hayes, Middlesex	His Master's Voice	B-1061	HO-5234ae
c 02/20	Selvin's Novelty Orchestra	–	New York City	Emerson	10133	4888-2
c 12/15/24	Nettie Potter	V	New York City	Banner	1483	5786-1
c 09/16/27	The Red Heads	–	New York City	Pathe Actuelle	36701	107782-1-2
09/27/27	Bessie Smith	V	New York City	Columbia	14250-D	144797-3
10/12/27	Original Wolverines	–	Chicago	Brunswick	3708	C-1303
10/25/27	Frankie Trumbauer's Augmented Orchestra	–	New York City	OKeh	40966	81571-B
11/01/27	Victoria Spivey	V	New York City	OKeh	8565	81599-A
11/03/27	Viola McCoy	V	New York City	Cameo	rejected	–
01/25/28	Frank Winegar and his Penn. Boys	–	Orange, NJ	Edison Diamond Disc	rejected	18191-A-B-C
02/29/28	Lizzie Miles	V	New York City	Conqueror	7185	7822- -3
03/22/28	Ted Lewis and his Band	V	New York City	Columbia	1428-D	145798-4
08–09/28	Bill Haid and his Cubs	V	Chicago	Paramount	20658	20829-1
09/11/31	Snooks and his Memphis Ramblers	V	New York City	Victor	22812	70225-1
01/28/35	The Wanderers	V	San Antonio	Bluebird	B-5834	87733-1
08/20/36	Wingy Manone and his Orchestra	V	New York City	Bluebird	B-6537	0221-1
01/19/39	Fats Waller	V	New York City	Bluebird	B-10143	031530-1
01/19/39	Fats Waller	V	New York City	RFW	3 (LP)	031530-2
07/12/39	Louis Prima and his New Orleans Gang	V	New York City	Decca	2660	65952-A
11/30/39	Jess Stacy and his Orchestra	–	New York City	Varsity	8140	US-1113-2
03/24/40	Jam Session at Commodore [4 parts]	–	New York City	Commodore	1504; 1505	76329–32-A
07/20/42	Les Brown and his Orchestra	V	Hollywood	Columbia	36688	HCO-859-1

Hallelujah!

Date	Performer	Vocal	Place	Label	Issue	Matrix
04/13/27	Cass Hagan and his Hotel Manger Orchestra	V	New York City	Columbia	966-D	144026-2-4

Date	Performer	Vocal	Place	Label	Issue	Matrix
05/03/27	California Ramblers	V	New York City	Edison Diamond Disc	52014	11681
06/27/27	Art Kahn and his Orchestra	V	New York City	Parlophone	E-5936	81114-B
07/15/27	Noble Sissle	V	New York City	OKeh	40859	81172-C
c 10–11/27	Arthur Briggs' Savoy Syncop's Orchestra	V	Berlin	Deutsche Grammophone/Polydor	21034	599bd
01/10/28	The Devillers	–	London	Regal	G-9049	WA-6789-1-2
c 10/24/29	Sam Wooding and his Orchestra	V	Paris	Pathe	X-8696	300481-1
01/24/30	Red Nichols and his Five Pennies	–	New York City	Brunswick	4701	E-31904-
03/11/35	Fats Waller	–	New York City	Victor	LPT-6001	–
11/29/36	Fats Waller and his Rhythm	V	Chicago	Victor	25478	01801-1
11/29/36	Fats Waller and his Rhythm	–	Chicago	Victor	25489	01802-1
11/02/37	Chick Webb and his Little Chicks	–	New York City	Decca	rejected	62743-A-B
12/07/37	Benny Goodman and his Orchestra	–	New York City	MGM	E/X-3789	–
12/17/37	Chick Webb and his Little Chicks	V	New York City	Decca	15039	62889-A
06/13/39	Fats Waller	–	London	His Master's Voice	rejected	OEA-7884-1-2
08/07/39	Fats Waller and his Rhythm	–	New York City	Ember	CJS-839	–
09/12/39	Teddy Wilson and his Orchestra	–	New York City	Columbia	35298	26060-A
11/22/39	Will Bradley and his Orchestra	–	New York City	Columbia	35333	25588-1
06/01/40	Tommy Dorsey and his Orchestra	–	New York City	Victor	LPM-6003	–
08/19/41	Tommy Dorsey and his Orchestra	–	New York City	Victor	27591	067655-1
02/27/42	Hazel Scott	–	New York City	Decca	18342	70413-A
08/20/42	Stephane Grappelly and his Quintet	–	London	Decca	rejected	DR-6931-1-2

High Society

Date	Performer	Vocal	Place	Label	Issue	Matrix
05/06/11	Prince's Band	–	New York City	Columbia	A-1038	19337-1
01–02/20	Benny Peyton's Jazz Kings	–	London	Columbia	rejected	–
06/22/23	King Oliver's Jazz Band	–	Chicago	OKeh	4933	8393-B
c 02/01/24	[Oliver] Naylor's Seven Aces	–	New York City	Gennett	5392	8740,-A
c 09/24	Jelly Roll Morton's Kings of Jazz	–	Chicago	Autograph	606	636
12/28	Monk Hazel and his Bienville Roof Orchestra	–	New Orleans	Brunswick	4181	NO-748-A
07/02/29	Clarence Williams' Washboard Band	–	New York City	OKeh	8706	404289-A
07/02/29	Clarence Williams' Washboard Band	–	New York City	OKeh	8706	404289-C
07/23/30	Clarence Williams and his Jazz Kings	–	New York City	Columbia	14555-D	150569-2
05/02/32	Abe Lyman and his Orchestra	–	New York City	Brunswick	6325	B-11766-A
08/30/32	Gene Kardos and his Orchestra	–	New York City	Melotone	M-12491	12225-1
09/09/32	Gene Kardos and his Orchestra	–	New York City	Melotone	rejected?	12225-
01/26/33	Louis Armstrong and his Orchestra	–	Chicago	Victor	24232	74895-1
06/16/33	Clarence Williams' Jug Band	–	New York City	Vocalion?	rejected	13473-
06/16/33	Clarence Williams' Jug Band	–	New York City	Vocalion?	rejected	13474-
07/14/33	Clarence Williams and his Orchestra	–	New York City	Vocalion	25010	13546-1
08/07/33	Clarence Williams' Jug Band	V	New York City	Columbia	2806-D	152466-2
08/07/33	Clarence Williams' Jug Band	V	New York City	Columbia	2806-D	152466-3

Date	Performer	Vocal	Place	Label	Issue	Matrix
08/17/34	Georgia Washboard Stompers	–	New York City	Decca	7002	38340-A
12/12/35	Mound City Blue Blowers	–	New York City	Champion	40103	60223-A
10/07/36	Sharkey [Bonano] and his Sharks of Rhythm	–	New York City	Vocalion	3380	20014-1
08/30/38	Bluebird Military Band	–	New York City	Bluebird	B-3201	026679-1
09/13/38	Bunny Berigan and his Orchestra	–	New York City	Victor	26068	026874-1
04/03/39	Lionel Hampton and his Orchestra	–	New York City	Victor	26209	035393-1
09/14/39	Jelly Roll Morton's New Orleans Jazzmen	–	New York City	Bluebird	B-10434	041457-1
10/02/39	Bob Crosby and his Orchestra	–	New York City	Decca	2848	66701-A
10/19/39	Jack Jenney and his Orchestra	–	New York City	Vocalion	5223	26184-A
12/39	Roy Eldridge and his Orchestra	–	New York City	Varsity	8154	US-1189-1
08/21/40	Henry "Kid" Rena's Jazz Band	–	New Orleans	Delta	804	804
01/28/41	Kid Punch Miller Trio	–	Chicago	Paramount	CJS-102 (LP)	–
03/29/42	Lu Watters' Yerba Buena Jazz Band	–	San Francisco	Jazz Man	15	MLB-129

Honeysuckle Rose

Date	Performer	Vocal	Place	Label	Issue	Matrix
02/03/30	McKinney's Cotton Pickers	V	New York City	Victor	LPM-10020	58546-1
02/03/30	McKinney's Cotton Pickers	V	New York City	Pirate	MPC-518	58546-2
04/10/31	Frankie Trumbauer and his Orchestra	V	Chicago	Brunswick	rejected	C-7695-
06/24/31	Frankie Trumbauer and his Orchestra	V	Chicago	Brunswick	6159	C-7880-A
12/09/32	Fletcher Henderson and his Orchestra	–	New York City	Columbia	2732-D	152324-1
03/09/33	Claude Hopkins and his Orchestra	–	New York City	Jazz Archive	4 (LP)	B-13135-A
09/26/33	Joe Sullivan	–	New York City	Columbia	2876-D	265139-2
05–06/34	Herman Chittison	–	Paris	Brunswick	A-500438	1224wpp
08/23/34	Dorsey Brothers Orchestra [2 parts]	V	New York City	Decca	296	38409/10-A
11/07/34	Fats Waller and his Rhythm	V	New York City	Victor	24826	84921-1
11/18/34	Coleman Hawkins	–	London	Parlophone	R-2041	CE-6742-1
11/22/34	Dick McDonough	–	New York City	CBS	AL-33457 (LP)	TO-1483-1
01/25/35	Red Norvo and his Swing Octet	–	New York City	Columbia	3059-D	CO-16703-2
03/11/35	Fats Waller	V	New York City	Victor	LPT-6001	–
04/10/35	Joe Haymes and his Orchestra	–	New York City	Bluebird	B-5920	89543-1
06/14/35	Adrian [Rollini] and his Tap Room Gang	V	New York City	Victor	25208	92267-1
12/06/35	Mildred Bailey and her Alley Cats	V	New York City	Decca	18108	60202-A
03/02/36	Putney Dandridge and his Orchestra	V	New York City	Vocalion	3190	18744-1
01/19/37	Eddie Carroll and his Swing Music	–	London	Parlophone	R-2326	CE-8045-1
01/21/37	Count Basie and his Orchestra	–	New York City	Decca	1141	61542-A
02/10/37	Earl Hines and his Orchestra	–	Chicago	Vocalion	3586	C-1819-1
02/22/37	Gerry Moore and his Chicago Brethern	–	London	Decca	F-6347	TB-2854-1
04/09/37	Fats Waller and his Rhythm	–	New York City	Victor	36206	07755-1
04/28/37	Coleman Hawkins and his All-Star Jam Band	–	Paris	Swing	1	OLA-1742-1
05/10/37	Frank Dailey and his Orchestra	–	New York City	Vri	?	M-459

Date	Performer	Vocal	Place	Label	Issue	Matrix
05/12/37	Eddie Stone and his Orchestra	–	New York City	Vocalion	3585	21126-2
07/12/37	Eric Siday	–	London	Parlophone	R-2466	CE-8497-2
07/12/37	Max Abrams and his Rhythm Makers	–	London	Parlophone	rejected	CE-8497-1
09/05/37	Teddy Wilson Quartet	–	Los Angeles	Brunswick	7964	LA-1431-A
c 10/07/37	Philippe Brun	–	Paris	His Master's Voice	rejected	OLA-1962-1-2
12/10/37	Chick Webb and his Orchestra	V	New York City	Jazz Archives	JA-33 (LP)	–
12/15/37	Artie Shaw and his New Music	–	New York City	Thesaurus	482	017810-1
01/16/38	Benny Goodman group	–	New York City	Columbia	A-1049	–
01/31/38	Quintette of the Hot Club of France	–	London	Decca	F-6639	DTB-3523-1
03/13/38	Eddie South and his Quintet	V	Hilversum	Brunswick	A-81504	AM-750
c 08/38	Jelly Roll Morton	–	Baltimore	Swaggie	S-1213 (LP)	–
c 08/38	Jelly Roll Morton	–	Baltimore	Swaggie	JCS-116 (LP)	–
10/19/38	Louis Armstrong and Fats Waller	–	New York City	Palm Club	10	–
08/07/39	Fats Waller and his Rhythm	V	New York City	Victor	RD-7552	–
11/14/39	Louis Jordan and his Tympany Five	V	New York City	Decca	7675	66872-A
11/22/39	Benny Goodman and his Orchestra	–	New York City	Columbia	35319	WCO-26290-A
05/08/40	Horace Henderson and his Orchestra	V	Chicago	Vocalion/OKeh	5579	WC-3049-A
11/07/40	Fats Waller and his Rhythm	V	New York City	RFW	2	–
12/06/40	King Cole Trio	–	Los Angeles	Decca	8535	DLA-2256-A
05/13/41	Fats Waller	–	New York City	Victor	20-1580	063890-1
07/17/41	Jimmie Noone Quartet	–	Chicago	Swaggie	S-1210	–
c 07/41	Earl Hines and his Orchestra	–	London, Ontario	Almanac	QSR-2418 (LP)	–
11/16/41	First English Public Jam Session	–	London	His Master's Voice	C-3269	2EA-9449-1
12/21/41	Fats Waller, his Rhythm and his Orchestra	V	New York City	Palm Club	13	–
42	Andy Anderson	V	New York City	Mono	MNLP-12-B	–
01/14/42	Fats Waller, his Rhythm and his Orchestra	V	New York City	Palm Club	09	–
03/25/42	Joe Daniels and his Hotshots	–	London	Parlophone	F-1939	CE-10922-1

Hot Lips

Date	Performer	Vocal	Place	Label	Issue	Matrix
c 05/22/22	Synco Jazz Band	–	New York City	Pathe Actuelle	020770	69708
06/17/22	California Ramblers	–	New York City	Vocalion	14384	9298
06/23/22	Paul Whiteman and his Orchestra	–	New York City	Victor	18920	26650-2
06/29/22	Paul Specht's Jazz Outfit	–	New York City	Banner	1090	1101-1-2
07/22	Cotton Pickers	–	New York City	Brunswick	2292	8270
c 07/22	Bobby Lee and his Music Landers	–	New York City	C & S	5012	J-112
07/19/22	California Ramblers	–	New York City	Cameo	rejected	–
08/22	Jazzbo's Carolina Serenaders	–	New York City	Cameo	257	248-A
c 08/10/22	Tampa Blue Jazz Band	–	New York City	Apex	4559	70773-B
c 08/10/22	Tampa Blue Jazz Band	–	New York City	OKeh	4663	70773-C
c 08/17/22	Bailey's Lucky Seven	–	New York City	Gennett	4935	7993-A-B
09/22	Eddie Davis and his Orchestra	–	New York City	Grey Gull	1120	633-A-C

Date	Performer	Vocal	Place	Label	Issue	Matrix
c 10/18/22	Lizzie Miles	V	New York City	OKeh	8040	70936-B
c 02/23	[Victor Vorzanger] Broadway Band	–	London	Aco	G-15162	C-5439
03/17/27	Bill Brown and his Brownies	–	New York City	Brunswick	7003	E-21989/90
06/07/27	Boyd Senter	–	New York City	OKeh	40888	80986-A
c 09/15/27	Henry Lange and his Orchestra	–	Richmond, IN	Gennett	6263	13077
c 09/15/27	Henry Lange and his Orchestra	–	Richmond, IN	Superior	306	13077-A
c 09/15/27	Henry Lange and his Orchestra	–	Richmond, IN	Gennett Special	40102	13077-B
07/15/35	Nat Gonella and his Georgians	V	London	Parlophone	F-193	CE-7063-1
12/03/36	Harry Roy and his Orchestra	V	London	Parlophone	F-624	CE-7967-1
04/22/37	Quintette of the Hot Club of France	–	Paris	His Master's Voice	B-8690	OLA-1707-1
11/12/37	Scott Wood and his Six Swingers [medley]	–	London	Columbia	FB-1832	CA-16699-1
12/17/37	Richard Himber and his Essex House Orchestra [medley]	–	New York City	Victor	25754	017732-1
06/21/39	Red Nichols and his Orchestra	–	New York City	Bluebird	B-10360	037670-1

How Come You Do Me Like You Do

Date	Performer	Vocal	Place	Label	Issue	Matrix
02/28/24	Marjorie Royce	V	New York City	OKeh	40094	72420-B
04/03/24	Rosa Henderson	V	New York City	Vocalion	14795	12971
c 05/20/24	Viola McCoy	V	New York City	Banner	1371	5509-2
c 05/21/24	Red Flame Kazoo Travelers	–	New York City	Cameo	569	1007-D
06/18/24	Edith Wilson	V	New York City	Columbia	14027-D	81831-4
c 08/19/24	Saxi Holtsworth's Harmony Hounds	V	New York City	Gennett	5530	9045-A
c 08/28/24	Jack Linx and his (Birmingham) Society Serenaders	–	Atlanta	OKeh	40192	8720-A
c 09/11/24	Original Memphis Five	–	New York City	Pathe Actuelle	036141	105548
10/01/24	Original Memphis Five	–	New York City	Victor	19480	30876-5
c 11/24	Florence Bristol	V	New York City	Up-To-Date	2019	T-2018-2
c 11/17/24	Fletcher Henderson and his Orchestra	–	New York City	Banner	1445	5728-1-2-3
12/04/24	Original Memphis Five	–	New York City	Columbia	250-D	140164-4
01/25	Fletcher Henderson and his Orchestra	V	New York City	Paramount	rejected	1996-1-2
01/25	Original Memphis Five	V	New York City	Paramount	12249	1996-6-7
01/23/25	Tennessee Tooters	–	New York City	Vocalion	14967	259
08/16/27	Original Memphis Five	–	New York City	Brunswick	3713	E-6538; E-24251
08/16/27	Original Memphis Five	–	New York City	Brunswick	3630	E-6539; E-24252
08/27/30	Red Nichols and his Five Pennies	–	New York City	Brunswick	rejected	E-34110-
12/10/30	Red Nichols and his Five Pennies	V	New York City	Brunswick	6149	E-35735-A
06/07/32	Cab Calloway and his Orchestra	V	New York City	Banner	32540	11911-1
05/19/33	Spike Hughes and his Negro Orchestra	V	New York City	Decca	F-3972	B-13363-A
04/35	Freddy Taylor and his Swing Men from Harlem	V?	Paris	Ultraphon	rejected	–
12/11/36	Milt Herth	–	Chicago	Decca	1300	91049-A
02/19/37	Artie Shaw and his Orchestra	–	New York City	Thesaurus	385	06234-1
09/11/37	Ocie Stockard and the Wanderers	–	Dallas	Bluebird	B-7459	014029-1

Date	Performer	Vocal	Place	Label	Issue	Matrix
03/02/39	George Shearing	–	London	Decca	F-7102	DR-3370-1
03/11/41	Maurice Rocco and his Rockin' Rhythm	V	Chicago	Decca	8558	93583-A

I Ain't Got Nobody

Date	Performer	Vocal	Place	Label	Issue	Matrix
06/02/19	L'Orchestre Scrap Iron Jazzerinos	–	Paris	His Master's Voice	K-1318	20539b
12/16/24	Goofus Five	V	New York City	OKeh	40261	73021-C
12/23/24	Tennessee Tooters	–	New York City	Vocalion	14952	155
06/03/25	Virginia Liston	V	New York City	OKeh	8223	73395-A
08/19/25	Bessie Smith	V	New York City	Columbia	14095-D	140858-3
09/25	Ida Cox	V	Chicago	Paramount	12334	2292-2
09/15/25	Tennessee Tooters	–	New York City	Vocalion	15135	1348
c 09/25/25	Fred Hall's Sugar Babies	–	New York City	OKeh	40496	73653-B
10/27/25	California Ramblers	–	New York City	Pathe Actuelle	36361	106353
08/02/26	University Six	–	New York City	Harmony	230-H	142492-2
04/11/27	Sophie Tucker	V	New York City	OKeh	40837	80717-C
06/10/27	Boyd Senter	–	New York City	OKeh	40861	81004-B
06/25/27	Coon-Sanders Orchestra	V	Chicago	Victor	20785	39064-2
08/04/27	Jay C. Flippen	V	New York City	Pathe Actuelle	32294	107700
08/12/27	California Ramblers	V	New York City	Banner	6082	7458-3
09–10/27	Fred Elizalde	–	London	Brunswick	138	–
09/14/27	Arkansas Travelers	–	New York City	Harmony	505-H	144669-2
10/02/27	Ray Miller and his Hotel Gibson Orchestra	V	Chicago	Brunswick	3677	C-1150
11/03/27	Viola McCoy	V	New York City	Cameo	rejected	–
c 11/11/27	Sam Lanin's Troubadours	V	New York City	Cameo	1267	2690-B
12/01/27	Fats Waller	–	Camden, NJ	Victor	21127	40094-2
02/21/28	Nat Star and his Dance Orchestra	–	Hayes, Middlesex	Homochord	D-1231	HH-12746-1
02/23/28	The Rhythmic Eight	–	Hayes, Middlesex	Zonophone	4097	Yy-12760-2
03/21/28	Bob Fuller	–	New York City	Brunswick	7006	E-22045
03/23/28	Ted Lewis and his Band	V	New York City	Columbia	1428-D	145799-3
06/12/28	Emmett Miller	V	New York City	OKeh	41062	400782-C
06/18/28	Roy Evans	V	New York City	Columbia	15272-D	146553-1
07/28	Bill Haid and his Cubs	V	Chicago	Paramount	20658	20755-1
07/02/28	Stovepipe Johnson	V	Chicago	Vocalion	1211	C-2114-
11/28	Meyer Davis Orchestra	V	New York City	Duophone	D-4020	E-28681-B
12/12/28	Earl Hines/Red McKenzie	V	Chicago	OKeh	8653	402218-A
01/18/29	Ray Miller and his Hotel Gibson Orchestra	V	Chicago	Sunny Meadows	D	XC-2826-
12/10/29	Louis Armstrong and his Orchestra	V	New York City	OKeh	8756	403493-A
01/27/30	California Ramblers	–	New York City	Edison Diamond Disc	52206	18198
01/14/31	Dave Nelson and the King's Men	V	New York City	Victor	22639	64849-2
06/10/31	Henny Hendrickson's Louisville Serenaders	V	Camden, NJ	Timely Tunes	C-1585	68228-2

Date	Performer	Vocal	Place	Label	Issue	Matrix
08/15/31	Stanley Black and his Oriole Modernists	V	London	Oriole	P-101	92
03/08/34	Coleman Hawkins	–	New York City	Parlophone	R-1825	265173-2
08/24/34	Art Tatum	–	New York City	Decca?	rejected	38428-A-B
10/03/34	Tiny Bradshaw and his Orchestra	V	New York City	Decca	456	38786-A
10/09/34	Art Tatum	–	New York City	Decca	741	38428-C
12/28/34	Lew Stone and his Band	V	London	Regal Zonophone	MR-1561	CAR-3144-1
01/28/35	The Wanderers	V	San Antonio	Bluebird	B-5869	87734-1
03/06/35	Fats Waller and his Rhythm	V	New York City	Victor	24888	88777-1
03/06/35	Fats Waller and his Rhythm	–	New York City	Victor	25026	88778-1
07/02/35	Cab Calloway and his Orchestra	V	Chicago	Brunswick	7530	C-1054-A
11/06/35	Joe Daniels and his Hot Shots	–	London	Parlophone	rejected	CE-7244-1-2
02/05/36	Joe Daniels and his Hot Shots	–	London	Parlophone	F-405	CE-7244-3
06/04/36	Bob Howard [medley]	–	London	Brunswick	02230	TB-2212-1
07/16/36	Joe Paradise and his Music	–	London	Parlophone	F-580	CE-7733-1
09/01/36	Scott Wood and his Six Swingers [medley]	–	London	Columbia	FB-1503	CA-15894-1
10/20/36	Buck and Bubbles	V	London	Columbia	FB-1561	CA-15988-1
c 02/37	Count Basie Ensemble	–	New York City	Vanguard	VRS-8524	–
06/11/37	Fats Waller	–	New York City	Victor	25631	010656-1
06/23/37	Teddy Weatherford	–	Paris	Swing	58	OLA-1876-1
08/17/37	Benny Carter and his Orchestra	–	The Hague	Brunswick	03311	AM-395-2
08/17/37	Benny Carter and his Orchestra	–	The Hague	Decca	F-42125	AM-395-1
09/21/37	Chick Webb and his Little Chicks	–	New York City	Decca	1513	62620-A
09/28/37	Wingy Manone and his Orchestra	V	New York City	Bluebird	B-7198	013880-1
11/37	Adelaide Hall [medley]	V	Copenhagen	Tono	K-6001	D-599
11/19/37	Bill Coleman et son Orchestre	–	Paris	Swing	14	OLA-1979-1
c 08/38	Jelly Roll Morton	V	Baltimore	Swaggie	S-1213 (LP)	–
02/13/39	Basie's Bad Boys	–	New York City	Tax	8000 (LP)	24510-1
01/23/40	Hot Lips Page and his Band	V	New York City	Decca	7714	67092-A
06/19/41	Willie Lewis and his Negro Band	V	Zurich	Elite Special	4071	1894-
07/30/41	Bing Crosby [w/Woody Herman's Woodchoppers]	V	Los Angeles	Decca	3971	DLA-2600-A

I Can't Believe That You're in Love with Me

Date	Performer	Vocal	Place	Label	Issue	Matrix
03/28/27	Warner's Seven Aces	V	Atlanta	Columbia	1001-D	143789-2
c 08/27	The Savile Dance Orchestra	–	London	Duophone/Aerial	UB-2127	DU-8431
04/05/30	Louis Armstrong and his Orchestra	V	New York City	OKeh	41415	403897-A
06/30/31	Mound City Blue Blowers	V	New York City	OKeh	41515	404967-B
09/14/32	Nat Gonella and his Trumpet	V	London	Decca	F-3176	GB-4888-3
08/29/35	Phil Green	–	London	Parlophone	R-2280	CE-7126-1
02/10/37	Earl Hines and his Orchestra	V	Chicago	Vocalion	3467	C-1818-2
03/08/37	Cootie Williams and his Rug Cutters	–	New York City	Vri	555	M-185-1
07/14/37	Valaida	V	London	Parlophone	F-923	CE-8492-1

Date	Performer	Vocal	Place	Label	Issue	Matrix
11/23/37	Eddie South and his Orchestra	–	Paris	Swing	31	OLA-1985-1
12/17/37	Teddy Wilson and his Orchestra	V	New York City	Brunswick	rejected	B-22195-1-2
01/06/38	Teddy Wilson and his Orchestra	V	New York City	Columbia	36335	B-22195-3
01/06/38	Teddy Wilson and his Orchestra	V	New York City	Brunswick	8070	B-22195-4
07/24/38	Artie Shaw and his Orchestra	–	New York City	Bluebird	B-7772	024084-1
05/24/39	Andre Ekyan	–	Paris	Swing	67	OSW-74-1
08/04/39	Count Basie and his Orchestra	V	New York City	Vocalion	5036	24980-A
09/28/39	Adrian Rollini Trio	–	Hollywood	Vocalion/OKeh	5621	WM-1084-A
11/30/39	Jess Stacy and his Orchestra	–	New York City	Varsity	8132	US-1112-2
05/25/40	Chocolate Dandies	–	New York City	Commodore	1506	R-2997-1
01/13/41	Bud Jacobson's Jungle Kings	–	Chicago	Signature	rejected	–
03/09/41	Bud Jacobson's Jungle Kings	–	Chicago	Signature	103	1614
07/31/41	Ella Fitzgerald and her Orchestra	V	Los Angeles	Decca	18421	DLA-2607-A
03/02/42	Lionel Hampton Sextet	–	New York City	Brunswick	87526-LPBM (LP)	70417-A

I Can't Give You Anything But Love

Date	Performer	Vocal	Place	Label	Issue	Matrix
05/24/28	The Rhythmic Eight	V	Hayes, Middlesex	Zonophone	5148	Yy-12994-2
05/26/28	Martha Copeland	V	New York City	Columbia	14327-D	146348-3
05/31/28	Red Nichols and his Five Pennies	–	New York City	Vocalion	15710	E-27624
06/01/28	Sid Roy's Lyricals	V	London	Imperial	1906	4862-2
06/08/28	Seger Ellis	V	New York City	OKeh	41077	400769-A
06/18/28	Seger Ellis	V	New York City	OKeh	rejected	400769-D-E-F
06/27/28	Goofus Five	V	New York City	OKeh	41069	400834-A-B
07/03/28	Cliff Edwards	V	New York City	Columbia	1471-D	146622-3
07/24/28	Annette Hanshaw	V	New York City	Harmony	706-H	14691-3
08/28	Bill Haid and his Cubs	V	Chicago	Banner	7193	20790-2
08/02/28	Rube Bloom	–	New York City	OKeh	41117	401049-A
09/21/28	Paul Whiteman and his Orchestra	V	New York City	Columbia	50103-D	98589-3
09/22/28	Shilkret's Rhyth-Melodists	–	Camden, NJ	Victor	21688	47413-2
10/30/28	Duke Ellington and his Cotton Club Orchestra	V	New York City	Victor	V-38008	48102-2
11/12/28	"Kenn" Sisson and his Orchestra	V	New York City	Duophone	D-4018	E-28668-A
11/29/28	Carroll Gibbons	–	London	His Master's Voice	B-2971	Bb-14797-2
12/28	Marek Weber und sein Orchester	–	Berlin	Electrola	EG-1131	BLR-4839-2
12/11/28	Lillie Delk Christian	V	Chicago	OKeh	8650	402206-A
03/29	Jazz-Orchester Lud Gluskin	–	Berlin	Artiphon	D-03512	03512
03/05/29	Louis Armstrong and his Savoy Ballroom Five	V	New York City	OKeh	8669	401690-C
07/29	Maestro Sam Wooding y sus Chocolate Kiddies	V	Barcelona	Parlophone	B-25423	76517-2
12/22/32	Ethel Waters [w/Duke Ellington and his Orchestra]	V	New York City	Brunswick	6517	B-12783-A

Date	Performer	Vocal	Place	Label	Issue	Matrix
02/17/33	Duke Ellington and his Famous Orchestra [medley]	–	New York City	Brunswick	6516	B-13079-A
07/29/33	King's Jesters	V	Chicago	Bluebird	B-6517	75982-1
11/09/34	Pat Hyde	V	London	Parlophone	R-1973	CE-6714-1
06/06/35	[Benny Goodman] Rhythm Makers Orchestra	–	New York City	NBC Thesaurus	165	92211-1
08/26/35	Connie Boswell	V	Larem, Holland	Decca	F-42108	AM-181-1
09/13/35	Ramona and her Gang	–	New York City	Victor	25156	95026-2
01/25/36	Val Rosing and his Swing Stars	V	London	Regal Zonophone	MR-2186	CAR-3889-1
05/04/36	Quintette of the Hot Club of France	V	Paris	His Master's Voice	K-7706	OLA-1058-1
06/04/36	Bob Howard [medley]	–	London	Brunswick	02230	TB-2212-1
09/01/36	Scott Wood and his Six Swingers [medley]	V	London	Columbia	FB-1504	CA-15896-1
10/21/36	Joe Daniels and his Hotshots	–	London	Parlophone	F-656	CE-7898-1
11/19/36	Teddy Wilson and his Orchestra	V	New York City	Brunswick	7781	B-20293-1
12/17/36	Dude Skiles and his Vine Street Boys	–	Hollywood	Vri	516	L-0367
03/08/37	Cootie Williams and his Rug Cutters	–	New York City	Vri	555	M-185-1
09/06/37	Benny Goodman and his Orchestra	V	Hollywood	Victor	25678	09690-2
06/24/38	Louis Armstrong and his Orchestra	V	New York City	Decca	2042	64229-A
08/28/38	Adelaide Hall [w/Fats Waller]	V	London	His Master's Voice	B-8849	OEA-6392-2
02/27/39	Gene Austin [w/Fats Waller]	V	New York City	RFW	2	033994-1
09/28/39	Adrian Rollini Trio	–	Hollywood	Vocalion/OKeh	5621	WM-1084-A
11/03/39	Fats Waller and his Rhythm	V	New York City	Bluebird	B-10573	043351-1
11/03/39	Fats Waller and his Rhythm	V	New York City	RFW	3	043351-2
02/05/40	Caspar Reardon	V	New York City	Schirmer	511	2015
02/09/40	Joe Sullivan and his Cafe Society Orchestra	V	New York City	Vocalion/OKeh	5496	26503-A
07/26/40	Miss Valaida Med Winstrup Olesens Swingband	V	Copenhagen	Tono	21166	1064-A-B
12/19/40	Benny Goodman and his Sextet	–	New York City	Columbia	36755	CO-29260-1
05/03/42	Tommy Dorsey and his Orchestra	V	New York City	Victor	LPM-6003	–

If I Could Be with You

Date	Performer	Vocal	Place	Label	Issue	Matrix
12/15/26	Eva Taylor	V	New York City	OKeh	rejected	80252-A
02/10/27	Eva Taylor	V	New York City	OKeh	8444	80413-B
c 11/06/29	George E. Lee and his Orchestra	V	Kansas City	Brunswick	7132	KC-583-
01/31/30	McKinney's Cotton Pickers	V	New York City	Victor	V-38118	58545-2
06/23/30	Ben Pollack and his Orchestra	V	New York City	Banner	0747	9819-2-3-4
06/25/30	Lazy Levee Loungers	V	New York City	Columbia	2243-D	150612-1
08/19/30	Louis Armstrong and his Sebastian New Cotton Club Orchestra	V	Los Angeles	OKeh	41448	404406-A
c 09/30	Gil Rodin and his Orchestra	V	New York City	Crown	3016	1011-2
09/16/30	Seger Ellis	V	New York City	OKeh	41452	404453-A
09/18/30	Ruth Etting	V	New York City	Columbia	2300-D	150826-3

Date	Performer	Vocal	Place	Label	Issue	Matrix
10/01/30	Chick Bullock	V	New York City	Banner	0861	10106-3
c 10/13/30	Alabama Washboard Stompers	V	New York City	Vocalion	1546	E-34908-A
10/15/30	Jack Payne and his BBC Dance Orchestra	V	London	Columbia	CB-155	WA-10775-1
06/06/35	[Benny Goodman] Rhythm Makers Orchestra	–	New York City	NBC Thesaurus	123	92213-1
11/22/35	Benny Goodman and his Orchestra	–	Chicago	Victor	25290	96504-1
01/29/36	Dick Stabile and his Orchestra	V	New York City	Decca	977	60414-A
05/27/37	Hudson-DeLange Orchestra	–	New York City	Brunswick	8016	M-503-2
03/19/39	Count Basie and his Orchestra	V	New York City	Vocalion	4748	24241-1
07/12/39	Louis Prima and his New Orleans Gang	V	New York City	Decca	2660	65953-A
02/40	Jack Teagarden and his Orchestra	V	New York City	Varsity	8209	US-1356-1
03/28/40	Dick Robertson and his Orchestra	V	New York City	Decca	3141	67420-A
04/06/40	Bechet-Spanier Big Four	–	New York City	Hot Record Society	2002	2801-1
01/21/41	Nat Gonella and his New Georgians	V	London	Columbia	FB-2570	CA-18292-1

I Got Rhythm

Date	Performer	Vocal	Place	Label	Issue	Matrix
10/20/30	Fred Rich and his Orchestra	V	New York City	Columbia	2328-D	150885-3
10/23/30	Red Nichols and his Five Pennies	V	New York City	Brunswick	4957	E-34959-
10/24/30	Luis Russell and his Orchestra	V	New York City	Melotone	M-12000	E-35025
10/29/30	Fred Rich and his Orchestra	V	New York City	Harmony	1233-H	150908-2
10/29/30	Fred Rich and his Orchestra	V	New York City	OKeh	41465	404534-A
11/18/30	Ethel Waters	V	New York City	Columbia	2346-D	150966-2
12/17/30	Cab Calloway and his Orchestra	V	New York City	American Record Corp.	rejected	10330-1-2
10/31	Adelaide Hall	V	London	Oriole	P-109	R-229
11/06/31	Louis Armstrong and his Orchestra	V	Chicago	OKeh	41534	405065-3
04/13/32	Billy Banks	V	New York City	Victor	test	1129
05/10/32	Bobby Howes	V	London	Columbia	DB-824	CA-12689-2
05/19/32	Roy Fox and his Band	V	London	Decca	F-3014	GB-4490-3
06/18/32	The Blue Mountaineers	V	London	Broadcast	3213	1151-1
06/30/32	Don Redman and his Orchestra	–	New York City	Brunswick	6354	B-12007-A
08/12/32	Ray Starita and his Ambassadors	V	London	Sterno	1023	S-2526
c 06/33	Arthur Briggs and his Boys	V	Paris	Brunswick	A-500262	6433bkp
09/29/33	The Spirits of Rhythm	V	New York City	American Record Corp.	rejected	14095-A-B
c 10/33	Freddy Johnson and his Harlemites	–	Paris	Brunswick	A-500341	6576bkp
10/24/33	Five Spirits of Rhythm	V	New York City	Brunswick	01715	B-14095-C
12/07/33	Freddy Johnson and his Harlemites	–	Paris	Brunswick	A-500341	6645 1/2 bkp
12/30/33	Casa Loma Orchestra	–	New York City	Brunswick	6800	B-14504-A
12/26/34	Joe Venuti and his Orchestra	–	New York City	London	HMG-5023 (LP)	–
10/35	Stephane Grappelly and his Hot Four	–	Paris	Decca	F-5780	2036 1/2 hpp
11/25/35	Garnet Clark	–	Paris	His Master's Voice	K-7645	OLA-733-1
12/04/35	Fats Waller and his Rhythm	V	New York City	His Master's Voice	HE-2902	98198-1

Date	Performer	Vocal	Place	Label	Issue	Matrix
03/16/36	Red Norvo and his Swing Sextette	–	New York City	Decca	779	60898-A
04/02/36	Ballyhooligans	V	London	His Master's Voice	BD-5056	OEA-2755-1
07/15/36	Joe Daniels and his Hot Shots	–	London	Parlophone	F-629	CE-7766-1
03/03/37	Jimmy Dorsey and his Orchestra	–	Los Angeles	Decca	1508	DLA-740-A
04/26/37	Lionel Hampton and his Orchestra	–	New York City	Victor	25586	07865-1
04/29/37	Benny Goodman Quartet	–	New York City	MGM	E/X-3789	–
06/09/37	Glenn Miller and his Orchestra	–	New York City	Brunswick	7915	B-21234-3
06/30/37	Count Basie and his Orchestra	–	New York City	Collector's Corner	8 (LP)	–
07/07/37	Dicky Wells and his Orchestra	–	Paris	Swing	27	OLA-1886-1
07/09/37	Valaida [Snow]	V	London	Parlophone	F-1048	CE-8491-1
09/21/37	Chick Webb and his Little Chicks	–	New York City	Decca	1759	62619-A
11/05/37	Emilio Caceres Trio	–	New York City	Victor	25710	015751-1
11/12/37	Scott Wood and his Six Swingers [medley]	–	London	Columbia	FB-1832	CA-16698-1
01/16/38	Benny Goodman Quartet	–	New York City	Columbia	A-1817	–
01/17/38	Bud Freeman Trio	–	New York City	Commodore	502	22313-1
05/31/38	Larry Adler	–	Paris	Columbia	DF-2427	CL-6719-1
05/31/38	Larry Adler	–	Paris	Columbia	DB/MC-5037	CL-6719-2
10/19/38	Louis Armstrong and Fats Waller	V	New York City	Palm Club	10	–
02/15/39	Clarence Profit Trio	–	New York City	Epic	LN-24028 (LP)	B-24124-1
12/24/39	Benny Goodman Sextet	–	New York City	Vanguard	VRS-8523 (LP)	–
02/05/40	Caspar Reardon and his Orchestra	V	New York City	Schirmer	512	2016
02/27/40	Fletcher Henderson conducts Horace Henderson and his Orchestra	V	Chicago	Vocalion/OKeh	5518	WC-2966-A
05/06/40	Sid Phillips Trio	–	London	Parlophone	F-1803	CE-10471-1
07/26/40	Max Geldray Quartet	–	London	Decca	F-7736	DR-4896-1
10/28/40	Felix Mendelssohn and his Hawaiian Serenaders	–	London	Columbia	FB-2667	CA-18195-1
01/16/42	Metronome All-Star Leaders	–	New York City	Columbia	C-601	32261-1
01/16/42	Metronome All-Star Leaders	–	New York City	Columbia	36499	32261-2

I'm Coming Virginia

Date	Performer	Vocal	Place	Label	Issue	Matrix
09/18/26	Ethel Waters	V	New York City	Columbia	14170-D	142649-2-3
04/29/27	Paul Whiteman and his Orchestra	V	New York City	Victor	LPM-2071	38135-7
04/29/27	Paul Whiteman and his Orchestra	V	New York City	Victor	20751	38135-9
05/11/27	Fletcher Henderson and his Orchestra	V	New York City	Columbia	1059-D	144133-3
05/13/27	Frankie Trumbauer and his Orchestra	–	New York City	OKeh	40843	81083-B
09/28/27	Original Indiana Five	–	New York City	Harmony	501-H	144806-3
10/27	Fred Spinelly and his Lido Venice Band	–	London	Edison Bell Electron	0188	11230-5
c 12/27	Arthur Briggs' Savoy Syncop's Orchestra	V	Berlin	Deutsche Grammophone/Polydor	21125	701bd
03/29/28	Noble Sissle and his Orchestra	–	London	Parlophone	R-3522	E-1815-4
12/13/35	Bunny Berigan and his Blue Boys	–	New York City	Decca	18116	60231-A
c 04–05/37	Fats Waller	V	New York City	Ristic	22 (LP)	–

Date	Performer	Vocal	Place	Label	Issue	Matrix
04/23/37	Teddy Wilson and his Orchestra	–	New York City	Brunswick	7893	B-21037-1
08/06/37	Maxine Sullivan	V	New York City	Vocalion/OKeh	3654	21473-1
c 09/13/37	Les Brown and his (Duke) University Blue Devils	–	New York City	Thesaurus	473	013395-1
c 10/07/37	Philippe Brun	–	Paris	His Master's Voice	rejected	OLA-1961-1-2
01/16/38	Benny Goodman and his Orchestra	–	New York City	Columbia	A-1049	–
03/07/38	Benny Carter and his Orchestra	–	Paris	Swing	20	OSW-4-1
09/09/38	Paul Whiteman and his Swing Wing	V	New York City	Decca	2145	64616-A
03/12/39	Artie Shaw and his Orchestra	–	New York City	Bluebird	B-10320	032965-1
08/39	Art Tatum	–	Hollywood	Polydor	623274 (LP)	–
09/26/39	Woody Herman and his Orchestra	V	New York City	Decca	2817	66673-A
10/16/39	Will Bradley and his Orchestra	–	New York City	Columbia	36345	26176-A
09/11/41	Charlie Barnet and his Orchestra	V	Hollywood	Bluebird	B-11417	061632-1
09/13/41	Sidney Bechet and his New Orleans Feetwarmers	–	New York City	Victor	27904	067791-2
02/17/42	Stephane Grappelly and his Quintet	–	London	Decca	rejected	DR-6688-1-2

Indiana

Date	Performer	Vocal	Place	Label	Issue	Matrix
01/30/17	Original Dixieland Jazz Band	–	New York City	Columbia	A-2297	77087-2-3
07/29/17	Original Dixieland Jazz Band	–	New York City	Aeolian Vocalion	rejected	–
07/28/28	Eddie Condon Quartet	V	New York City	Parlophone	R-2932	401035-A
04/18/29	Red Nichols and his Five Pennies	–	New York City	Brunswick	4373	E-29708-A
04/18/29	Red Nichols and his Five Pennies	–	New York City	Brunswick	80006	E-29708-B
08/19/29	Mound City Blue Blowers	V	New York City	Columbia	1946-D	148895-3
06/13/32	Casa Loma Orchestra	–	New York City	Brunswick	6337	B-11931-A
c 12/32	Joel Shaw and his Orchestra	V	New York City	Crown	3451	1979-2
01/29/35	KXYZ Novelty Band	–	San Antonio	Bluebird	B-5868	87761-1
05/09/35	Mound City Blue Blowers	V	New York City	Vocalion	2973	17518-1
06/06/35	[Benny Goodman] Rhythm Makers Orchestra	–	New York City	NBC Thesaurus	165	92214-1
10/20/36	Buck and Bubbles	V	London	Columbia	FB-1602	CA-15986-1
03/23/37	Chu Berry and his Stompy Stevedores	–	New York City	Vri	587	M-294-1-2
11/12/37	Bill Coleman et son Orchestre	V	Paris	Swing	42	OLA-1974-1
04/06/39	Harry James and his Orchestra	–	New York City	Brunswick	8366	B-24347-C
07/12/39	Earl Hines and his Orchestra	–	New York City	Bluebird	B-10391	038255-1
08/39	Art Tatum	–	Hollywood	Jazz Panorama	LP-15	–
07/26/40	Art Tatum	–	Los Angeles	Decca	8550	DLA-2071-A
12/06/40	Chick Bullock	V	New York City	OKeh	6261	29224-1
01/10/41	Royal Air Force Dance Orchestra	–	London	Decca	F-7782	DR-5235-1
07/22/41	Red Allen and his Orchestra	–	New York City	OKeh	6357	30896-1
03/17/42	Art Hodes and his Orchestra	–	New York City	Decca	18438	70521-A
03/17/42	Art Hodes and his Orchestra	–	New York City	Decca	18438	70521-B

I Never Knew

Date	Performer	Vocal	Place	Label	Issue	Matrix
11/24/25	Ross Gorman and his Earl Carroll Orchestra	–	New York City	Columbia	516-D	141307-4
02/01/29	Red Nichols and his Five Pennies	–	New York City	Brunswick	4243	E-29209-
05/17/32	Casa Loma Orchestra	V	New York City	Brunswick	6337	B-11853-A
07/11/33	Joe Haymes and his Orchestra	V	Camden, NJ	Bluebird	B-5178	76725-1
10/10/33	Chocolate Dandies	–	New York City	Columbia	2875-D	265157-1
01/29/35	KXYZ Novelty Band	–	San Antonio	Bluebird	B-5832	87760-1
04/11/35	Claude Bampton and his Bandits	–	London	Decca	F-5515	GB-7069; EXP-76
06/06/35	[Benny Goodman] Rhythm Makers Orchestra	–	New York City	NBC Thesaurus	125	92212-1
08/14/35	Joe Kennedy and his Rhythm Orchestra	–	San Antonio	Bluebird	B-6102	94514-1
10/24/35	Mike Riley, Eddie Farley and their Onyx Club Boys	–	New York City	Decca	619	60109-A
11/22/35	Lew Davis	–	London	Parlophone	rejected	CE-7300-1-2
12/16/35	Lew Davis	–	London	Parlophone	R-2152	CE-7300-3
01/24/36	Darktown Strutters	V	London	His Master's Voice	BD-5050	OEA-2681-1
06/20/36	Hudson-DeLange Orchestra	–	New York City	Brunswick	7708	B-19488-1
07/02/36	Five Bright Sparks	–	London	Columbia	FB-1517	CA-15837-1
03/25/37	Carolina Cotton Pickers	–	Birmingham, AL	Vocalion	rejected	B-28-
05/27/37	Hudson-DeLange Orchestra	–	New York City	Brunswick	8090	M-504-2
06/18/37	Joe Sodja's Swingtette	–	New York City	Vri	609	M-531-1
07/02/37	Nat Gonella and his Georgians [medley]	V	London	Parlophone	F-832	CE-8457-1
07/20/37	Teddy Foster and his Kings of Swing	V	London	His Master's Voice	BD-5253	OEA-5069-1
03/10/38	Tommy Dorsey and his Orchestra	–	New York City	Victor	25813	021140-1
04/08/38	Benny Goodman and his Orchestra	–	New York City	Victor	26089	022416-1
08/16/38	Harry Bluestone	–	Los Angeles	Decca	rejected	DLA-1415-A-B
05/08/39	Charlie Barnet and his Orchestra	–	New York City	Bluebird	B-10285	036924-1
12/20/39	Joe Daniels and his Hot Shots	–	London	Parlophone	F-1637	CE-10230-1
03/19/40	Count Basie and his Orchestra	–	New York City	Columbia	35521	26655-1
05/06/40	Sid Phillips Trio	–	London	Parlophone	F-1803	CE-10472-2
07/30/40	Stephane Grappelly and his Musicians	–	London	Decca	rejected	DR-4902-1-2
12/09/40	Teddy Wilson and his Orchestra	–	New York City	Columbia	35905	29233-1
02/28/41	Stephane Grappelly and his Musicians	–	London	Decca	F-8128	DR-4902-3
04/17/42	Louis Armstrong and his Orchestra	V	Los Angeles	Decca	4229	DLA-2977-A

I've Found a New Baby

Date	Performer	Vocal	Place	Label	Issue	Matrix
01/20/26	[Fletcher Henderson] Dixie Stompers	V	New York City	Harmony	121-H	141526-3
c 01/22/26	Clarence Williams Blue Five	V	New York City	OKeh	8286	73957-A
c 01/22/26	Clarence Williams Blue Five	V	New York City	OKeh	8286	73958-B
01/22/26	Ethel Waters	V	New York City	Columbia	561-D	141542-1

Date	Performer	Vocal	Place	Label	Issue	Matrix
01/26/26	Lou Gold and his Orchestra	V	New York City	Pathe Actuelle	36403	106575
04/07/26	Georgia Melodians	–	New York City	Edison Diamond Disc	rejected	10913
05/26	Dixie Washboard Band	V	New York City	Oriole	rejected?	6552-1-2-3
06/11/26	Ben Finger's Parady Club Orchestra	V	New York City	Gennett	rejected	X-179, -A
02/03/27	Andy Preer and the Cotton Club Orchestra	–	New York City	Gennett	6056	GEX-513,-A-C
04/06/28	Chicago Rhythm Kings	V	Chicago	Brunswick	4001	C-1886-A
04/08/29	McKinney's Cotton Pickers	V	New York City	Victor	V-38061	51086-2
01/31/30	James P. Johnson and Clarence Williams	V	New York City	Columbia	14502-D	149952-2
11/12/30	Joe Venuti's Blue Four	–	New York City	OKeh	41469	404549-B
09/15/32	[Sidney Bechet] New Orleans Feetwarmers	–	New York City	Victor	24150	73400-1
03/24/33	Alphonse Trent and his Orchestra	V	Richmond, IN	Champion	16587	19081
09/08/33	Three Keys	–	New York City	Vocalion	2569	13973-1
02/05/34	Paul Cornelius and his Orchestra	–	Richmond, IN	Champion	16734	19481
08/31/34	Isham Jones and his Orchestra	–	New York City	Decca	262	38497-A
01/29/35	KXYZ Novelty Band	–	San Antonio	Bluebird	B-5868	87763-1
08/35	Frank "Big Boy" Goudie	–	Paris	Ultraphon	AP-1527	P-77468
10/21/35	Stephane Grappelly and his Hot Four	–	Paris	Decca	F-5943	2079hpp
06/15/36	Benny Goodman and his Orchestra	–	New York City	Victor	25355	102215-1
06/18/36	Jimmie Gunn and his Orchestra	–	Charlotte, NC	Bluebird	B-6500	102689-1
10/08/36	Harry Roy's Tiger-Ragamuffins	V	London	Parlophone	F-589	CE-7874-1
04/11/37	Bob Pope and his Orchestra	–	Birmingham, AL	American Record Corp.	rejected	B-123-1-2
04/15/37	Frank Newton	–	New York City	Vri	571	M-402-2
04/27/37	Stephane Grappelly	–	Paris	Swing	rejected	OLA-1738-1
06/01/37	Teddy Wilson and his Orchestra	–	New York City	Brunswick	7926	B-21220-1
06/01/37	Teddy Wilson and his Orchestra	–	New York City	Tax	8000 (LP)	B-21220-3
08/12/37	Erskine Hawkins and his 'bama State Collegians	–	New York City	Vocalion	3668	21507-1
09/29/37	Stephane Grappelly [trio]	–	Paris	Swing	21	OLA-1738-2
03/08/38	Kenny Clarke's Kvintett	–	Stockholm	Odeon	A-255509	Sto-6318-1
08/31/38	Pee Wee [Russell], Zutty, and James P.	–	New York City	Hot Record Society	1002	23395-1
05/24/39	Harry James and his Orchestra	–	New York City	Brunswick	8406	B-24691-A
06/06/39	Paul Whiteman's Bouncing Brass	–	New York City	Decca	2466	65360-A
07/19/39	Bud Freeman and his Summa Cum Laude Orchestra	–	New York City	Bluebird	B-10370	038291-1
08/10/39	Bob Zurke and his Delta Rhythm Band	–	New York City	Victor	26355	041539-1
09–10/39	Larry Breese and his Orchestra	–	Los Angeles	Ammor	100	AM-501
10/30/39	Lionel Hampton and his Orchestra	–	New York City	Victor	26447	043247-1
01/16/40	George Wettling's Chicago Rhythm Kings	–	New York City	Decca	18045	67059-A
01/16/40	George Wettling's Chicago Rhythm Kings	–	New York City	Decca	18045	67059-B
c 05/40	Art Hodes' Blue Three	–	New York City	Signature	101	1600
11/30/40	Jay McShann Combo	–	Wichita, KS	Victor	LP-7334	–

Date	Performer	Vocal	Place	Label	Issue	Matrix
01/15/41	Benny Goodman Sextet Featuring Count Basie	–	New York City	Columbia	36039	CO-29514-1
06/27/41	Willie Lewis and his Negro Band	–	Zurich	Elite Special	4078	1923-
11/16/41	First English Public Jam Session	–	London	His Master's Voice	C-3269	2EA-9701-1
03/13/42	Royal Air Force Dance Orchestra	–	London	Decca	F-8180	DR-6733-2

I Wish I Could Shimmy Like My Sister Kate

Date	Performer	Vocal	Place	Label	Issue	Matrix
06/14/22	Original Memphis Five	–	New York City	Arto	9153	20170-3
c 08/22	Mary Straine	V	Long Island City	Black Swan	14123	–
08/22	Original Memphis Five	–	New York City	Paramount	20161	1169-1-2-3
08/22	Jazzbo's Carolina Serenaders	–	New York City	Cameo/Muse	269	260-C-G
08/21/22	Ladd's Black Aces	–	New York City	Gennett	4938	8006-A
09/22	The Cotton Pickers	–	New York City	Brunswick	2338	8923, 8925
09/11/22	Original Memphis Five	–	New York City	Pathe Actuelle	020825	69846
09/13/22	California Ramblers	–	New York City	Vocalion	14436	9849
09/19/22	Leona Williams and her Dixie Band	V	New York City	Columbia	A-3713	80556-3
10/02/22	Virginians	–	New York City	Victor	18965	26917-3
10/23/22	The Southland Five	–	New York City	Columbia	rejected	80621-1-2-3
c 11/25/22	Eva Taylor	V	New York City	OKeh	4740	71056-B
c 12/22	Southern Five	–	New York City	Melody/LaBelle	1410	–
12/01/22	The Georgians	–	New York City	Columbia	A-3775	80695-2
c 01/23	Bessie Smith	V	New York City	OKeh	rejected	–
01/23	Abe Small and his Melody Boys	–	New York City	Strong	10002	002-1
04/23	Savoy Havana Band	–	London	Columbia	3276	73353
05/22/23	Original Capitol Orchestra	–	Hayes, Middlesex	Zonophone	2355	Yy-3007-2
c 07/23	Anna Jones [w/Fats Waller]	V	New York City	Paramount	12052	1468-1-2
11/17/25	Bessie Smith	V	New York City	Columbia	rejected	141275-1-2-3-4-5
12/27/26	University Six	–	New York City	Harmony	414-H	143221-1
02/08/27	Goofus Five	–	New York City	OKeh	40767	80403-B
11/03/27	Viola McCoy	V	New York City	Cameo	rejected	–
12/01/27	Varsity Eight	–	New York City	Cameo	1280	2717-C
c 02/01/28	Ray Miller and his Hotel Gibson Orchestra	–	Chicago?	Brunswick	3829	E-7105
02/14/28	Jan Garber and his Orchestra	–	New York City	Columbia	1306-D	145633-3
c 03/28	Charles Pierce and his Orchestra	–	Chicago	Paramount	12640	20470-4
03/23/28	Boyd Senter and his Senterpedes	–	New York City	OKeh	41018	400168-A
c 04/28	Charles Pierce and his Orchestra	–	Chicago	Paramount	12640	20470-7
09/25/28	Whoopee Makers	–	New York City	Columbia	14367-D	147057-4
12/28	Clarence Williams and his Orchestra	–	Long Island City	QRS	R-7044	309-A
02/15/29	Earl Hines and his Orchestra	V	Chicago	Victor	22683	48888-3
11/17/32	Edgar Jackson and his Dance Band	–	London	Decca	F-3307	GB-5199-1
03/27/33	Henry Allen/Coleman Hawkins and their Orchestra	–	New York City	Pirate	MPC-513	13184-A
09/05/34	Alabama Jug Band	V	New York City	Decca	7001	38552

Date	Performer	Vocal	Place	Label	Issue	Matrix
07/27/36	Joe Haymes and his Orchestra	–	New York City	Vocalion	3307	19620-1
09/28/38	Bill Coleman et son Orchestre	V	Paris	Swing	214	OSW-44-1
12/23/38	New Orleans Feetwarmers	–	New York City	Vanguard	8523	–
11/10/39	Muggsy Spanier and his Ragtime Band	V	New York City	Bluebird	B-10506	043376-1
01/16/40	George Wettling's Chicago Rhythm Kings	–	New York City	Decca	18044	67061-A
12/40	Art Hodes' Columbia Quintet	–	New York City	Jazz Records	rejected	–

I Would Do Anything for You

Date	Performer	Vocal	Place	Label	Issue	Matrix
07/02/29	California Ramblers	V	New York City	Harmony	959-H	148777-1
05/24/32	Claude Hopkins and his Orchestra	–	New York City	Columbia	2665-D	152199-1
05/25/32	Claude Hopkins and his Orchestra	–	New York City	Jazz Archives	4 (LP)	B-11894-A
07/26/32	[Billy Banks] The Rhythmakers	V	New York City	Melotone	M-12457	12119-1
07/26/32	[Billy Banks] The Rhythmakers	V	New York City	Banner	32530	12119-2
07/26/32	Joe Haymes and his Orchestra	V	Camden, NJ	Victor	24083	58942-1
10/12/32	The Three Keys	V	New York City	Brunswick	6522	B-12466-A
08/24/33	Joseph Robechaux and his New Orleans Rhythm Boys	–	New York City	Vocalion	2646	13877-1
08/22/34	Art Tatum	–	New York City	Decca	1373	38388-A
10/09/34	Art Tatum	–	New York City	Decca	1373	38388-C
11/23/34	Jimmy Noone and his Orchestra	–	Chicago	Vocalion	2862	C-859-A
03/27/35	Zutty [Singleton] and his Band	V	Chicago	Decca	432	C-9879-A
06/06/35	[Benny Goodman] Rhythm Makers Orchestra	–	New York City	NBC Thesaurus	165	92211-1
09/35	Art Tatum	–	Hollywood	Jazz Panorama	LP-15	–
02/15/36	Locke Brothers Rhythm Orchestra	V	Charlotte, NC	Bluebird	B-6316	99148-1
05/27/36	Benny Goodman and his Orchestra	–	New York City	Victor	25350	101258-1
08/21/36	Tempo King and his Kings of Tempo	–	New York City	Bluebird	B-6534	0234-1
03/22/37	Red Norvo and his Orchestra	–	Chicago	Brunswick	7868	C-1855-1
03/25/37	Carolina Cotton Pickers	–	Birmingham, AL	Vocalion	rejected	B-27
05/20/38	Una Mae Carlisle and her Jam Band	V	London	Vocalion	S-199	DTB-3655-1
c 08/38	Jelly Roll Morton [trio]	–	Baltimore	Swaggie	S-1213 (LP)	–
10/24/38	Three's a Crowd	–	New York City	Bluebird	B-10160	027976-1
01/23/40	Hot Lips Page and his Band	V	New York City	Decca	7699	67091-A
02/02/40	Duke Derbigny's Orchestra	–	New Orleans	Mono	MNLP-12 (LP)	–
01/15/42	Casa Loma Orchestra	V	New York City	Decca	rejected	70171-A

The Jazz Me Blues

Date	Performer	Vocal	Place	Label	Issue	Matrix
c 11/20	Lucille Hegamin	V	New York City	Arto	9045	18004-1
05/21	Tim Brymn and his Black Devil Orchestra	–	New York City	OKeh	8005	7899-B
05/03/21	Original Dixieland Jazz Band	V	New York City	Victor	rejected	25072-1-2-3

Date	Performer	Vocal	Place	Label	Issue	Matrix
05/03/21	Original Dixieland Jazz Band	–	New York City	Victor	18772	25072-5
c 05/09/21	Lillyn Brown	V	New York City	Emerson	10384	41797-2
02/18/24	Wolverine Orchestra	–	Richmond, IN	Gennett	5408	11754-A
10/05/27	Bix Beiderbecke and his Gang	–	New York City	OKeh	40923	81520-A
01/16/28	Old Gold Serenaders	–	Richmond, IN	Gennett	rejected	13362
c 03/28	Charles Pierce and his Orchestra	–	Chicago	Paramount	12640	20469-3
c 04/28	Charles Pierce and his Orchestra	–	Chicago	Paramount	12640	20469-5
04/28/28	Frank Teschmacher's Chicagoans	–	Chicago	UHCA	61	C-1906-A
c 10/30/28	Harry King and his Royalists	–	New York City	Gennett	rejected	GEX-2128,-A
04/05/29	Bert Lown and his Loungers	–	New York City	Harmony	974-H	148180-3
11/24/31	Original Memphis Five	–	New York City	Columbia	2588-D	151887-2
10/02/33	Joe Venuti and his Blue Six	–	New York City	Columbia	CB-686	265148-2
09/12/34	New Orleans Rhythm Kings	–	New York City	Decca	162	38611-A
10/03/34	Alabama Jug Band	V	New York City	Decca	7041	38781-A
01/04/35	Hal Kemp and his Orchestra	–	New York City	Brunswick	7458	B-16615-A
08/06/35	Arthur Young and his Youngsters [medley]	–	London	Decca	F-5709	TB-1859-1
11/19/35	Gene Krupa and his Chicagoans	–	Chicago	Parlophone	R-2268	90461-A
04/15/36	Harry Roy's Tiger-Ragamuffins	V	London	Parlophone	F-458	CE-7578-1
12/11/36	Milt Herth	–	Chicago	Decca	1727	91046-B
09/28/37	Wingy Manone and his Orchestra	V	New York City	Bluebird	B-7198	013884-1
01/11/38	Danny Polo and his Swing Stars	–	London	Decca	F-6615	DTB-3483-2
03/15/39	Bunny Berigan and his Orchestra	–	New York City	Victor	26244	035032-1
06/26/39	Glenn Hardman and his Hammond Five	–	Chicago	Columbia	35263	WC-2641-A
10/11/39	Jimmy McPartland and his Orchestra	–	Chicago	Decca	18042	91832-A
02/06/40	Bob Crosby's Bob Cats	–	New York City	Decca	3040	67175-A
c 03/14/41	George Hartmann and his Orchestra	–	New Orleans	Keynote	K-601	GH-2-A
05/13/41	Larry Clinton and his Orchestra	–	New York City	Bluebird	B-11240	065254-1
05/26/41	Ted Lewis and his Band	–	Los Angeles	Decca	4272	DLA-2410-A
10/14/42	Joe Daniels and his Hotshots	–	London	Parlophone	F-1956	CE-11015-1

King Porter Stomp

Date	Performer	Vocal	Place	Label	Issue	Matrix
07/17/23	Jelly Roll Morton	–	Richmond, IN	Gennett	5289	11537
c 10/24	Al Turk's Princess Orchestra	–	New York City?	Olympic	1463	B-1641
11/03/24	Benson Orchestra of Chicago	–	St. Louis	Victor	rejected	31143-1-2-3-4
c 12/24	King Oliver [and Jelly Roll Morton]	–	Chicago	Autograph	617	685
c 02/03/25	Johnny Sylvester and his Orchestra	–	New York City	Pathe Actuelle	036211	105826
02/20/25	Fletcher Henderson and his Orchestra	–	New York City	Vocalion	rejected	399 1/2/401
02/26/25	Lanin's Red Heads	–	New York City	Columbia	327-D	140398-2
03/25	Charles Creath's Jazz-o-maniacs	–	St. Louis	Okeh	8210	9019-A
04/20/26	Jelly Roll Morton	–	Chicago	Vocalion	1020	C-166; E-2869
03/14/28	Fletcher Henderson and his Orchestra	–	New York City	Columbia	1543-D	145763-3
12/09/32	Fletcher Henderson and his Orchestra	–	New York City	OKeh	41565	152325-1

Date	Performer	Vocal	Place	Label	Issue	Matrix
08/18/33	Fletcher Henderson and his Orchestra	–	New York City	Vocalion	2527	13828-1
08/18/33	Fletcher Henderson and his Orchestra	–	New York City	Brunswick	A-9771	13828-2
09/14/34	Claude Hopkins and his Orchestra	–	New York City	Decca	184	38671-A
06/06/35	[Benny Goodman] Rhythm Makers Orchestra	–	New York City	NBC Thesaurus	127	92219-1
07/01/35	Benny Goodman and his Orchestra	–	New York City	Victor	25090	92547-1
11/06/35	Blanche Calloway and her Band	–	New York City	Vocalion	3112	18241-1
02/36	Chick Webb and his Orchestra	–	New York City	Polydor	423248	–
05/17/37	Teddy Hill and his NBC Orchestra	–	New York City	Bluebird	B-6988	101210-1
07/13/37	Benny Goodman and his Orchestra	–	Los Angeles	Columbia	ML-4591	–
12/16/37	Harry Roy and his Orchestra	–	London	Parlophone	F-1158	CE-8815-1
05–07/38	Jelly Roll Morton	–	Washington, DC	Circle	23-24	1639
05–07/38	Jelly Roll Morton	–	Washington, DC	Circle	73-69	1674
08/38	Jelly Roll Morton	–	Baltimore	Swaggie	rejected	–
09/12/38	Erskine Hawkins and his Orchestra	–	New York City	Bluebird	B-7839	026860-1
04/06/39	Harry James and his Orchestra	–	New York City	Brunswick	8366	B-24349-C
12/14/39	Jelly Roll Morton	–	New York City	General	4005	R-2565
02/07/40	Metronome All-Star Band	–	New York City	Columbia	36389	26489-A
03/28/40	Teddy Bunn	–	New York City	Blue Note	503	RS-713-A
05/28/40	Zutty Singleton and his Orchestra	–	New York City	Decca	18093	67841-A
07/14/40	Jelly Roll Morton	–	New York City	Pirate	MPC-502	–
07/27/40	Cab Calloway and his Orchestra	–	Cedar Grove, NJ	Jazz Panorama	LP-16	–
01/27/42	Bob Crosby and his Orchestra	–	Los Angeles	Decca	4390	DLA-2852-A

Limehouse Blues

Date	Performer	Vocal	Place	Label	Issue	Matrix
c 04/24	New Orleans Jazz Band	–	New York City	Dominion	338	10083-1-2
04/02/24	California Ramblers	–	New York City	Bell	P-278	–
06/22/24	Romance of Harmony Orchestra	–	Richmond, IN	Gennett	rejected	11920
05/24/28	Original Wolverines	–	Chicago	Vocalion	15708	C-1971-; E-7353
05/31/28	Red Nichols and his Five Pennies	V	New York City	Brunswick	20070	XE-27622-
05/31/28	Red Nichols and his Five Pennies	–	New York City	Brunswick	A-5081	XE-27622-G
12/11/28	Ted Lewis and his Band	–	New York City	Columbia	1789-D	147416-4
01/10/30	Jack Hylton and his Orchestra	–	London	His Master's Voice	B-5789	Bb-18542-3
05/18/31	Garland Wilson	–	New York City	Columbia	Special	230205-1
06/16/31	Duke Ellington and his Orchestra	–	Camden, NJ	Victor	22743	68237-1
02/18/32	Casa Loma Orchestra	–	New York City	Brunswick	advertisement	B-11318-A
03/30/32	Spike Hughes and his Orchestra	–	London	Decca	F-3004	GB-4145-3
07/11/33	Joe Haymes and his Orchestra	–	Camden, NJ	Bluebird	B-5133	76722-1
02/24/34	Casa Loma Orchestra	–	New York City	Brunswick	6886	B-14855-A
08/17/34	Georgia Washboard Stompers	–	New York City	Decca	7005	38344
09/11/34	Fletcher Henderson and his Orchestra	–	New York City	Decca	157	38598-A
09/28/34	Arthur Schutt	–	New York City	American Record Corp.	rejected	16073-1-2

Date	Performer	Vocal	Place	Label	Issue	Matrix
08/06/35	Arthur Young and his Youngsters [medley]	–	London	Decca	F-5709	TB-1858-1
09/35	Andre Ekyan and his Orchestra	–	Paris	Ultraphon	AP-1546	77526
09/13/35	Scott Wood and his Six Swingers [medley]	–	London	Regal Zonophone	MR-1909	CAR-3588-1
09/24/35	Joe Paradise and his Music	–	London	Parlophone	F-288	CE-7165-1
10/35	Stephane Grappelly	–	Paris	Decca	F-5780	2035hpp
12/11/35	Black Hand Gang	–	London	Parlophone	R-2154	CE-7360-1
01/02/36	Mustang Band of Southern Methodist University	–	Los Angeles	Decca	706	DLA-291-
05/04/36	Quintette of Hot Club of France	–	Paris	His Master's Voice	K-7706	OLA-1062-1
06/04/36	Bob Howard and his Orchestra [medley]	–	London	Brunswick	02230	TB-2213-2
03/09/37	Harry Roy and his Orchestra	–	London	Parlophone	F-1132	CE-8086-1
03/11 & 16/37	Benny Goodman Quartet	–	New York City	MGM	E/X-3789	–
03/23/37	Chu Berry and his Stompy Stevedores	–	New York City	Vri	587	M-296-1
06/18/37	Joe Sodja's Swingtette	–	New York City	Vri	609	M-530-1-2
12/37	Freddy Gardner and his Swing Orchestra	–	London	Rex	9225	R-2538-1
08/03/38	Earl Hines and his Orchestra	–	Chicago	Jazz Panorama	JP-19	–
08/31/38	Joe Daniels and his Hot Shots	–	London	Parlophone	F-1214	CE-9302-1
12/05/38	Danish Jam Session	–	Copenhagen	His Master's Voice	X-6212	OCS-1084-2
12/06/38	Nat Gonella and his Georgians	–	London	Parlophone	F-1302	CE-9463-1
c 02/39	Max Geldray	–	Paris	Swing	49	OSW-61-1
06/19/39	Wingy Manone and his Orchestra	–	New York City	Bluebird	B-10432	037734-1
02/20/40	Larry Clinton and his Orchestra	–	New York City	Victor	26523	047078-1
c 03/40	Ella Fitzgerald and her Famous Orchestra	–	New York City	Jazz Trip	5 (LP)	–
03/22/40	Django Reinhardt and his Music	–	Paris	Swing	82	OSW-119-1
07/27/40	Cab Calloway and his Orchestra	–	Cedar Grove, NJ	Jazz Panorama	LP-16	–
09/13/41	Sidney Bechet and his New Orleans Feetwarmers	–	New York City	Victor	27600	067792-1
10/28/41	Benny Goodman Sextet	–	New York City	OKeh	6486	CO-31610-1

Liza

Date	Performer	Vocal	Place	Label	Issue	Matrix
07/16/29	Sammy Fain	V	New York City	Harmony	993-H	148816-1
08/24/34	Art Tatum	–	New York City	Decca	1373	38432-A
09/25/34	Fletcher Henderson and his Orchestra	–	New York City	Decca	555	38728-A
10/09/34	Art Tatum	–	New York City	Decca	1373	38432-D
11/23/34	Jimmy Noone and his Orchestra	–	Chicago	Vocalion	2862	C-861-A
08/01/35	Willie Bryant and his Orchestra	–	New York City	Victor	25160	92911-1
10/07/35	Teddy Wilson and his Orchestra	–	New York City	Brunswick	7563	B-18131-1
01/36	Joe Turner	–	Paris	Ultraphon	AP-1573	77604
11/18/36	Don Albert and his Orchestra	–	San Antonio	Vocalion	3491	SA-2523-1
03/22/37	Red Norvo and his Orchestra	–	Chicago	Brunswick	7868	C-1854-2

Date	Performer	Vocal	Place	Label	Issue	Matrix
c 05/37	James P. Johnson	–	New York City	Ristic	22 (LP)	–
08/02/37	Benny Goodman Quartet	–	Hollywood	Victor	25660	09634-3
08/17/37	Benny Goodman Quartet	–	Los Angeles	Columbia	ZLP-12609	–
05/03/38	Chick Webb and his Orchestra	–	New York City	Decca	1840	63708-A
05/24/38	Clarence Williams' Trio	–	New York City	Vocalion	4169	22980-1
08/13/38	Chick Webb with the Saturday Night Swing Club Band	–	New York City	Jazz Archive	JA-33 (LP)	–
01/09/39	Chick Webb and his Orchestra [medley]	–	New York City	Polydor	423248 (LP)	–
09/14/39	Jimmie Lunceford and his Orchestra	–	New York City	Vocalion/OKeh	5276	26069-A
12/11/39	Teddy Wilson and his Orchestra	–	New York City	Columbia	35711	25738-1
04/09/41	Stephane Grappelly and his Quartet	–	London	Decca	rejected	DR-5580-1-2
08/20/42	Stephane Grappelly and his Quintet	–	London	Decca	F-8204	DR-6930-2

Loveless Love (Careless Love)

Date	Performer	Vocal	Place	Label	Issue	Matrix
01–02/21	Noble Sissle and his Sizzling Syncopators	V	New York City	Pathe Actuelle	020493	–
c 01/22	Katherine Handy	V	New York City	Paramount	12011	B-102-1
02/23	Alberta Hunter	V	New York City	Paramount	12019	1327-2
01/23/25	Oscar Celestin	–	New Orleans	OKeh	8198	8907-A
05/15/25	Bessie Smith	V	New York City	Columbia	rejected	140604-1-2-3
05/26/25	Bessie Smith	V	New York City	Columbia	14083-D	140626-1
05/26/25	Bessie Smith	V	New York City	Columbia	14083-D	140626-2
01/14/27	Fats Waller	–	Camden, NJ	Victor	20470	37359-3
c 04/27	Johnny Dodds	–	Chicago	Paramount	12483	4413-1
c 04/28	Novelty Blue Boys	–	New York City	Grey Gull	1522	2910-A-B
06/09/30	Fred Gardner's Texas University Troubadours	V	San Antonio	OKeh	41440	404099-A
c 01/31	Jack Teagarden and his Orchestra	V	New York City	Crown	3051	1120-1-2
01/31	Ruth Johnson	V	Grafton, WI	Paramount	rejected	L-724
02/06/31	Seger Ellis	V	New York City	Brunswick	rejected	E-36085-A
02/17/31	Seger Ellis	V	New York City	Brunswick	6050	E-36085-A
c 03/31	Ruth Johnson	V	Grafton, WI	Paramount	13060	L-816-2
03/13/31	State Street Ramblers	V	Richmond, IN	Champion	16464	17622
03/27/31	Blanche Calloway	V	Camden, NJ	Victor	22659	68942-2
04/15/31	King Oliver and his Orchestra	–	New York City	Vocalion	1610	E-36474-A
06/09/31	Dave's [Nelson] Harlem Highlights	V	New York City	Timely Times	C-1577	69907-2
08/13/34	Lee Wiley	V	New York City	Decca	132	38298-B
08/15/34	Noble Sissle and his International Orchestra	V	Chicago	Decca	154	C-9297-A
02/25/35	Bobby Gordon's Rhythm	V	Los Angeles	Vocalion	2926	LA-1009-B
07/31/35	Little Ramblers	V	New York City	Bluebird	B-6043	92797-1
10/08/36	Ballyhooligans	–	London	His Master's Voice	rejected	OEA-3788-1
10/21/36	Joe Daniels and his Hotshots	–	London	Parlophone	F-741	CE-7894-2

Date	Performer	Vocal	Place	Label	Issue	Matrix
03/24/37	Carolina Cotton Pickers	–	Birmingham, AL	Vocalion	rejected	B-17
11/09/37	Georgia White	V	Chicago	Decca	7419	91351-A
38	W. C. Handy	V	Washington, DC	[Library of Congress]	none	1620-B-3
10/28/38	Boots and his Buddies	–	San Antonio	Bluebird	B-10036	028745-1
12/26/39	W. C. Handy Orchestra	V	New York City	Varsity	8162	US-1224-1
10/15/40	Billie Holiday	V	New York City	OKeh	6064	28875-1
11/15/40	Lew Stone and his Stone-Crackers	V	London	Decca	F-7685	DR-5114-1
11/26/40	Joe Turner	V	New York City	Decca	7827	68395-B
06/23/41	[Henry Levine] Dixieland Jazz Group of NBC . . .	V	New York City	Victor	27545	066128-1
04/42	Lu Watters' Yerba Buena Jazz Band	V	San Francisco	Jazz Man	rejected	–

Maple Leaf Rag

Date	Performer	Vocal	Place	Label	Issue	Matrix
c 03–04	Wilbur Sweatman and his Band	–	Minneapolis	Metropolitan Music Store	none	–
10/15/06	U. S. Marine Band	–	Washington, DC	Victor	4911	3887-2
c 03/07	Vess Ossman	–	New York City	Columbia	3626	3626-1
c 05/07	Vess Ossman	–	New York City	Imperial	45600	–
02/18/09	U. S. Marine Band	–	Washington, DC	Victor	16792	3887-3
c 10	W. G. "Gus" Haenschen's Banjo Orchestra of St. Louis	–	New York City	Columbia	61070	M-61070
03/13/23	New Orleans Rhythm Kings	–	Richmond, IN	Gennett	5104	11358-B
05/20/24	Herb Wiedoeft's Cinderella Roof Orchestra	–	Los Angeles	Brunswick	rejected	A-115/8
10/21/24	Herb Wiedoeft's Cinderella Roof Orchestra	–	New York City	Brunswick	2795	14060
09/25/25	Halfway House Orchestra	–	New Orleans	Columbia	476-D	140998-1
05/19/26	Vera Guilaroff	–	Montreal	Pathe Actuelle	rejected	E-2378/81
06/22/26	Harry Snodgrass	–	New York City	Brunswick	3239	E-19646
07/12/26	Vera Guilaroff	–	Montreal	Pathe Actuelle/Supertone	21178	E-2453
08–10/27	Jazz Kings	–	Berlin	Tri-Ergon	TE-5064	MO-862
06/27/28	G. G. McBrayer	–	Richmond, IN	Gennett	20335	13935
10/24/30	Victor Arden	–	New York City	Victor	rejected	63168-1-2-3
12/10/30	Victor Arden	–	New York City	Victor	22608	63168-4
09/15/32	[Sidney Bechet] New Orleans Feetwarmers	–	New York City	Victor	23360	73502-1
09/12/34	Earl Hines and his Orchestra	–	Chicago	Decca	218	C-9463-A-B
01/07/35	Paul Mares and his Friars Society Orchestra	–	Chicago	OKeh	rejected	C-872-1-2
01/26/35	Paul Mares and his Friars Society Orchestra	–	Chicago	OKeh	41574	C-872-C
07/05/35	Clyde McCoy and his Orchestra	–	Chicago	Decca	681	C-90074-A
10/18/36	Tommy Dorsey and his Orchestra	–	New York City	Victor	25496	02172-1
03/14/37	Ike Ragon and his Orchestra	–	Hot Springs, AR	Vocalion	03513	HS-56

Date	Performer	Vocal	Place	Label	Issue	Matrix
06/23/37	Teddy Weatherford	–	Paris	Swing	315	OLA-1879-2
12/16/37	Harry Roy and his Orchestra	–	London	Parlophone	F-1133	CE-8811-1
05–07/38	Jelly Roll Morton	–	Washington, DC	Circle	21-22	1654
05–07/38	Jelly Roll Morton	–	Washington, DC	Circle	22	1653
07/18/38	Ozzie Nelson and his Orchestra	–	New York City	Bluebird	B-7726	024054-1
08/30/38	Bluebird Military Band	–	New York City	Bluebird	B-3201	026678-1
12/19/41	Lu Watters' Yerba Buena Jazz Band	–	San Francisco	Jazz Man	1	MLB-109

Margie

Date	Performer	Vocal	Place	Label	Issue	Matrix
11/24/20	Original Dixieland Jazz Band	–	New York City	Victor	rejected	24581-1-2-3-4
12/01/20	Original Dixieland Jazz Band	–	New York City	Victor	18717	24581-5
06/01/28	Red Nichols and his Five Pennies	–	New York City	Brunswick	3961	E-27625
09/21/28	Bix Beiderbecke and his Gang	–	New York City	Parlophone	R-2833	401140-A
07/16/30	Spike Hughes and his Orchestra	–	London	Decca	F-1815	MB-1632-1
04/18/32	Billy Banks and his Orchestra	V	New York City	Banner	32462	11718-1
c 08/32	Joel Shaw and his Orchestra	V	New York City	Crown	3382	1853-2
09/21/32	Duke Ellington and his Orchestra	V	New York City	?	rejected	73560-1
09/24/33	Billy Cotton and his Band	–	London	Regal Zonophone	MR-1061	CAR-2217-1
01/23/34	Cab Calloway and his Orchestra	V	New York City	Victor	24659	81094-1
05/03/34	Claude Hopkins and his Orchestra	V	New York City	Brunswick	6916	B-15164-A
12/18/34	Scott Wood and his Six Swingers [medley]	–	London	Regal Zonophone	MR-1675	CAR-3125-1
03/05/35	Duke Ellington and his Orchestra	–	New York City	Brunswick	7526	B-16973-1
11/08/35	Harry Roy and his Orchestra	–	London	Parlophone	F-483	CE-7267-1
03/18/37	Billy Kyle and his Swing Club Band	–	New York City	Vri	531	M-281-1
11/37	Adelaide Hall [medley]	V	Copenhagen	Tono	K-6001	D-599
01/06/38	Jimmie Lunceford and his Orchestra	V	New York City	Decca	1617	63133-A
06/13/38	Eddie Brunner and his Orchestra	–	Paris	Swing	41	OSW-31-2
09/13–14/38	Jan Savitt and his Top Hatters [medley]	–	New York City	Thesaurus	594	026876-1
09/14/38	Benny Goodman and his Orchestra	–	Chicago	Victor	26060	025476-1
12/06/38	Don Redman and his Orchestra	V	New York City	Bluebird	B-10061	030360-1
10/12/39	Mary Lou Williams	–	New York City	Columbia	rejected	25471
03/22/40	Andre Ekyan et son Orchestre	–	Paris	Swing	194	OSW-117-1
09/25/40	Casa Loma Orchestra	–	New York City	Decca	3639	68142-A
10/22/40	Noel Chiboust and his Orchestra	–	Paris	Swing	97	OSW-141-1
10/24/40	Tommy Dorsey and his Orchestra	V	Hollywood	Victor	LPM-6003	–
06/27/41	Willie Lewis Presents	–	Zurich	Elite Special	4081	1926-
02/17/42	Stephane Grappelly and his Quintet	–	London	Decca	F-8175	DR-6685-2

The Memphis Blues

Date	Performer	Vocal	Place	Label	Issue	Matrix
07/15/14	Victor Military Band	–	New York City	Victor	17619	15065-3

Date	Performer	Vocal	Place	Label	Issue	Matrix
07/24/14	Prince's Band	–	New York City	Columbia	A-5591	37010
c 03/07/19	Lt. Jim Europe's 369th Infantry Band	–	New York City	Pathe	22085	67486
05/21	Tim Brymn and his Black Devil Orchestra	–	New York City	OKeh	4339	7873-B
c 07/21	Lanin's Southern Serenaders	–	New York City	Arto	9097	–
10/21	Esther Bigeou	V	New York City	OKeh	8026	70223-C
03/22/22	Virginians	–	New York City	Victor	18895	26266-4
01/23	Isham Jones and his Orchestra	–	New York City	Brunswick	2423	9791
01/04/23	Ted Lewis and his Band	–	Chicago	Columbia	A-3813	80763-3
c 06/04/23	Handy's Orchestra	–	New York City	OKeh	4896	71601-B
c 02/25	Monette Moore	V	New York City	Ajax	17124	–
03/25	Twin Six Guitar Jack Penewell	–	New York City	Paramount	20467	2049
12/06/26	Johnny Marvin	–	New York City	Victor	20386	37103-4
04/27	Original Indiana Five	–	New York City	Cameo	1138	2408-C
04/21/27	Ted Lewis and his Band	–	New York City	Columbia	1050-D	143997-1
05/27	Al Bernard	V	New York City	Brunswick	3553	E-22870
c 05/02/27	Six Hottentots	–	New York City	Banner	1986	7241-2
12/07/27	Ben Pollack and his Californians	–	Chicago	Victor	X LX-3003	41343-1
12/07/27	Ben Pollack and his Californians	–	Chicago	Victor	21184	41343-2
c 02/28	Devine's Wisconsin Roof Orchestra	–	Chicago	Paramount	20651	20393-2
04/24/28	Art Gillham	–	New Orleans	Columbia	rejected	146182-1-2
04/05/29	Original Memphis Five	V	New York City	Vocalion	15805	E-29579
09/12/34	Fletcher Henderson and his Orchestra	–	New York City	Decca	158	38605-B
03/20/35	Ambrose and his Orchestra	V	London	Decca	F-5489	GB-7020-1
06/11/36	Ern Pettifer	–	London	Parlophone	F-517	CE-7687-1
08/29/36	Benny Carter w/Kai Ewans' Orchestra	V	Copenhagen	His Master's Voice	X-4698	OCS-450-2
12/11/36	Milt Herth	–	Chicago	Decca	1183	91047
03/09/37	Harry Roy and his Orchestra	–	London	Parlophone	F-1110	CE-8087-1
05/04/38	Willie Lewis and his Orchestra	–	Hilversum	Panachord	H-1036	AM-486-2
06/25/38	Leith Stevens and his Saturday Night Swing Club Orchestra	–	New York City	Vocalion	4210	23163-1
09/19/39	Will Bradley and his Orchestra	–	New York City	Vocalion	5130	26088-A
06/23/41	Dixieland Jazz Group of NBC . . .	–	New York City	Victor	27542	066125-1
12/19/41	Lu Watters and his Yerba Buena Jazz Band	–	San Francisco	Jazz Man	2	MLB-113
07/31/42	Harry James and his Orchestra	–	Hollywood	Columbia	36713	HCO-913-1
c 08/42	Teddy Weatherford	–	Calcutta	Columbia	FB-40225	CEI-22184-1

Milenberg Joys

Date	Performer	Vocal	Place	Label	Issue	Matrix
07/18/23	New Orleans Rhythm Kings	–	Richmond, IN	Gennett	3076	11551
07/18/23	New Orleans Rhythm Kings	–	Richmond, IN	Gennett	5217	11551-A
07/18/23	New Orleans Rhythm Kings	–	Richmond, IN	Gennett	5217	11551-C
06/09/24	Jelly Roll Morton	–	Richmond, IN	Gennett	rejected	11916

Date	Performer	Vocal	Place	Label	Issue	Matrix
10/24	Jimmy Joy's St. Anthony's Hotel Orchestra	–	Dallas	OKeh	40251	8754-A
06/22/25	Ted Lewis and his Band	–	New York City	Columbia	439-D	140709-2
06/23/25	Tennessee Tooters	–	New York City	Vocalion	15068	922
c 07/25	Carlyle Stevenson's El Patio Orchestra	–	Los Angeles	Sunset	1117	829
c 07/21/25	Seven Missing Links	–	New York City	Banner	1618	6136-1
c 07/21/25	Seven Missing Links	–	New York City	Pathe Actuelle	36299	106159
c 08/25	Boyd Senter and his Zo-Bo-Ka-Zoos	–	Chicago	Pathe Actuelle	36320	874-1-2
08/10/25	[Jack Hylton's] Kit-Kat Band	–	Hayes, Middlesex	His Master's Voice	B-2101	Bb-6479-2
08/21/25	Cotton Pickers	–	New York City	Brunswick	2937	16191
09/01/25	Slim Perkins [Bob Fuller]	–	New York City	Banner	1612	6158
09/14/25	Busse's Buzzards	–	New York City	Victor	19782	33379-2
c 10/25	Joseph Gish and his Orchestra	–	Chicago	New Flexo	311	271
10/20/25	Varsity Eight	–	New York City	Cameo	817	1668-B
09/26	Sam Wooding Band	–	Berlin	Deutsche Grammophon/Polydor	20691	604bk
10/28/26	Wen Talbert	V	New York City	Vocalion	rejected	E-4018/9
05/26/27	Devonshire Restaurant Dance Orchestra	–	Hayes, Middlesex	Zonophone	2964	Yy-10761-3
10/14/27	Rodney Rogers' Red Peppers	–	Chicago	Brunswick	3744	C-1318
01/10/28	Husk O'Hare's Wolverines	V	Chicago	Vocalion	15646	C-1423; E-6870
07/11/28	McKinney's Cotton Pickers	–	Chicago	Victor	21611	46096-2
07/11/28	McKinney's Cotton Pickers	–	Chicago	Victor	X LVA-3031	46096-3
07/28/28	Lil Hardaway's Orchestra	V	Chicago	Vocalion	rejected	C-2156-
09/22/28	Lil Hardaway's Orchestra	V	Chicago	Vocalion	1252	C-2336-
c 03/29	Lud Gluskin Ambassadonians	–	Berlin	Tri-Ergon	TE-5543	MO-2425
c 12/29	Bill Carlsen and his Orchestra	–	Grafton, WI	Paramount	20797	L-56-2
c 10/31	[Fletcher Henderson] Connie's Inn Orchestra	–	New York City	Crown	3212	1506-3
05/02/32	Abe Lyman's California Orchestra	–	New York City	Brunswick	6325	B-11764-A
08/09/32	Paul Whiteman's Rhythm Boys	–	New York City	Victor	rejected	73181-1
10/04/32	Gene Kardos and his Orchestra	–	New York City	Perfect	15693	12419-1
12/13/32	Benny Moten's Kansas City Orchestra	–	Camden, NJ	Victor	24381	74852-1
03/16/34	Lew Stone and his Band	–	London	Decca	F-3953	TB-1131-2
05/09/34	Casa Loma Orchestra	–	New York City	Brunswick	6922	B-15185-A
08/23/34	Dorsey Brothers Orchestra	–	New York City	Decca	119	38407-A
04/29/37	Artie Shaw and his New Music	–	New York City	Thesaurus	395	07884-1
05/27/37	Harry Roy and his Orchestra	–	London	Parlophone	F-1109	CE-8375-1
08/01/38	Larry Clinton and his Orchestra	–	New York City	Victor	26018	024426-1
12/06/38	Don Redman and his Orchestra	–	New York City	Bluebird	B-10071	030361-1
01/19/39	Tommy Dorsey and his Orchestra [2 parts]	–	New York City	Victor	26437	031805-1; 031806-1
08/01/39	Johnny Williams and his Boys	–	New York City	Vocalion	5077	24955-A
08/11/39	Redd Evans and his Billy Boys	V	New York City	Vocalion	5173	25189-1
08/21/40	Henry "Kid" Rena's Jazz Band	–	New Orleans	Delta	802	802
01/27/42	Bob Crosby and his Orchestra	–	Los Angeles	Decca	25293	DLA-2855-A
03/29/42	Lu Watters' Yerba Buena Jazz Band	–	San Francisco	Jazz Man	13	MLB-126

Mood Indigo

Date	Performer	Vocal	Place	Label	Issue	Matrix
10/14/30	[Duke Ellington] Harlem Footwarmers	–	New York City	OKeh	rejected	404481-A
10/17/30	[Duke Ellington] Jungle Band	–	New York City	Brunswick	4952	E-34928-A
10/30/30	[Duke Ellington] Harlem Footwarmers	–	New York City	Columbia	C3L-27 (LP)	480023-A
10/30/30	[Duke Ellington] Harlem Footwarmers	–	New York City	OKeh	8840	480023-B
11/21/30	Duke Ellington and his Cotton Club Orchestra	–	New York City	Victor	20-1532	64811-1
12/10/30	Duke Ellington and his Cotton Club Orchestra	–	New York City	Victor	22587	64811-4
03/09/31	Cab Calloway and his Orchestra	–	New York City	Banner	32152	10482-2-3
08/18/31	Henry Lange and his Orchestra	–	Richmond, IN	Champion	16332	17944
02/03/32	Duke Ellington and his Orchestra [medley]	–	New York City	Victor	L-16006 (LP)	71812-2-3
08/18/32	Three Keys	V	New York City	Columbia	rejected	152270-1-2
08/29/32	Three Keys	V	New York City	Columbia	2706-D	152270-3
01/09/33	Boswell Sisters	V	New York City	Brunswick	6470	B-12860-A
06/24/33	Billy Cotton and his Band	–	London	Regal Zonophone	MR-996	CAR-2068-1
11/18/33	Jack Hylton and his Orchestra [medley]	–	London	Decca	F-3764	GB-6351-2
c 12/33	Garland Wilson	–	Paris	Brunswick	A-500358	5747bdp
09/04/34	Jimmie Lunceford and his Orchestra	–	New York City	Decca	BM-1109	38532-A
09/04/34	Jimmie Lunceford and his Orchestra	–	New York City	Decca	131	38532-B
06/06/35	[Benny Goodman] Rhythm Makers	–	New York City	NBC Thesaurus	165	92211-1
08/06/35	Arthur Young and his Youngsters	–	London	Decca	F-5709	TB-1858-1
07/16/36	Joe Paradise and his Music	–	London	Parlophone	F-533	CE-7736-1
12/21/36	Duke Ellington	–	Hollywood	Brunswick	7990	LO-377-1
04/13/38	Nat Gonella and his Georgians	V	London	Parlophone	F-1205	CE-9082-1
05/09/39	Joe Daniels and his Hot Shots	–	London	Parlophone	F-1468	CE-9783-1
02/14/40	Duke Ellington and his Famous Orchestra	V	New York City	Columbia	35427	WM-1137-A
10/04/40	Ambrose and his Orchestra	–	London	Decca	F-7641	DR-5039-1
11/07/40	Duke Ellington and his Famous Orchestra	–	Fargo, ND	Palm	30-03	–
10/24/41	Sidney Bechet and his New Orleans Feetwarmers	–	New York City	His Master's Voice	JK-2718	068113-1

Moonglow

Date	Performer	Vocal	Place	Label	Issue	Matrix
09/25/33	Joe Venuti and his Orchestra	–	New York City	Banner	32883	14080-1
10/13/33	Joe Venuti and his Orchestra	–	New York City	Bluebird	B-5520	78189-1
01/22/34	Cab Calloway and his Orchestra	–	New York City	Victor	24690	81089-1
05/14/34	Benny Goodman and his Orchestra	–	New York City	Columbia	2927-D	152738-1
07/19/34	Casa Loma Orchestra	V	New York City	Brunswick	6937	B-15434-A
08/20/34	Ethel Waters	V	New York City	Decca	140	38352-A
08/20/34	Ethel Waters	V	New York City	Brunswick	01848	38352-C
08/22/34	Art Tatum	–	New York City	Decca	155	38387-A

Date	Performer	Vocal	Place	Label	Issue	Matrix
09/12/34	Duke Ellington and his Orchestra	–	New York City	Brunswick	6987	B-15912-A
11/02/34	Nat Gonella and his Georgians	V	London	Parlophone	R-1983	CE-6703-1
05/35	Nane Cholet	V	Paris	Ultraphon	AP-1314	77374
05/22/35	Louis De Vries and his Rhythm Boys	V	London	Decca	rejected	GB-7149-1-2
06/05/35	Louis De Vries and his Rhythm Boys	V	London	Decca	F-5566	GB-7148-3
09/35	Andre Ekyan and his Orchestra	–	Paris	Ultraphon	AP-1546	77525
10/21/35	Stephane Grappelly and his Hot Four	–	Paris	Decca	F-5831	2082hpp
11/29/35	Joe Paradise and his Music	V	London	Parlophone	F-406	CE-7321-1
08/21/36	Benny Goodman Quartet	–	Hollywood	Victor	25398	97752-1
07/08/37	Joe Daniels and his Hot Shots	–	London	Parlophone	F-860	CE-8465-1
10/04/37	Gerry Moore and his Band	–	London	Parlophone	F-1046	CE-8634-1
11/30/37	Benny Goodman Quartet	–	New York City	Columbia	ML-4590	–
10/05/39	Adrian Rollini Trio	–	Hollywood	Vocalion/OKeh	5200	WM-1089
02/22/40	Art Tatum	–	Los Angeles	Decca	155	DLA-1944-A
01/23/41	Artie Shaw and his Orchestra	–	Hollywood	Victor	27405	055258-1

My Blue Heaven

Date	Performer	Vocal	Place	Label	Issue	Matrix
09/09/27	Don Voorhees and his Orchestra	V	New York City	Columbia	1129-D	144651-3
11/02/27	Rube Bloom	–	New York City	OKeh	40931	81768-B
12/12/27	Lillie Delk Christian	V	Chicago	OKeh	8536	82046-A
08/08/34	Luis Russell and his Orchestra	V	New York City	Banner	33399	15572-1
12/23/35	Jimmie Lunceford and his Orchestra	V	New York City	Decca	712	60274-A
06/18/36	Jimmie Gunn and his Orchestra	V	Charlotte, NC	Bluebird	B-6469	102687-1
12/23/36	Artie Shaw and his Orchestra	–	New York City	Brunswick	7827	B-20451-1-3
02/19/37	Artie Shaw and his Orchestra [medley]	–	New York City	Thesaurus	377	06233-1
03/05/37	Original Yellow Jackets	V	Hot Springs, AR	Vocalion	rejected	HS-29-
07/20/37	Teddy Weatherford	–	Paris	Swing	38	OLA-1918-1
04/29/38	Teddy Wilson	–	New York City	Brunswick	rejected	B-22827-1
05/13/38	Teddy Wilson	–	New York City	Teddy Wilson School	none	P-22827-2
Summer/38	Roy Peyton [medley]	–	Oslo	Rex	EB-385	RP-06
09/19/38	Siday-Simpson Quartet	–	London	Parlophone	rejected	CE-9327-1
11/11/39	Artie Shaw and his Orchestra	–	New York City	Victor	LPT-6000 (LP)	–
c 12/39	Stuff Smith and his Orchestra	V	New York City	Varsity	8081	US-7794-2
01/03/40	Coleman Hawkins' All-Star Octet	–	New York City	Bluebird	B-10770	046158-1
06/07/40	Jimmie Lunceford and his Orchestra	V	New York City	Privateer	103	–
12/05/40	Artie Shaw and his Gramercy Five	–	Hollywood	Victor	27405	055197-1
06/17/41	Maxine Sullivan	V	New York City	Decca	4154	69370-A-B
06/27/41	Willie Lewis Presents	V	Zurich	Elite Special	4082	1929-

My Melancholy Baby

Date	Performer	Vocal	Place	Label	Issue	Matrix
07/19/27	Original Indiana Five	V	New York City	Banner	6032	7392-2-3

Date	Performer	Vocal	Place	Label	Issue	Matrix
01/03/28	All Star Orchestra	V	New York City	Victor	21212	41512-2
03/07/28	Charleston Chasers	V	New York City	Columbia	1335-D	145726-2
04/24/28	Dorsey Brothers' Orchestra	V	New York City	OKeh	41032	400634-C
05/15/28	Paul Whiteman and his Orchestra	V	New York City	Columbia	50068-D	98537-4
10/21/29	Jimmy Noone and his Apex Club Orchestra	–	Chicago	Brunswick	7124	C-4687-
09/04/34	Isham Jones and his Orchestra	–	New York City	Decca	754	38526
04/10/35	Joe Haymes and his Orchestra	V	New York City	Bluebird	B-5918	89544-1
05/10/35	Chick Bullock	V	New York City	Banner	33467	17529-1
02/05/36	Roy Eldridge and his Orchestra	–	Chicago	Decca	rejected	90603-A
03/17/36	Teddy Wilson and his Orchestra	V	New York City	Brunswick	7729	B-18830-1
06/15/36	Benny Goodman and his Orchestra	–	New York City	Victor	rejected	102216-1
11/18/36	Benny Goodman Quartet	–	New York City	Victor	25473	03063-1
04/12/38	Jimmie Lunceford and his Orchestra	V	New York City	Decca	1808	63586-A
05/09/38	Mildred Bailey and her Orchestra	V	New York City	Vocalion	4474	22906-1
05/28/38	Benny Goodman and his Orchestra	–	New York City	Victor	25880	023509-1
05/31/38	Larry Adler	–	Paris	Columbia	DF-2444	CL-6718-1
06/13/38	Herman Chittison	–	Paris	Swing	33	OSW-38-1
c 08/38	Jelly Roll Morton	–	Baltimore	Swaggie	JCS-116 (LP)	–
01/12/39	Dick Robertson and his Orchestra	–	New York City	Decca	2276	64888-A
03/22/39	Quintette of the Hot Club of France	–	Paris	Decca	23261	4973hpp
05/17/39	Quintette of the Hot Club of France	–	Paris	Decca	F-7198	5080hpp
05/26/39	Jack Hylton and his Orchestra [w/Coleman Hawkins]	–	London	His Master's Voice	BD-5550	OEA-7954-2
10/06/39	Red Nichols and his Five Pennies	–	New York City	Bluebird	B-10593	041717-1
02/40	Jack Teagarden and his Orchestra	V	New York City	Varsity	8209	US-1357-1
02/15/40	Arthur Briggs and his Swing Band	–	Paris	Swing	72	OSW-95-1
03/26/40	Doris Rhodes	V	New York City	Columbia	35548	27093-
06/07/40	Jimmie Lunceford and his Orchestra	–	New York City	Privateer	103	–
07/26/40	Max Geldray Quartet	–	London	Decca	F-7736	DR-4897-1
11/06/40	Fats Waller and his Rhythm	V	New York City	RFW	1 (LP)	057089-1
12/06/40	Chick Bullock	V	New York City	OKeh	6261	29223-1
04/03/41	Earl Hines and his Orchestra	–	New York City	Victor	27562	063334-1
04/03/41	Earl Hines and his Orchestra	–	New York City	Victor	X LVA-3023	063334-2
10/06/41	Harry James and his Orchestra	–	New York City	Columbia	36434	31410-1
03/25/42	Joe Daniels and his Hot Shots	–	London	Parlophone	F-1945	CE-10916-1
05/03/42	Tommy Dorsey and his Orchestra	V	New York City	Victor	LPM-6003	–

Nagasaki

Date	Performer	Vocal	Place	Label	Issue	Matrix
06/29/28	Ipana Troubadours	V	New York City	Columbia	1463-D	146602-2
09/14/28	Seven Blue Babies	V	New York City	Edison Diamond Disc	rejected	N-431-A-B
09/14/28	Seven Blue Babies	V	New York City	Edison Diamond Disc	52405	18726
10/05/32	Three Keys	V	New York City	Brunswick	6411	B-12424-A

Date	Performer	Vocal	Place	Label	Issue	Matrix
10/06/32	Don Redman and his Orchestra	V	New York City	Brunswick	6429	B-12447-A
05/03/33	Eddie South and his Orchestra	V	Chicago	Victor	24383	75497-1
09/22/33	Fletcher Henderson and his Orchestra	V	New York City	Columbia	2825-D	265138-2
10/24/33	Lew Stone and his Monseigneur Band	V	London	Decca	F-3821	TB-1098-1
05–06/34	Herman Chittison	–	Paris	Brunswick	A-500440	1228wpp
09/17/34	Casa Loma Orchestra	–	New York City	Decca	200	38678-A
01/07/35	Paul Mares and his Friars Society Orchestra	–	Chicago	OKeh	rejected	C-870-1-2
01/21/35	Charlie Barnet and his Orchestra	V	New Orleans	Bluebird	B-5815	87643-1
01/26/35	Paul Mares and his Friars Society Orchestra	–	Chicago	OKeh	41574	C-870-C
04/23/35	Willie Lewis and his Orchestra	–	Paris	Pathe Actuelle	PA-591	CPT-1983-
05/03/35	Nat Gonella and his Georgians	V	London	Parlophone	F-161	CE-6968-1
06/14/35	Adrian [Rollini] and his Tap Room Gang	V	New York City	Victor	25085	92266-1
06/25/35	Putney Dandridge and his Orchestra	–	New York City	Vocalion	3024	17729-1
07/02/35	Cab Calloway and his Orchestra	V	Chicago	Brunswick	7504	C-1055-A
07/19/35	Washboard Serenaders	V	London	Parlophone	F-358	CE-7113-1
02/13/36	Albert Ammons and his Rhythm Kings	–	Chicago	Decca	749	90567-A
07/02/36	Five Bright Sparks	–	London	Columbia	FB-1473	CA-15838-1
09/01/36	Scott Wood and his Six Swingers [medley]	V	London	Columbia	1504	CA-15896-1
09/19/36	Billy Costello	V	London	Decca	F-6100	TB-2481-1
10/15/36	Quintette of the Hot Club of France	V	Paris	His Master's Voice	K-7843	OLA-1290-1
01/11–16/37	Benny Carter and his Orchestra	–	London	Vocalion	S-69	S-141-1
07/08/37	Valaida	V	London	Parlophone	F-952	CE-8489-1
08/02/37	Dixieland Swingsters	–	Charlotte, NC	Bluebird	B-7258	011855-1
11/16/37	Benny Goodman Quartet	–	New York City	Columbia	ML-4590	–
07/19/38	Gene Krupa and his Swing Band	V	New York City	Brunswick	8188	B-23256-1
08/07/39	Fats Waller and his Rhythm	–	New York City	Jazz Society	AA-536	–
02/17/42	Stephane Grappelly and his Quintet	–	London	Decca	rejected	DR-6687-1-2

Nobody's Sweetheart

Date	Performer	Vocal	Place	Label	Issue	Matrix
c 02/24	Harvey Brooks' Quality Four	–	Hollywood	Hollywood	1021	42
c 03/03/24	OKeh Syncopators	–	New York City	OKeh	40072	72383-B
c 03/11/24	Lanin's Jazz Band	–	New York City	Pathe Actuelle	036075	105195
c 03/13/24	Six Black Diamonds	–	New York City	Banner	1349	5452-2
c 03/19/24	Ladd's Black Aces	–	New York City	Gennett	5422	8801-A
12/16/27	McKenzie and Condon's Chicagoans	–	Chicago	OKeh	40971	82082-B
12/27/27	Claire Hull and his Wanderers	–	Richmond, IN	Gennett	6356	13325-A
01/24/28	Louisiana Rhythm Kings	V	Chicago	Vocalion	15657	C-1667
c 02/16/28	Original Indiana Five	V	New York City	Cameo	8154	2895-A-C
02/25/28	Red Nichols and his Five Pennies	–	New York City	Brunswick	3854	E-7168; E-26749
c 04/28	Charles Pierce and his Orchestra	–	Chicago	Paramount	20616	20534-2

Date	Performer	Vocal	Place	Label	Issue	Matrix
07/12/28	McKinney's Cotton Pickers	V	Chicago	Victor	V-38000	46400-2
11/06/28	Jack Pettis and his Pets	V	New York City	Historical	HLP-33 (LP)	48126-1
01/11/29	Maurice [Elwin] and Sidney [Nesbitt]	V	Hayes, Middlesex	Zonophone	5260	Yy-15377-2
04/12/29	Fred Elizalde and his Music	–	London	Parlophone	R-1201	E-2404-1
10/09/29	Paul Whiteman and his Orchestra	–	New York City	Columbia	2098-D	149123-2
01/04/30	Hotel Pennsylvania Music	V	New York City	Harmony	1086-H	149733-1
01/21/30	Adrian Schubert and his Salon Orchestra	V	New York City	Oriole	1854	9299-1
12/23/30	Cab Calloway and his Orchestra	V	New York City	Brunswick	6105	E-35881-A
04/31	Eubie Blake and his Orchestra	V	New York City	Crown	3130	1296-2
11/13/31	Billy Cotton and his Band	V	London	Regal	MR-450	CAR-887-1
12/02/31	[Harry Hudson] Radio Rhythm Boys	V	London	Edison Bell Radio	1581	90291-2
12/02/31	Roy Fox and his Band	V	London	Decca	F-2716	GB-3664-1
12/11/31	Fred Elizalde	–	London	Decca	rejected	GB-3707-1-2
04/05/32	Frankie Trumbauer and his Orchestra [medley]	V	New York City	Columbia	18002-D	255004-1
06/15/32	Fred Elizalde	–	London	Decca	F-3229	GB-4574-2
11/28/32	Jimmy Raschel and his Orchestra	V	Richmond, IN	Champion	rejected	18912
12/21/32	Louis Armstrong and his Orchestra [medley]	V	Camden, NJ	Victor	40-0104	74878-2
05/26/33	Nat Gonella and his Trumpet	V	London	Brunswick	01537	GB-5920-1
c 06/33	Arthur Briggs and his Boys	V	Paris	Brunswick	A-500262	6431bkp
06/01/33	Washboard Rhythm Kings	V	Camden, NJ	Victor	23403	76251-1
08/22/33	Clyde McCoy and his Drake Hotel Orchestra	–	Chicago	Columbia	2808-D	152477-2
09/29/33	Spirits of Rhythm	V	New York City	American Record Corp.	rejected	14094-
10/31/33	Five Spirits of Rhythm	V	New York City	American Record Corp.	rejected	B-14094-
12/18/34	Scott Wood and his Six Swingers [medley]	–	London	Regal Zonophone	MR-1675	CAR-3125-1
03/28/35	Brian Lawrance and the Quaglino Quartet	V	London	Decca	rejected	GB-7027-1-2
04/04/35	Brian Lawrance and his Quartet	V	London	Panachord	25723	GB-7027-4
07/09/35	Paul Whiteman and his Orchestra	–	New York City	Victor	25319	92579-1
11/19/35	Rhythm Rascals	V	London	Crown	89	H-318
02/27/36	Ballyhooligans	–	London	His Master's Voice	BD-5041	OEA-2707-1
04/27/36	Benny Goodman Trio	–	Chicago	Victor	25345	100501-1
05/16/36	Billy Cotton's Cotton Pickers	V	London	Regal Zonophone	MR-2119	CAR-4070-1
05/25/36	Max Abrams and his Rhythm Makers	–	London	Parlophone	F-512	CE-7651-2
06/04/36	Bob Howard [medley]	–	London	Brunswick	02239	TB-2214-1
09/19/36	Billy Costello	V	London	Decca	F-6148	TB-2482-1
07/08/37	Joe Daniels and his Hot Shots	–	London	Parlophone	F-860	CE-8464-1
04/26/38	Benny Goodman Trio	–	New York City	MGM	E/X-3789	–
12/05/38	Oscar Aleman	–	Copenhagen	His Master's Voice	X-6213	OCS-1085-1
08/11/39	Eddie Condon and his Chicagoans	–	New York City	Decca	18040	66073-A
08/22/40	Connie Boswell	V	New York City	Decca	3425	68002-A

Oh, Lady Be Good

Date	Performer	Vocal	Place	Label	Issue	Matrix
12/18/24	Ben Bernie and his Hotel Roosevelt Orchestra	–	New York City	Vocalion	14955	14068
01/28/25	California Ramblers	–	New York City	Columbia	293-D	140368-2
05/17/26	Gilt-Edged Four	V	London	Columbia	3981	WA-3257-1
01/20/30	Louisiana Rhythm Kings	–	New York City	Brunswick	4706	E-31945-
12/26/33	Buck and Bubbles	V	New York City	Columbia	rejected	152661-1-2-3
01/04/34	Buck and Bubbles	V	New York City	Columbia	2873-D	152661-5
11/18/34	Coleman Hawkins and his Rhythm	–	London	Parlophone	R-2007	CE-6740-1
12/34	Quintette of the Hot Club of France	–	Paris	Ultraphon	AP-1422	P-77163
12/20/34	Arthur Young and his Youngsters [medley]	V	London	Regal Zonophone	MR-1568	CAR-3128-1
09/24/35	Joe Paradise and his Music	–	London	Parlophone	F-327	CE-7167-1
03/16/36	Red Norvo and his Swing Sextette	–	New York City	Decca	779	60899-A
04/36	Larry Adler	V	London	Vocalion	536	S-112-2
04/27/36	Benny Goodman Trio	–	Chicago	Victor	25333	100500-1
10/05/36	Buck and Bubbles	V	London	Columbia	FB-1524	CA-15958-1
10/08/36	Nat Gonella and his Georgians	–	London	Parlophone	F-639	CE-7883-1
10/09/36	Jones-Smith Incorporated [Basie]	–	Chicago	Vocalion	3459	C-1660-1
02/22/37	Gerry Moore and his Chicago Brethren	–	London	Decca	F-6347	TB-2853-1
03/11/37	Brian Lawrance and his Lansdowne House Sextet	V	London	Decca	F-6383	TB-2910-1
05/05/37	Red Jessup and his Melody Makers	V	New York City	American Record Corp.	7-07-15	21100-1
05/10/37	Frank Dailey and his Orchestra	–	New York City	Vri	?	M-460
07/12/37	Dicky Wells and his Orchestra	–	New York City	Swing	10	OLA-1898-1
08/04/37	Frankie Reynolds and his Orchestra	V	Charlotte, NC	Bluebird	B-7241	011947-1
09/29/37	Eddie South	V	Paris	Swing	45	OLA-2147-1
11/26/37	Larry Clinton and his Orchestra	V	New York City	Victor	25724	017418-1
05/03/38	Slim [Gaillard] and Slam [Stewart]	V	New York City	Vocalion	4163	22849-1
05/26/38	Trixie Smith	V	New York City	Ace of Hearts	158 (LP)	63872-A
07/23/38	Count Basie and his Orchestra	–	New York City	Jazz Panorama	LP-2	–
02/04/39	Count Basie and his Orchestra	–	New York City	Decca	2631	64985-A
08/27/39	Artie Shaw and his Orchestra	–	New York City	Bluebird	B-10430	042609-1
12/24/39	Jam Session: Basie and Goodman groups	–	New York City	Vanguard	8524	–
02/09/40	Joe Sullivan and his Cafe Society Orchestra	–	New York City	Vocalion/OKeh	5496	26501-A
03/40	Frankie Trumbauer and his Orchestra	–	New York City	Varsity	8269	US-1418-1
07/12/40	Felix Mendelssohn and his Hawaiian Serenaders	–	London	Columbia	FB-2525	CA-18068-1
12/09/40	Teddy Wilson and his Orchestra	–	New York City	Columbia	36084	29236-1
03/12/41	Eddie South and his Orchestra	–	New York City	Columbia	36193	29927-1
06/19/41	Willie Lewis Presents	V	Zurich	Elite Special	4072	1896
07/17/41	Jimmie Noone Quartet	–	Chicago	Swaggie	S-1210	–

Date	Performer	Vocal	Place	Label	Issue	Matrix
10/24/41	Sidney Bechet and his New Orleans Feetwarmers	–	New York City	Victor	27707	068115-1
03/25/42	Joe Daniels and his Hot Shots	–	London	Parlophone	F-1909	CE-10917-1

Old Fashioned Love

Date	Performer	Vocal	Place	Label	Issue	Matrix
10/03/23	Ambassadors	–	New York City	Vocalion	14686	12062
10/10/23	Arthur Gibbs and his Gang	–	New York City	Victor	19165	28730-3
c 11/10/23	Clarence Williams' Blue Five	–	New York City	OKeh	4993	72041-B
c 11/10/23	Eva Taylor	V	New York City	OKeh	8114	72028-C
11/17/23	Georgians	–	New York City	Columbia	30-D	81361-1
01/08/24	Noble Sissle/Eubie Blake	V	New York City	Victor	19253	29189-2
02/24	Alberta Hunter	V	New York City	Paramount	12093	1666-1-3
05/04/32	Joe Haymes and his Orchestra	V	Camden, NJ	Victor	24007	72617-1
10/04/32	Gene Kardos and his Orchestra	–	New York City	Melotone	M-12500	12418-1
09/24/33	Billy Cotton and his Orchestra	–	London	Regal Zonophone	MR-1061	CAR-2218-1
03/08/34	Floyd "Buck" Washington	–	New York City	Columbia	2925-D	265174-1
05/07/34	Mezz Mezzrow and his Orchestra	–	New York City	Victor	25202	82392-1
09/26/34	Red Norvo and his Swing Septet	–	New York City	Columbia	3059-D	CO-16021-A
07/02/35	Jimmy Grier and his Orchestra	V	Los Angeles	Brunswick	7528	LA-1051-A
08/26/35	Freddy Jenkins and his Harlem Seven	V	New York City	Bluebird	B-6129	94133-1
03/17/37	[Adrian Rollini] Roly's Tap Room Gang	–	New York City	Vri	rejected	M-273-1-2
04/01/37	Midge Williams and her Jazz Jesters	V	New York City	Vri	rejected	M-347-1-2
c 04–05/37	Fats Waller	–	New York City	Ristic	22 (LP)	–
04/06/39	Benny Goodman Quartet	V	New York City	Victor	rejected	035709-1
06/15/39	James P. Johnson and his Orchestra	–	New York City	Columbia	DZ-545	24777
10/04/40	Eddy Howard	V	New York City	Columbia	35771	28794-1

Ol' Man River

Date	Performer	Vocal	Place	Label	Issue	Matrix
01/07/28	Don Vorhees and his Orchestra	V	New York City	Columbia	1284-D	145486-3
01/11/28	Paul Whiteman and his Orchestra	V	New York City	Victor	21218	41607-2
03/03/28	Lou Raderman and his Pelham Heath Inn Orchestra	V	New York City	Harmony	607-H	145722-2
c 05/23/28	Noble Sissle and his Sizzling Syncopators	V	London	Parlophone	R-145	E-1955-2
07/02–11/28	Fred Elizalde	–	London	Brunswick	187	–
07/07/28	Bix Beiderbecke and his Gang	–	Chicago	OKeh	41088	400994-A
08/28	Castle Farms Serenaders	V	Chicago	Paramount	20656	20827-1
09/06/28	Sammy Stewart and his Orchestra	–	Chicago	Vocalion	15724	C-2304
Late 28–early 29	Jack Hamilton and his Entertainers	–	Paris	Azurephone	1011	4758
10/03/33	Horace Henderson and his Orchestra	V	New York City	Parlophone	R-1766	265152-1

Date	Performer	Vocal	Place	Label	Issue	Matrix
02/03/34	Casa Loma Orchestra	–	New York City	Brunswick	6800	B-14774-A
08/08/34	Luis Russell and his Orchestra	V	New York City	Banner	33179	15576-1
10/03/34	Tiny Bradshaw and his Orchestra	V	New York City	Decca	236	38785-A
01/10/36	Nat Gonella and his Georgians	V	London	Parlophone	F-370	CE-7384-1
06/01/36	Putney Dandridge and his Orchestra	V	New York City	Vocalion	3269	19354-1
10/18/37	Willie Lewis and his Orchestra	–	Paris	Pathe Actuelle	PA-1297	CPT-3474-1
04/04/38	Cootie Williams and his Rug Cutters	–	New York City	Vocalion	4086	M-804-1
03/11/40	Snub Mosely and his Band	V	New York City	Decca	7768	67289-A
01/22/41	Harry James and his Orchestra	V	New York City	Columbia	36023	29543-1
04/17/41	Red Allen and his Orchestra	V	New York City	OKeh	6281	30273-2
06/27/41	Willie Lewis and his Negro Band	–	Zurich	Elite Special	4079	1921

On the Sunny Side of the Street

Date	Performer	Vocal	Place	Label	Issue	Matrix
04/18/30	Casa Loma Orchestra	V	New York City	Odeon	ONY-36080	403965-B
06/27/30	The Rhythmic Eight	V	Hayes, Middlesex	Zonophone	5649	Yy-19483-2
12/20/33	Chick Webb's Savoy Orchestra	V	New York City	Columbia	2875-D	152658-1
01/10/34	Clarence Williams and his Orchestra	V	New York City	Vocalion	2630	14571-1
01/10/34	Clarence Williams and his Orchestra	–	New York City	Vocalion	rejected	14571-2
03/08/34	Coleman Hawkins and his Orchestra	–	New York City	Parlophone	R-1825	265175-1
09/10/34	Chick Webb and his Orchestra	V	New York City	Decca	172	38594-A
10/34	Louis Armstrong and his Orchestra [2 parts]	V	Paris	Brunswick	A-500491	1481 1/2wpp; 1482 1/2wpp
11/18/36	Don Albert and his Orchestra	V	San Antonio	Vocalion	3423	SA-2522-1
04/26/37	Lionel Hampton and his Orchestra	V	New York City	Victor	25592	07864-1
05/28/37	Don Redman and his Orchestra	V	New York City	Vri	580	M-508-1
11/15/37	Louis Armstrong and his Orchestra	–	Los Angeles	Decca	1560	DLA-1085-A
11/15/37	Louis Armstrong and his Orchestra	–	Los Angeles	Decca	3794	DLA-1085-B
03/13/38	Eddie South and his Quintet	V	Hilversum	Brunswick	A-81505	AM-751-
04/12/38	Nat Gonella and his Georgians	V	London	Parlophone	F-1206	CE-9076-1
10/19/38	Louis Armstrong and Fats Waller	V	New York City	Palm Club	10	–
06/26/39	Glenn Hardman and his Hammond Five	–	Chicago	Columbia	35341	WC-2638-A
07/26/40	Max Geldray Quartet	–	London	Decca	F-7626	DR-4894-1
04/03/41	Earl Hines	–	New York City	Victor	X LVA-3023	063333-1
04/03/41	Earl Hines	–	New York City	Victor	27562	063333-2
09/41	Chu Berry and his Jazz Ensemble	–	New York City	Commodore	1508	R-4179-
c 11/41	Nat King Cole Quartet	V	New York City	Varsity	8340	522; 5899
12/24/41	Benny Goodman Sextet	V	New York City	Columbia	36617	CO-32053-1

Panama

Date	Performer	Vocal	Place	Label	Issue	Matrix
00c	Ossman-Dudley Trio	–	New York City	Columbia	85109	85109
02/04/07	Vess L. Ossman	–	New York City	Victor	rejected	4238-1-2-3

Date	Performer	Vocal	Place	Label	Issue	Matrix
02/04/07	Vess L. Ossman	–	New York City	Victor	rejected	4238-4-5
08/30/22	New Orleans Rhythm Kings	–	Richmond, IN	Gennett	4968	11182-B
03/23	Handy's Orchestra	–	New York City	OKeh	8059	71349-B
c 03/15/24	Johnny DeDroit and his New Orleans Jazz Orchestra	–	New Orleans	OKeh	40240	8556-B
06/20/24	Henry Halstead and his Orchestra	–	Oakland, CA	Victor	19514	PB-40-4
12/12/24	McKenzie's Candy Kids	–	New York City	Vocalion	14977	14472; 290
12/22/25	[Fletcher Henderson] Dixie Stompers	–	New York City	Harmony	92-H	141424-3
04/25/28	Johnnie Miller's New Orleans Frolickers	–	New Orleans	Columbia	1546-D	146193-3
05/29/28	Red Nichols and his Five Pennies	–	New York City	Brunswick	3961	E-27605
09/05/30	Luis Russell and his Orchestra	–	New York City	OKeh	8849	404429-A
07/19/34	Casa Loma Orchestra	–	New York City	Brunswick	7325	B-15433-A
09/12/34	New Orleans Rhythm Kings	–	New York City	Decca	162	38610-A
04/25/36	Jimmy McPartland's Squirrels	–	Chicago	Hot Record Society	1003	90700-A
05/08/36	Wingy Manone and his Orchestra	–	New York City	Bluebird	B-6411	101578-1
11/16/37	Bob Crosby and his Orchestra	–	Los Angeles	Decca	1615	DLA-1094
05–07/38	Jelly Roll Morton	–	Washington, DC	Circle	2	1641
07/11/38	Tommy Dorsey and his Orchestra	–	Hollywood	Victor	26185	019425-1
06/30/39	Louis Bacon and his Orchestra	–	Paris	Swing	185	OSW-93-1
01/04/40	Jelly Roll Morton's Seven	–	New York City	General	1703	R-2583
08/21/40	Henry "Kid" Rena's Jazz Band	–	New Orleans	Delta	800	800

Rockin' Chair

Date	Performer	Vocal	Place	Label	Issue	Matrix
02/19/29	Hoagy Carmichael and his Orchestra	V	Chicago	Victor	rejected	48897-1-2-3
12/13/29	Louis Armstrong and his Orchestra	V	New York City	OKeh	8756	403496-C
05/21/30	Hoagy Carmichael and his Orchestra	V	New York City	Victor	V-38139	59800-2
10/10/30	Bud Richie and his Boys	V	Richmond, IN	Champion	16109	17162
12/01/30	Red Nichols and his Five Pennies	V	New York City	Brunswick	6012	E-35619-A
c 01/31	Jack Teagarden and his Orchestra	V	New York City	Crown	3051	1119-1
c 01/31	Ruth Johnson	V	Grafton, WI	Paramount	rejected	L-723
01/10/31	[Duke Ellington] Whoopee Makers	V	New York City	Oriole	2191	10357-1
01/10/31	[Duke Ellington] Whoopee Makers	V	New York City	Banner	32070	10357-2
01/10/31	[Duke Ellington] Whoopee Makers	V	New York City	Banner	32070	10357-3
01/12/31	Chick Bullock	V	New York City	Banner	32080	10361
01/14/31	[Duke Ellington] Jungle Band	V	New York City	Brunswick	6732	E-35800-A
02/03/31	Alabama Washboard Stompers	–	New York City	Vocalion	1587	VO-1004-A-B
02/03/31	Alabama Washboard Stompers	V	New York City	Vocalion	rejected	VO-1001-A-B
02/19/31	Clarence Williams and his Jazz Kings	–	New York City	Harmony	rejected	404855-A-B
c 03/31	Ruth Johnson	V	Grafton, WI	Paramount	13060	L-815-1
03/18/31	Fred Rich and his Orchestra	V	New York City	Clarion	5273-C	100502-1-4
03/18/31	Fred Rich and his Orchestra	V	New York City	OKeh?	rejected	404882-A-B
06/09/31	Dave's [Nelson] Harlem Highlights	V	New York City	Timely Tunes	C-1576	69906-1

Date	Performer	Vocal	Place	Label	Issue	Matrix
12/17/31	Gilmore Sisters	–	New York City	Victor	23316	70981-1
02/02/32	Garland Wilson	–	New York City	OKeh	41556	405135-A
05/09/32	Hoagy Carmichael and his Orchestra [medley]	V	New York City	Victor	L-16009 (LP)	72558-1
08/18/32	Mildred Bailey	V	New York City	Victor	24117	73304-1
11/15/32	Nat Gonella and his Trumpet	–	London	Decca	F-3292	GB-5174-2
12/26/34	Joe Venuti and his Orchestra [medley]	V	New York City	London	HMG-5023 (LP)	–
06/02/36	Scott Wood and his Six Swingers	V	London	Columbia	FB-1427	CA-15781-1
03/23/37	Mildred Bailey and her Orchestra	V	Chicago	Vocalion	3553	C-1859-1-2
04/11/37	Bob Pope and his Orchestra	V	Birmingham, AL	American Record Corp.	8-02-06	B-120-2
02/20/39	Louis Armstrong with the Casa Loma Orchestra	V	New York City	Decca	2395	65045-A
07/14/39	Larry Clinton and his Orchestra	V	New York City	Victor	26319	038274-1
01/08/41	Larry Clinton and his Orchestra	V	New York City	Bluebird	B-11018	058850-1
03/14/41	Mildred Bailey	V	New York City	Decca	3755	68820-A
05/13/41	Fats Waller	–	New York City	Victor	27765	063888-1
07/02/41	Gene Krupa and his Orchestra	V	New York City	OKeh	6352	30830-1
09/02/41	Artie Shaw and his Orchestra	–	New York City	Victor	27664	067738-1

Rosetta

Date	Performer	Vocal	Place	Label	Issue	Matrix
02/13/33	Earl Hines and his Orchestra	–	New York City	Columbia	35878	B-13060-A-C
02/13/33	Earl Hines and his Orchestra	–	New York City	Brunswick	6541	B-13060-B
05/22/34	Teddy Wilson	–	New York City	Columbia	rejected	152754-1-2
09/12/34	Earl Hines and his Orchestra	V	Chicago	Decca	337	C-9465-A
03/06/35	Fats Waller and his Rhythm	V	New York City	Victor	24892	88781-1
03/06/35	Fats Waller and his Rhythm	–	New York City	Victor	25026	88782-1
04/01/35	Ray Nichols and his Four Towers Orchestra	V	New York City	Bluebird	B-5902	89500-1
04/29/35	Henry Allen and his Orchestra	V	New York City	Vocalion	2965	17395-1
06/06/35	[Benny Goodman] Rhythm Makers Orchestra	–	New York City	NBC Thesaurus	124	92218-1
08/14/35	Joe Kennedy	V	San Antonio	Bluebird	B-6080	94512-1
09/35	Art Tatum	–	Hollywood	Jazz Panorama	LP-15	–
10/07/35	Teddy Wilson	–	New York City	Brunswick	7563	B-18132-1
11/25/35	Garnet Clark and his Hot Clubs Four	–	Paris	His Master's Voice	K-7618	OLA-730-1
01/14/37	Benny Goodman and his Orchestra	–	New York City	Victor	25510	04238-1
01/03/38	Gerry Moore	–	London	Parlophone	F-1014	CE-8835-1
10/12/38	George Chisholm and his Jive Five	–	London	Decca	F-7015	DR-2989-1
10/24/38	Three's a Crowd	–	New York City	Bluebird	B-10051	027974-1
01/13/39	Frankie Newton and his Orchestra	–	New York City	Bluebird	B-10176	031460-
08/02/39	Woody Herman and his Orchestra	V	New York City	Decca	2728	66051-A
10/06/39	Earl Hines	–	Chicago	Bluebird	rejected	040480-1-2
10/21/39	Earl Hines	–	Chicago	Bluebird	B-10555	040480-3

Date	Performer	Vocal	Place	Label	Issue	Matrix
03/22/40	Andre Ekyan and his Orchestra	–	Paris	Swing	98	OSW-114-1
07/26/40	Art Tatum	–	Los Angeles	Decca	8502	DLA-2070-A
11/05/40	Fred Boehler and his Orchestra	–	Zurich	Columbia	ZZ-1006	CZ-928-1
04/07/41	Teddy Wilson [trio]	–	Chicago	Columbia	36632	CCO-3654-1
04/07/41	Teddy Wilson [trio]	–	Chicago	Columbia	36632	CCO-3654-2
04/28/42	George Shearing	–	London	ACL	1161 (LP)	DR-6799-

Royal Garden Blues

Date	Performer	Vocal	Place	Label	Issue	Matrix
04/02/20	Morrison's Jazz Orchestra	–	New York City	Columbia	rejected	79097-1-2-3
04/13/20	Morrison's Jazz Orchestra	–	Camden, NJ	Victor	tests	–
01/21	Mamie Smith's Jazz Hounds	–	New York City	OKeh	4254	7724-B
01–02/21	Noble Sissle	V	New York City	Pathe Actuelle	020493	–
01/05/21	Mary Stafford	V	New York City	Columbia	A-3365	79628-3
c 02/02/21	Noble Sissle	V	New York City	Emerson	10367	41633-2-3-4
03–04/21	Daisy Martin	V	New York City	Gennett	4712	7466-A
05/25/21	Original Dixieland Jazz Band	V	New York City	Victor	18798	25413-4
c 09/21	Ethel Waters' Jazz Masters	–	New York City	Black Swan	2035	P-161-1-2
08/17/23	Benson Orchestra of Chicago	–	Camden, NJ	Victor	rejected	28433-1-2-3
05/06/24	Wolverine Orchestra	–	Richmond, IN	Gennett	rejected	11856
06/20/24	Wolverine Orchestra	–	Richmond, IN	Gennett	20062	11931-C
10/05/27	Bix Beiderbecke and his Gang	–	New York City	OKeh	8544	81519-B
10/12/27	Original Wolverines	–	Chicago	Brunswick	3708	C-1290
12/06/30	Casa Loma Orchestra	–	New York City	Columbia	2884-D	404573-B
03/06/31	Ted Lewis and his Band	V	New York City	Columbia	2527-D	151398-2
08/01/33	Buddy Featherstonhaugh and his Cosmopolitans	–	London	Decca	F-3649	TB-1022
01/20/34	Brad Gowans' New Orleans Rhythm Kings	–	New York City	American Record Corp.	rejected	14653
10/03/34	Wingy Manone and his Orchestra	–	New York City	OKeh	41570	16086-1
03/27/35	Zutty [Singleton] and his Band	–	Chicago	Decca	465	C-9882-A
06/06/35	[Benny Goodman] Rhythm Makers Orchestra	–	New York City	NBC Thesaurus	295	92216-1
04/03/36	Tommy Dorsey and his Orchestra	–	New York City	Victor	25326	99950-1
06/10/36	Casa Loma Orchestra	–	New York City	Decca	986	61154-A
08/19/36	Bob Crosby and his Orchestra	–	New York City	Decca	1850	61217-A
10/19/36	Benny Carter and his Swing Quintet	–	London	Vocalion	S-46	S-132-1
06/25/38	Leith Stevens and his Swing Club Orchestra	–	New York City	Vocalion	4210	23163-1
12/19/38	Mezzrow-Ladnier Quintet	–	New York City	Bluebird	B-10087	030450-1
12/19/38	Mezzrow-Ladnier Quintet	–	New York City	Victor	X LVA-3027	030450-2
06/19/39	Wingy Manone and his Orchestra	–	New York City	Bluebird	B-10331	037729-1
07/28/39	John Kirby and his Orchestra	–	New York City	Vocalion/OKeh	5187	24946-A
11/07/40	Benny Goodman and his Sextet featuring Count Basie	–	New York City	Columbia	35810	CO-29028-1

Date	Performer	Vocal	Place	Label	Issue	Matrix
12/40	Art Hodes' Columbia Quintet	–	New York City	Jazz Records	1001	HS-1201
05/06/41	Sid Phillips Quintet	–	London	Decca	F-7972	DR-5681-1
07/24/42	Count Basie and his All-American Rhythm Section	–	Hollywood	Columbia	36710	HCO-874-1

Runnin' Wild

Date	Performer	Vocal	Place	Label	Issue	Matrix
12/22	Cotton Pickers	–	New York City	Brunswick	2382	9487
12/22	Joseph Samuels' Jazz Band	–	New York City	Paramount	20190	1263-1-3
12/22	Original Memphis Five	–	New York City	Banner	1143	5025-1-2-3
12/22	Nathan Glantz	–	New York City	Pathe Actuelle	020883	69966
12/02/22	Southland Six	–	New York City	Vocalion	14476	10393
12/05/22	Ted Lewis and his Band	–	Chicago	Columbia	A-3790	80703-3
12/27/22	Virginians	V	New York City	Victor	19027	27263-1-3
c 01/16/23	Ladd's Black Aces	V	New York City	Gennett	5035	8173-A-B
03/16/23	Original Capitol Orchestra	–	Hayes, Middlesex	Zonophone	rejected	Yy-2711-1-2
c 07/23	[Billy Arnold] Novelty Jazz Band	–	Paris	Pathe	6616	6965
11/07/23	Savoy Havana Band	–	London	Columbia	952	AX-210
10/24	Neger-Jazz-Orchester	–	Berlin	Vox	01637	–
04/01/29	Southern Blues Singers	V	Richmond, IN	Gennett	6845	14981-A
10/17/30	[Duke Ellington] Jungle Band	V	New York City	Brunswick	4952	E-34927-A
10/27/30	James Cole's Washboard Band	–	Richmond, IN	Champion	16150	17204
06/18/34	Red Nichols and his World-Famous Pennies	V	Chicago	Bluebird	B-5553	80642-1
03/29/35	Nat Gonella and his Georgians [medley]	V	London	Parlophone	F-148	CE-6907-1
05/29/35	Jimmie Lunceford and his Orchestra	V	New York City	Decca	503	39554-A
02/03/37	Benny Goodman Quartet	–	New York City	Victor	25529	04561-1
03/25/37	Benny Goodman Quartet	–	New York City	Columbia	ML-4591	–
04/26/37	Quintette of the Hot Club of France	–	Paris	His Master's Voice	B-8614	OLA-1712-1
07/06/37	Joe Daniels and his Hot Shots	–	London	Parlophone	F-889	CE-8478-1
11/05/37	Emilio Caceres Trio	–	New York City	Victor	26109	015750-1
11/30/39	Raymond Scott and his New Orchestra	–	New York City	Columbia	rejected	26316-A-B
12/21/39	Raymond Scott and his New Orchestra	–	New York City	Columbia	rejected	26316-C-D
11/11/40	Maestro Paul Laval and his Woodwindy Ten	–	New York City	Victor	27303	057615-1
09/12/41	Sid Phillips Quintet	–	London	Decca	F-8147	DR-6231-1

St. James Infirmary

Date	Performer	Vocal	Place	Label	Issue	Matrix
12/12/28	Louis Armstrong and his Savoy Ballroom Five	V	Chicago	OKeh	8657	402225-A
c 11/29	Kansas City Frank and his Footwarmers	–	Chicago	Paramount	12898	21470-1-2
c 11/06/29	George E. Lee and his Orchestra	V	Kansas City	Brunswick	4684	KC-586-

Date	Performer	Vocal	Place	Label	Issue	Matrix
c 01/30	Carl Fenton and his Orchestra	V	Long Island City	QRS	Q-1023	2002-3
01/16/30	Rube Bloom and his Bayou Boys	V	New York City	Columbia	2103-D	149772-2
01/27/30	Mattie Hite	V	New York City	Columbia	14503-D	149914-3
01/28/30	King Oliver and his Orchestra	V	New York City	Victor	22298	58527-3
01/28/30	Gene Austin	V	New York City	Victor	22299	58530-3
01/29/30	[Duke Ellington] Ten Black Berries	V	New York City	Conqueror	7486	9319-1
01/29/30	[Duke Ellington] Ten Black Berries	V	New York City	Banner	0594	9319-2
01/29/30	[Duke Ellington] Ten Black Berries	V	New York City	Banner	0594	9319-3
01/31/30	Mills' Merry Makers	V	New York City	Harmony	1104-H	149953-1
02/08/30	Alex Hill and his Orchestra	V	Chicago	Vocalion	1465	C-5273-
02/14/30	Chick Bullock	V	New York City	Banner	0647	9367-2-3
02/24/30	California Ramblers	V	New York City	Grey Gull/Radiex	1843	3912-C-E
03/30	[Duke Ellington] Harlem Hot Chocolates	V	New York City	Hit of the Week	1046	1046
03/05/30	Alphonse Trent and his Orchestra	V	Richmond, IN	Gennett	7161	16350-A
04/29/30	Spike Hughes and his Dance Orchestra	V	London	Decca	F-1787	MB-1251-1
12/23/30	Cab Calloway and his Orchestra	V	New York City	Brunswick	6105	E-35882-A
c 05/31	Emmett Matthews	V	Grafton, WI	Paramount	13087	L-905-2
05/18/31	Garland Wilson	V	New York City	Columbia	Special	230206-2
09/30/31	Spike Hughes and his Three Blind Mice	V	London	Decca	F-2584	GB-3345-3
12/21/32	Louis Armstrong and his Orchestra [medley]	V	Camden, NJ	Victor	36084	74877-3
12/15/40	Jack Teagarden's Big Eight	V	New York City	Hot Record Society	2006	3414
05/26/41	Jack Teagarden and his Orchestra	V	Los Angeles	Decca	3844	DLA-2414-A
07/03/41	Cab Calloway and his Orchestra	V	New York City	OKeh	6391	30838-1
07/24/41	Cab Calloway and his Orchestra	V	New York City	OKeh	6391	30838-4
11/12/41	Artie Shaw and his Orchestra [2 parts]	V	New York City	Victor	27895	068195-1-2; 068196-2
04/42	Lu Watters' Yerba Buena Jazz Band	–	San Francisco	Jazz Masters	rejected	–

The St. Louis Blues

Date	Performer	Vocal	Place	Label	Issue	Matrix
12/18/15	Prince's Band	–	New York City	Columbia	A-5772	37476-3
09/17	Ciro's Club Coon Orchestra	V	London	Columbia	699	76007-1
03/03–07/19	Lt. Jim Europe's 369th Infantry Band	–	New York City	Pathe	22087	67471
c 04/19	[Yerkes] Novelty Five	–	New York City	Aeolian Vocalion	12148	–
c 11/20	Al Bernard	V	New York City	Brunswick	2062	4607
c 04/21	The Scandalous Syncopators	–	New York City	Grey Gull	1065	1251-B
05/03/21	Original Dixieland Jazz Band	V	New York City	Victor	rejected	25073-1-2-3-4
05/25/21	Original Dixieland Jazz Band	V	New York City	Victor	18772	25412-2
c 07/21	Lanin's Southern Serenaders	V	New York City	Arto	9097	–
10/21	Esther Bigeou	V	New York City	OKeh	8026	70224-A
01/22	Handy's Memphis Blues Band	–	New York City	Paramount	200983	970-2-3
12/07/22	Ted Lewis and his Band	–	Chicago	Columbia	A-3790	80711-1-2
07/18/23	K. K. Pierce	–	Richmond, IN	Gennett	rejected	11549

Date	Performer	Vocal	Place	Label	Issue	Matrix
c 08/23	Jimmy's Joys	–	Los Angeles	Golden	B-1865	G-1865
04/14/24	Bernie Cummins and his Orchestra	–	Richmond, IN	Gennett	rejected	11840
05/19/24	Bernie Cummins and his Orchestra	–	Richmond, IN	Gennett	5466	11879
06–07/24	Boyd Senter	–	Chicago	Autograph	none	545
c 11/24	Kansas City Five	–	New York City	Ajax	17078	31711
01/14/25	Bessie Smith	V	New York City	Columbia	14064-D	140241-1
10/14/25	Eddie Peabody	–	New York City	Banner	1646	6240-3
c 10/19/25	Jimmy Joy's Baker Hotel Orchestra	–	Dallas	OKeh	40539	9377-A
c 11/13/25	Boyd Senter	–	New York City	Pathe Actuelle	36397	106399
03/29/26	Paul Whiteman and his Orchestra	–	New York City	Victor	20092	35251-2
04/11/26	Paul Whiteman and his Orchestra	–	London	His Master's Voice	rejected	CR-261-1
06/03/26	Ted Lewis and his Band	–	New York	Columbia	697-D	142276-2
06/18/26	Gus Mulcay	–	New York City	Harmony	408-H	142316-1
08/19/26	Virginia Childs	V	New York City	Columbia	rejected	142541-1-2-3
09/26	Joe Candullo and his Everglades Orchestra	–	New York City	Banner	1839	6806-1
09/26	Joe Candullo and his Everglades Orchestra	–	New York City	Regal	8310	6806-2
09/26	Joe Candullo and his Everglades Orchestra	–	New York City	Banner	1839	6806-3
09/26	Joe Candullo and his Everglades Orchestra	–	New York City	Regal	8150	6806-5
09/26	Bessie Brown	V	New York City	Banner	1859	6814-2
09/26	Bessie Brown	V	New York City	Oriole	746	6814-3
09/09/26	Abe Lyman and his Orchestra	–	New York	Brunswick	3316	E-21036/7
11/15/26	Gilbert Watson and his Orchestra	–	New York City	Domino	21563	E-2586-1
11/17/26	Fats Waller	–	Camden, NJ	Victor	20357	36773-1
c 27	Nashville Jazzers	–	New York City	Van Dyke/Madison	5001	102-A-B
c 01/27	Original Indiana Five	–	New York City	Emerson	3119	31075-1-2
c 02/22/27	Lanin's Broadway Broadcasters	–	New York City	Cameo	1149	2357-A-B
04/05/27	Al Bernard	V	New York City	Brunswick	3547	E-22629
04/07/27	Johnny Sylvester and his Playmates	–	New York City	Gennett	6099	GEX-583-A
05/07/27	Alex Jackson's Plantation Orchestra	–	New York City	Vocalion	rejected	E-4939/40
05/12/27	[Fletcher Henderson] Dixie Stompers	–	New York City	Harmony	451-H	144136-1
c 06/27	Novelty Blue Boys	–	New York City	Grey Gull	1464	2507-A-B
11/14/27	Al Bernard	V	New York City	OKeh	409962	81820-B
12/27	Devine's Wisconsin Roof Orchestra	–	Chicago	Paramount	20582	20270-1
01/12/28	Sonny Clay and his Orchestra	–	Los Angeles	Vocalion	rejected	LAE-6; E-6840
02/23/28	Leroy Smith and his Orchestra	–	Camden, NJ	Victor	21328	43429-2
04/02/28	Sidney Williams	–	Chicago	Vocalion	15691	C-1858; E-7285
04/24/28	Barrel-House Pete [Art Gillham]	–	New Orleans	Columbia	rejected	146181-1-2
05/01/28	Irene Beasley	V	New York City	Victor	21467	43935-3
06/15/28	Roy Evans	V	New York City	Columbia	rejected	146529-1-2-3
06/23/28	Roy Evans	V	New York City	Columbia	1697-D	146529-5
08/09/28	Emmett Miller	V	New York City	OKeh	41095	401061-B
08/28/28	Zaidee Jackson	V	Hayes, Middlesex	His Master's Voice	rejected	Bb-14926-1-2

Date	Performer	Vocal	Place	Label	Issue	Matrix
c 09/28	Katherine Henderson	V	Long Island City	QRS	R-7024	236-A
09/10/28	George C. Hill's Band	–	Richmond, IN	Gennett	rejected	14263
11/14/28	Lud Gluskin Ambassadonians	–	Paris	Pathe	35703	N-8902-1
12/20/28	Warren Mills and his Blues Serenaders [w/Ellington]	V	New York City	Jazz Archives	21 (LP)	49007-1
12/20/28	Warren Mills and his Blues Serenaders [w/Ellington]	V	New York City	Victor	35962	49007-2
01/17/29	Adrian Schubert and his Salon Orchestra	V	New York City	Banner	6323	8470-2-3
c 02/07/29	Harold "Scrappy" Lambert	V	New York City	Vocalion	15804	E-29241-
02/26/29	Jimmy Noone's Apex Club Orchestra	–	Chicago	Swaggie	JCS-33787 (LP)	C-3005-A
05/10/29	Tony Parenti	–	New York City	American Record Corp.	rejected	8743-1-2-3
05/24/29	Irving Mills and his Hotsy Totsy Gang	–	New York City	Banner	32701	E-29947-A
06/07/29	W.E. Burton	–	Richmond, IN	Paramount	12787	15159
c 06/24/29	Bessie Smith [4 parts]	V	New York City	Circle	J-1016; J-1017	NY-39-40-41-42
06/28/29	Tony Parenti	–	New York City	American Record Corp.	rejected	8743-4-5
10/29	Eddie Peabody	–	New York City	Banner	6564	4163-; 9081
12/13/29	Louis Armstrong and his Orchestra	V	New York City	OKeh	41350	403495-B
03/21/30	Fats Waller	–	New York City	Victor	22371	59720-1
03/21/30	Seger Ellis	–	New York City	OKeh	41447	403874-C
07/15/30	Jimmy Dorsey	–	London	Decca	F-6142	MB-1621-1
07/24/30	Cab Calloway and his Orchestra	V	New York City	Brunswick	4936	E-33355-A
10/01/30	Guy Lombardo and his Royal Canadians	V	New York City	Columbia	50256-D	98722-3
c 03/31	Laura Rucker	V	Grafton, WI	Paramount	13075	L-818-2
04/31	Eubie Blake and his Orchestra	V	New York City	Crown	3130	1298-3-4
06/09/31	Dave's [Nelson] Harlem Highlights	V	New York City	Timely Tunes	C-1588	69908-2
07/15/31	Ambrose and his Orchestra	–	London	His Master's Voice	rejected	OB-1291-1-2
08/31	Dixie Serenaders	V	Los Angeles	Champion	16365	18182
02/11/32	Duke Ellington and his Orchestra [w/Bing Crosby]	V	New York City	Brunswick	20105	BX-11263-A
02/11/32	Duke Ellington and his Orchestra [w/Bing Crosby]	V	New York City	Brunswick	20105	BX-11263-B
06/15/32	Fred Elizalde	–	London	Decca	rejected	GB-4570-1-2-3
10/05/32	Jack Hylton and his Orchestra	V	London	Decca	F-3239	GB-4985-2
12/23/32	Ethel Waters	V	New York City	Brunswick	6521	B-12790-A
03/21/33	Art Tatum	–	New York City	Brunswick	6543	B-13163-A
03/21/33	Art Tatum	–	New York City	Brunswick	6543	B-13163-B
04/26/33	Louis Armstrong and his Orchestra	–	Chicago	Victor	24320	75480-1
08/19/33	Washboard Rhythm Kings	V	New York City	Banner	32867	13839-1
08/22/33	Joseph Robechaux and his New Orleans Rhythm Boys	–	New York City	Vocalion	2539	13852-2
12/06/33	Clarence Williams and his Orchestra	–	New York City	Vocalion	2676	14424-1
06/34	Herman Chittison	–	Paris	Brunswick	A-500451	1246wpp
06/23/34	Pat Hyde	V	London	Parlophone	R-1898	CE-6585-1

Date	Performer	Vocal	Place	Label	Issue	Matrix
08/23/34	Dorsey Brothers Orchestra	–	New York City	Decca	119	38408-A-B
10/34	Louis Armstrong and his Orchestra	V	Paris	Brunswick	A-9683	1478wpp
12/07/34	Gladys Keep	V	London	Regal Zonophone	MR-1531	CAR-3099-1
12/18/34	Scott Wood and his Six Swingers [medley]	–	London	Regal Zonophone	MR-1567	CAR-3123-1
02/25/35	Billy Mason and his Orchestra	–	London	Decca	rejected	TB-1720-1
03/29/35	Nat Gonella and his Georgians [medley]	–	London	Parlophone	F-148	CE-6907-1
05/22/35	Louis DeVries and his Rhythm Boys	–	London	Decca	rejected	GB-7148-1-2
05/28/35	Boswell Sisters	V	New York City	Brunswick	7467	B-17646-2
05/28/35	Boswell Sisters	V	New York City	Brunswick	7467	B-17646-3
06/05/35	Louis DeVries and his Rhythm Boys	–	London	Decca	F-5566	GB-7148-5
06/06/35	[Benny Goodman] Rhythm Makers Orchestra	–	New York City	NBC Thesaurus	165	92214-1
06/10/35	Ray Noble and his Orchestra	V	New York City	Victor	25082	92232-1
06/28/35	Joe Daniels and his Hot Shots	–	London	Parlophone	rejected	CE-7068-1
07/01/35	Peggy Dell	V	London	Decca	F-5606	GB-7290-1
07/17/35	Joe Daniels and his Hot Shots	–	London	Parlophone	F-211	CE-7068-2
07/19/35	Washboard Serenaders	V	London	Parlophone	F-428	CE-7110-1
07/24/35	Nat Gonella and his Georgians [medley]	V	London	Parlophone	F-209	CE-7084-1
08/35	Frank "Big Boy" Goudie	–	Paris	Ultraphon	AP-1527	P-77469
08/06/35	Arthur Young and his Youngsters [medley]	–	London	Decca	F-5709	TB-1858-1
09/35	Andre Ekyan and his Orchestra	–	Paris	Ultraphon	AP-1545	77524
09/06/35	Larry Adler	V	London	Regal Zonophone	MR-1883	CA-15219-1
09/30/35	Stephane Grappelly and his Hot Four	–	Paris	Decca	F-5824	2009hpp
11/01/35	Joe Daniels and his Hot Shots	–	London	Parlophone	F-211	CE-7068-3
11/09/35	Lew Stone and his Band	–	London	Decca	F-5783	TB-2054-1
01/02/36	Mustang Band of SMU	–	Los Angeles	Decca	rejected	DLA-296
06/04/36	Bob Howard [medley]	–	London	Brunswick	02239	TB-2214-1
07/08/36	Ballyhooligans	–	London	His Master's Voice	BD-5089	OEA-3832-1
07/27/36	Joe Haymes and his Orchestra	–	New York City	Vocalion	3369	19618-1
08/21/36	Benny Goodman and his Orchestra	–	Hollywood	Victor	25411	97748-1
09/30/36	Teddy Foster and his Kings of Swing	V	London	Decca	F-6149	TB-2511-1
c 01/37	Larry Adler	–	London	Rex	8959	F-2123
03/11/37	Brian Lawrance and his Lansdowne House Sextet	V	London	Decca	F-6343	TB-2912-2
03/27/37	Rhythm Wreckers	V	Los Angeles	Vocalion	3566	LA-1291-A
04/14/37	Noble Sissle and his Orchestra	–	New York City	Vri	rejected	M-401-1-2
05/10/37	Frank Dailey and his Orchestra	–	New York City	Vri	?	M-458
09/09/37	Django Reinhardt	–	Paris	Swing	7	OLA-1952-1
11/30/37	Benny Goodman and his Orchestra	–	New York City	Columbia	ML-4590	–
38–40	Avery "Kid" Howard	V	New Orleans	Mono	MNLP-12 (LP)	–
06/29/38	Maxine Sullivan	V	New York City	Victor	25895	023752-1
07/08/38	Matty Malneck	–	Los Angeles	Decca	2182	DLA-1309-A
08/20/38	Bluebird Military Band	–	New York City	Bluebird	B-7816	026681-1

Date	Performer	Vocal	Place	Label	Issue	Matrix
09/29/38	Mildred Bailey and her Orchestra	V	New York City	CBS	CL-1861	23516-1
09/29/38	Mildred Bailey and her Orchestra	V	New York City	Vocalion	4801	23516-3
11/05/38	Jam Session	–	New York City	Jazz Panorama	LP-9	–
summer/38	Roy Peyton	–	Oslo	Rex	EB-385	RP-05
04/08/39	Albert Ammons	–	New York City	Solo Art	12003	R-2090
08/07/39	Fats Waller and his Rhythm	–	New York City	Victor	RD-7553	–
09–10/39	Pete Johnson and Albert Ammons	–	Chicago	Storyville	670184 (LP)	–
11/28/39	Artie Shaw and his Orchestra	–	New York City	Victor	LPT-6000 (LP)	–
12/26/39	W. C. Handy's Orchestra	–	New York City	Varsity	8163	US-1223-1
02/07/40	Billy Cotton and his Band	V	London	Rex	9796	R-4315-1
02/13/40	Earl Hines and his Orchestra	–	New York City	Victor	LPV-512	047055-2
02/13/40	Earl Hines and his Orchestra	–	New York City	Bluebird	B-10674	047055-1
05/01/40	Maxine Sullivan	V	New York City	Columbia	36341	26788-C
07/26/40	Valaida Med Winstrup Olesens Swingband	V	Copenhagen	Tono	21166	1065-B
07/26/40	Art Tatum	–	Los Angeles	Decca	8550	DLA-2068-A
07/28/40	Dr. Henry Levine's Barefoot Dixieland Philharmonic	–	New York City	Victor	PM-42409	–
08/06/40	Gene Krupa and his Orchestra	–	Chicago	OKeh	rejected	WC-3212-A
10/15/40	Billie Holiday	V	New York City	OKeh	6064	28874-1
10/15/40	Billie Holiday	V	New York City	OKeh	6064	28874-2
11/07/40	Duke Ellington and his Orchestra	–	Fargo, ND	Palm	30-11	–
04/09/41	Fred Boehler and his Band	V	Zurich	Columbia	ZZ-1019	–
c 05/41	Jack Teagarden and his Orchestra	V	Hollywood	[film: Birth of the Blues]	[promotional]	PP-306
06/23/41	Dixieland Jazz Group of NBC . . .	V	New York City	Victor	27542	066127-1
11/16/41	First English Public Jam Session [2 parts]	–	London	His Master's Voice	B-9250	OEA-9447; OEA-9448-1
11/27/41	Sid Phillips Quintet	–	London	Decca	rejected	DR-6496-1-2
02/11/42	John Kirby and his Orchestra	–	New York City	Victor	27926	071903-1
02/11/42	John Kirby and his Orchestra	–	New York City	Victor	LPM-10016 (LP)	071903-2
03/10/42	Benny Goodman Sextet	–	New York City	Epic	EE-22025 (LP)	CO-32595-1
07/17/42	Art Hodes	–	New York City	B & W	2	2B-4
07/24/42	Count Basie and his All-American Rhythm Section	–	Hollywood	Columbia	36711	HCO-880-1
c 08/42	Teddy Weatherford	V	Calcutta	Columbia	FB-40220	CEI-22185-1

San

Date	Performer	Vocal	Place	Label	Issue	Matrix
04/11/21	Benson Orchestra of Chicago	–	Camden, NJ	Victor	18779	25149-4
c 08/21	Lindsay McPhail	–	New York City	Pathe Actuelle	020623	–
c 08/21	Lindsay McPhail	–	New York City	Olympic	15122	–
03/10/22	Husk O'Hare's Super Orchestra of Chicago	–	Richmond, IN	Gennett	5009	11068
03/14/24	Mound City Blue Blowers	–	Chicago	Brunswick	2602	112-CH

Date	Performer	Vocal	Place	Label	Issue	Matrix
04/10/24	Ted Lewis and his Band	–	New York City	Columbia	122-D	81681-2
05/14/24	Varsity Eight	–	New York City	Cameo	556	1002-D
06/09/24	Paul Whiteman and his Orchestra	–	New York City	Victor	19381	30172-3
c 06/18/24	Lido Venice Dance Orchestra	–	New York City	Pathe Actuelle	036110	105395
07–08/24	Nathan Glantz	–	New York City	Banner	1399	5585-3
c 07/28/24	Ben Selvin and his Orchestra	–	New York City	Vocalion	14851	13430
08/24	Original Louisiana Five	–	New York City	Lyra/Pur/Tri	11413	1869-2
09/24/24	Georgia Melodians	–	New York City	Edison Diamond Disc	51412	9733
01/07/25	Oliver Naylor's Orchestra	–	New York City	Victor	test	–
04/25	"Alex Hyde" m. sein. New Yorker Original Jazz-Orchester	–	Berlin	Deutsche Grammophon/Polydor	20219	1902at
04/02/25	Barbary Coast Orchestra	–	New York City	Columbia	72-P	170032-1
09/25	Julian Fuhs Follies Band	–	Berlin	Homochord	B-1905	M-17993
05/12/26	University Six	–	New York City	Harmony	224-H	142196-2-3
c 03/07/27	John Williams' Synco Jazzers	–	Chicago	Gennett	rejected	12628
04/21/27	Johnny Dodds	–	Chicago	Brunswick	3574	C-775; E-22704
05/21/27	John Williams' Band	–	Chicago	Gennett	rejected	GEX-658, -A
c 01/02/28	Alabama Red Peppers	V	New York City	Cameo	8109	2788-A-C
01/12/28	Paul Whiteman and his Orchestra	–	New York City	Victor	24078	30172-6
01/12/28	Paul Whiteman and his Orchestra	–	New York City	Victor	25367	30172-7
05/21/28	Abe Lyman's Sharps and Flats	–	Chicago	Brunswick	3964	C-1954-A
[?] 06/28	Tub Jug Washboard Band	–	Chicago	Paramount	12671	20671-2
Late 28– early 29	Jack Hamilton and his Entertainers	–	Paris	Azurephone	1011	4761
01/08/30	Ted Lewis and his Band	–	New York City	Columbia	2113-D	149743-4
07/01/30	Jimmy Noone's Apex Club Orchestra	–	Chicago	Swaggie	JCS-33786 (LP)	C-5903-A
07/01/30	Jimmy Noone's Apex Club Orchestra	–	Chicago	Ace of Hearts	84 (LP)	C-5903-B
01/04/31	Jack Harris and his Orchestra	–	London	Decca	F-2174	GB-2489-2
03/05/32	Red Pepper Sam	–	New York City	Melotone	91295	11413-1
05/17/32	Pickens Sisters	V	New York City	Victor	24025	72593-1
08/04/32	Gene Kardos and his Orchestra	–	New York City	Victor	24122	73167-1
10/15/36	Ballyhooligans	–	London	His Master's Voice	BD-5168	OEA-3879-1
10/22/36	Scott Wood and his Six Swingers [medley]	–	London	Columbia	FB-1556	CA-15996-1

The Sheik of Araby

Date	Performer	Vocal	Place	Label	Issue	Matrix
11/17/21	California Ramblers	–	New York City	Vocalion	14275	8261
12/14/21	California Ramblers	–	New York City	Arto	9114	–
c 02/22	Mitchell's Jazz Kings	–	Paris	Pathe	6550	5926
07/03/30	Red Nichols and his Five Pennies	V	New York City	Brunswick	4885	E-33333-A
11/05/30	Spike Hughes and his Orchestra	–	London	Decca	F-2114	GB-2188-3
05/16/32	Duke Ellington and his Famous Orchestra	–	New York City	Brunswick	6336	B-11840-A

Date	Performer	Vocal	Place	Label	Issue	Matrix
08/01/33	Buddy Featherstonhaugh and his Cosmopolitans	–	London	Decca	F-3650	TB-1021-1
08/17/33	Buddy Featherstonhaugh and his Cosmopolitans	–	London	Decca	rejected	GB-6090-1-2
09/19/34	Tiny Bradshaw and his Orchestra	V	New York City	Decca	194	38696-A
01/29/35	KXYZ Novelty Band	–	San Antonio	Bluebird	B-5831	87762-1
05/08/35	Willie Bryant and his Orchestra	–	New York City	Victor	25038	89819-2
07/19/35	Washboard Serenaders	V	London	Parlophone	F-428	CE-7108-1
09/01/35	Alix Combelle	–	Paris	Ultraphon	AP-1544	77523
10/29/35	Nat Gonella and his Georgians	V	London	Parlophone	F-317	CE-7215-1
10/22/36	Scott Wood and his Six Swingers [medley]	–	London	Columbia	FB-1556	CA-15995-1
11/18/36	Don Albert and his Orchestra	V	San Antonio	Vocalion	3411	SA-2520-1
02/27/37	Three Peppers	V	New York City	Vri	rejected	M-139
03/26/37	Bogan's Birmingham Busters	V	Birmingham, AL	Vocalion	03570	B-38-1
04/27/37	Quintette of the Hot Club of France	–	Paris	His Master's Voice	B-8737	OLA-1737-1
06/15/37	Benny Goodman Quartet	–	New York City	Phillips	B-21208-H	–
06/18/37	Joe Sodja's Swingtette	–	New York City	Vri	rejected	M-529-1
07/08/37	Joe Daniels and his Hot Shots	–	London	Parlophone	F-844	CE-8463-1
11/29/37	Art Tatum	–	New York City	Decca	2052	62825-A
04/06/38	Ozzie Nelson and his Orchestra	–	Hollywood	Bluebird	B-7517	019194-1
04/12/38	Fats Waller, his Rhythm and his Orchestra	V	New York City	RFW	3 (LP)	022434-1
04/12/38	Fats Waller, his Rhythm and his Orchestra	V	New York City	Victor	25847	022434-2
07/09/38	Tommy Dorsey and his Clambake Seven	–	Hollywood	Victor	rejected	019418-1
07/15/38	Tommy Dorsey and his Clambake Seven	–	Hollywood	Victor	26023	019418-2
09/22/38	Ken "Snakehips" Johnson and his West Indian Dance Orchestra	–	London	Decca	F-6958	DR-2938-1
04/14/39	Jack Teagarden and his Orchestra	V	New York City	Brunswick	8370	B-24376-A
05/24/39	Woody Herman and his Orchestra	–	New York City	Decca	2539	65635-A
05/24/39	Andre Ekyan et son Orchestre	–	Paris	His Master's Voice	FELP-1120	OSW-72
08/07/39	Fats Waller	V	New York City	Victor	RD-7552	–
10/06/39	Benny Goodman Trio	–	New York City	Polygon	6007	–
01/03/40	Coleman Hawkins' All-Star Octet	–	New York City	Bluebird	B-10770	046157-1
c 04/40	Harry James and his Orchestra	–	New York City	Varsity	8270	US-1560-1-2
04/10/40	Benny Goodman Sextet	–	Los Angeles	Columbia	35466	WCO-26718-A
10/22/40	Noel Chiboust and his Orchestra	–	Paris	Swing	86	OSW-139-1
04/08/41	Nat Gonella and his New Georgians	V	London	Columbia	FB-2620	CA-18448-1
04/18/41	Sidney Bechet's One-Man Band	–	New York City	Victor	27485	063785-1
04/18/41	Sidney Bechet's One-Man Band	–	New York City	Victor	LPV-510 (LP)	063785-2
09/16/41	Teddy Wilson and his Orchestra	–	New York City	Columbia	rejected	31322-1

Shine

Date	Performer	Vocal	Place	Label	Issue	Matrix
04/18/24	California Ramblers	–	New York City	Columbia	127-D	81699-3
04/30/24	Virginians	–	New York City	Victor	19334	29953-3
05/01/24	Vagabonds	–	New York City	Gennett	5447	8859-A
06/24	Jeffries and his Rialto Orchestra	–	London	Aco	G-15472	C-6449
c 05/07/24	Original Memphis Five	–	New York City	Pathe Actuelle	036095	105306
04/25	Alex Hyde M. Sein. New Yorker Original Jazz-Orchester	–	Berlin	Deutsche Grammophon/Polydor	20218	1897at
07/28	Jesse Stafford and his Orchestra	–	Los Angeles	Brunswick	4048	LAE-219
03/13/29	Boyd Senter and his Senterpedes	V	New York City	Victor	21912	49781-3
11/25/29	Reuben "River" Reeves and his River Boys	–	Chicago	Vocalion	rejected	C-4746
03/09/31	Louis Armstrong and his Cotton Club Orchestra	V	Paris	OKeh	41486	404421-C
02/29/32	Bing Crosby	V	New York City	Brunswick	6276	B-11376-A
06/25/32	Chick Bullock	V	New York City	Oriole	2506	11972-1
07/29/33	King's Jesters	–	Chicago	Bluebird	B-5184	75980-1
06/18/34	Red Nichols and his World-Famous Pennies	V	Chicago	Bluebird	B-5553	80632-1
11/23/34	Jimmy Noone and his Orchestra	–	Chicago	Vocalion	2888	C-860-A
01/11/35	Pinky Tomlin [medley]	V	Los Angeles	Brunswick	7378	LA-318-A
02/01/35	Brian Lawrance and the Quaglino Quartet	V	London	Panachord	25685	GB-6922-1
08/09/35	Slim Green	V	New York City	Decca	7120	39844-A
11/18/35	Val Rosing and his Swing Stars	V	London	Columbia	FB-1236	CA-15457-1
01/18/36	Billy Cotton's Cotton Pickers	V	London	Regal Zonophone	MR-2161	CAR-3875-1
02/36	Chick Webb and his Orchestra [w/Ella Fitzgerald]	V	New York City	Jazz Archives	JA-33 (LP)	–
10/15/36	Quintette of the Hot Club of France	V	Paris	His Master's Voice	K-7790	OLA-1293-1
11/19/36	Ella Fitzgerald and her Savoy Eight	V	New York City	Decca	1062	61421-A
08/10/37	Benny Goodman Quartet	–	Los Angeles	Columbia	ML-4591	–
01/16/38	Benny Goodman and his Orchestra	–	New York City	Columbia	A-1049	–
06/30/39	Louis Bacon and his Orchestra	–	Paris	Swing	185	OSW-92-1
12/15/40	Jack Teagarden's Big Eight	–	New York City	Hot Record Society	2006	3417
01/28/41	Kid Punch Miller Trio	–	Chicago	Paramount	CJS-102 (LP)	–
02/04/42	Henry Levine and his Strictly from Dixie Jazz Band	–	New York City	Victor	27831	071766-1

Solitude

Date	Performer	Vocal	Place	Label	Issue	Matrix
01/10/34	Duke Ellington and his Orchestra	–	Chicago	Victor	24755	80149-1
09/11/34	Benny Goodman and his Music Hall Orchestra	–	New York City	Banner	33192	15583-1
09/12/34	Duke Ellington and his Orchestra	–	New York City	Brunswick	6987	B-15910-A

Date	Performer	Vocal	Place	Label	Issue	Matrix
10/06/34	Five Lucky Strikes	?	New York City	American Record Corp.	rejected	16116-
11/07/34	Jimmie Lunceford and his Orchestra	V	New York City	Decca	299	38969-A
12/05/34	Mills Blue Rhythm Band	V	New York City	Columbia	2994-D	CO-16272-1
12/28/34	Lew Stone and his Band	–	London	Regal Zonophone	MR-1561	CAR-3143-1
01/11/35	Dorsey Brothers Orchestra	V	New York City	Decca	15013	39243-A
01/17/35	Dorsey Borthers Orchestra	–	New York City	Design	DLP-20	–
03/11/35	Fats Waller [medley]	V	New York City	Victor	LPT-6001	–
04/26/35	Jack Hylton and his Orchestra	–	London	His Master's Voice	BD-5035	OEA-1856-2
07/02/35	Louis Prima and his New Orleans Gang	V	New York City	Brunswick	7531	B-17765-1
09/06/35	Larry Adler	–	London	Regal Zonophone	MR-1883	CA-15217-1
09/11/35	Nat Gonella and his Georgians	V	London	Parlophone	F-228	CE-7118-1
09/24/35	Joe Paradise and his Music	V	London	Parlophone	F-288	CE-7166-1
12/19/35	Louis Armstrong and his Orchestra	V	New York City	Decca	666	60251-A
12/19/35	Louis Armstrong and his Orchestra	V	New York City	Decca	666	60251-B
01/36	Adelaide Hall	V	Paris	Ultraphon	AP-1575	P-77618
06/04/36	Bob Howard [medley]	–	London	Brunswick	02239	TB-2214-1
12/21/36	Duke Ellington	–	Hollywood	Brunswick	7990	LO-377-1
04/21/37	Quintette of the Hot Club of France	–	Paris	His Master's Voice	B-8669	OLA-1706-1
12/14/38	Joe Daniels and his Hot Shots	–	London	Parlophone	F-1342	CE-9498-1
01/06/39	Meade Lux Lewis	–	New York City	Blue Note	1	443-12
09/28/39	Adrian Rollini Trio	–	Hollywood	Vocalion/OKeh	5376	WM-1085-A
02/09/40	Joe Sullivan and his Cafe Society Orchestra	–	New York City	Vocalion/OKeh	5531	26500-A
02/14/40	Duke Ellington and his Famous Orchestra	V	New York City	Columbia	35427	WM-1137-A
05/09/41	Billie Holiday	V	New York City	OKeh	6270	30460-1
05/14/41	Duke Ellington	–	New York City	Victor	27564	065605-1

Some of These Days

Date	Performer	Vocal	Place	Label	Issue	Matrix
c 11/23/22	Original Dixieland Jazz Band	–	New York City	OKeh	rejected	71043-A-B-C
01/03/23	Original Dixieland Jazz Band	–	New York City	OKeh	4738	71043-F
01/13/23	Paul Specht and his Orchestra	–	New York City	Columbia	rejected	80787-1-2
06/15/23	Art Landry's Call of the North Orchestra	–	Richmond, IN	Gennett	5189	11509
11/09/24	Coon-Sanders' Orchestra	V	Chicago	Victor	19600	31172-3
01/20/25	Art Kahn and his Orchestra	–	Chicago	Columbia	310-D	140268-2
05/06/25	New Orleans Jazz Band	–	New York City	Banner	1544	6006-1
05/06/25	New Orleans Jazz Band	–	New York City	Apex	8359	6006-2
01/19/27	Fletcher Henderson and his Orchestra	V	New York City	Vocalion	1079	E-4397/8
02/08/27	Goofus Five	–	New York City	OKeh	rejected	80404-A-B-C
04/27	Original Indiana Five	V	New York City	Cameo	1138	2407-D
05/27	Original Indiana Five	V	New York City	Banner	6006	7289-2
c 08/04/27	George H. Tremer	V	Birmingham, AL	Gennett	6242	GEX-778-A

Date	Performer	Vocal	Place	Label	Issue	Matrix
08–10/27	Jazz Kings	V	Berlin	Tri-Ergon	TE-5062	MO-859
10/14/27	Ethel Waters	V	New York City	Columbia	14264-D	144867-1
04/24/28	Art Gillham [Barrel-House Pete]	V	New Orleans	Columbia	rejected	146183-1-2
08/28	Black Pirates	–	Chicago	Broadway	1374	20822-2
09/28	Allister Wylie and his Coronado Hotel Orchestra	V	St. Louis	Brunswick	4143	STL-857
01/17/29	Adrian Schubert and his Salon Orchestra	V	New York City	Banner	6300	8471-2-3
01/28/29	Ray Miller and his Orchestra	V	Chicago	Sunny Meadows	F	XC-2882-
06/07/29	Red Nichols and his Five Pennies	V	New York City	Brunswick	20091	XE-29996-A
07/10/29	Sophie Tucker	V	New York City	Victor	22049	55602-2
09/10/29	Louis Armstrong and his Orchestra	V	New York City	OKeh	41298	402943-A
09/10/29	Louis Armstrong and his Orchestra	–	New York City	OKeh	8729	402923-B-C
12/23/30	Cab Calloway and his Orchestra	V	New York City	Brunswick	6020	E-35880-A
01/14/31	Dave Nelson and the King's Men	V	New York City	Victor	23039	64851-2
01/23/31	Spike Hughes and his Orchestra	–	London	Decca	F-2259	GB-2543-1
06/10/31	Snooks and his Memphis Ramblers	–	New York City	Timely Tunes	C-1583	69919-2
07/06/31	Julia Gerity	V	New York City	Victor	test	1119
12/17/31	Gilmore Sisters	–	New York City	Victor	23316	70980-1
32	French Hot Boys	–	Paris	Salabert	3166	SS-873-B
02–03/32	Joel Shaw and his Orchestra	V	New York City	Crown	3285	1670-1
03/05/32	Red Pepper Sam	V	New York City	Melotone	91295	11414-2
05/26/32	Bing Crosby	V	Chicago	Brunswick	6351	JC-8641-1
07/29/33	King's Jesters	–	Chicago	Bluebird	B-6517	75977-1
08/19/33	Washboard Rhythm Kings	V	New York City	Banner	32867	13841-1
09/16/33	Jack Hylton and his Orchestra	V	London	Decca	F-37675	TB-1077-2
06/13/34	Pat Hyde	V	London	Parlophone	R-1871	CE-6529-1
12/18/34	Scott Wood and his Six Swingers [medley]	–	London	Regal Zonophone	MR-1567	CAR-3122-1
02/04/35	Coleman Hawkins	V	The Hague	Decca	F-42052	AM-148-2
07/01/35	Peggy Dell	V	London	Decca	F-5606	GB-7288-1
07/05/35	Clyde McCoy and his Orchestra	–	Chicago	Champion	40108	C-90077-A
09/35	Quintette of the Hot Club of France	–	Paris	Ultraphon	AP-1548	P-77539
09/18/35	Billy Cotton and his Band	V	London	Regal Zonophone	MR-1946	CAR-3598-1
09/26/35	Mario "Harp" Lorenzi and his Rhythmics	V	London	Columbia	FB-1168	CA-15287-1
01/08/36	Ike "Yowse Suh" Hatch and his Harlem Stompers	–	London	Regal Zonophone	MR-2050	CAR-3844-1
02/15/36	Locke Brothers Rhythm Orchestra	V	Charlotte, NC	Bluebird	B-6316	99145-1
02/27/36	Ballyhooligans [medley]	–	London	His Master's Voice	BD-5049	OEA-2706-1
06/04/36	Bob Howard and his Orchestra [medley]	–	London	Brunswick	02230	TB-2213-2
08/07/36	Teddy Foster and his Kings of Swing	V	London	Decca	F-6049	TB-2334-1
09/10/36	Swing Rhythm Boys	V	London	Crown	236	H-623-1
09/12/36	Benny Carter Med Sonora Swing Band	–	Stockholm	Sonora	3188	1879-A-B
01/07/37	Nat Gonella and his Georgians	V	London	Parlophone	F-646	CE-8001-1

Date	Performer	Vocal	Place	Label	Issue	Matrix
03/11/37	Brian Lawrance and his Lansdowne House Sextet	–	London	Decca	F-6343	TB-2909-1
07/08/37	Valaida	V	London	Parlophone	F-952	CE-8486-1
09/13/38	Benny Goodman Quartet	–	Chicago	MGM	E/X-3790	–
10/24/38	Joe Daniels and his Hot Shots	–	London	Parlophone	F-1273	CE-9380-1
02/07/40	Billy Cotton and his Band	V	London	Rex	9796	R-4314-1
06/27/41	Willie Lewis Presents	V	Zurich	Elite Special	4082	1927-

Somebody Stole My Gal

Date	Performer	Vocal	Place	Label	Issue	Matrix
11/20/23	Ted Weems and his Orchestra	–	Camden, NJ	Victor	19212	29015-2
c 03/25/24	[Sam Lanin's] Broadway Broadcasters	–	New York City	Cameo	522	903-A-E
04/16/24	Fletcher Henderson and his Orchestra	–	New York City	Columbia	126-D	81692-3
c 09/11/24	Original Memphis Five	–	New York City	Pathe Actuelle	036141	105550
04/17/28	Bix Beiderbecke and his Gang	–	New York City	OKeh	41030	400616-B
05/28	Fred Elizalde and his Hot Music	–	London	Brunswick	177	575 ?
09/25/28	Whoopee Makers	–	New York City	Columbia	14367-D	147058-3
11/28	Harris Brothers' Texans	V	Dallas	Vocalion	15747	DAL-730
11/09/28	Sammy Stewart and his Orchestra	–	Chicago	Vocalion	rejected	C-2545-A-B-C
11/27/28	The Sizzlers	–	New York City	Edison Diamond Disc	rejected	N-599
11/27/28	The Sizzlers	–	New York City	Edison Diamond Disc	52463	18904
04/17/30	Ted Lewis and his Band	V	New York City	Columbia	2336-D	150478-2
10/31/30	Bennie Moten's Kansas City Orchestra	V	Kansas City	Victor	23028	62927-1
11/12/30	Frankie Franko and his Louisianians	V	Chicago	Melotone	M-12009	C-6179-
03/31	Fletcher Henderson and his Orchestra	V	New York City	Crown	3107	1233-3
06/09/31	Dave's [Nelson] Harlem Highlights	V	New York City	Timely Tunes	C-1587	69905-1
10/12/31	Cab Calloway and his Orchestra	V	New York City	Banner	32323	10868-1-2
05/19/33	Billy Cotton and his Band	V	London	Regal Zonophone	MR-958	CAR-1980-1
c 06/26/33	Blue Mountaineers	V	London	Broadcast	4-Tune 523	1394-2
10/03/34	Alabama Jug Band	–	New York City	Decca	7041	38782
04/04/35	Brian Lawrance and his Quartet	V	London	Panachord	25733	GB-7045-2
06/24/35	Fats Waller and his Rhythm	V	Camden, NJ	Victor	25194	88997-1
04/02/36	Ballyhooligans	–	London	His Master's Voice	BD-5065	OEA-2757-1
06/04/36	Bob Howard and his Orchestra [medley]	–	London	Brunswick	02230	TB-2213-2
09/10/36	Swing Rhythm Boys	V	London	Crown	236	H-622-1
07/26/37	Musical Maniacs	–	New York City	Vocalion	3655	21435-1
03/03/38	Joe Daniels and his Hot Shots	–	London	Parlophone	F-1099	CE-8982-1
02/09/40	Billy Cotton and his Band	V	London	Rex	9789	R-4323-1
03/20/40	Count Basie and his Orchestra	V	New York City	Columbia	35500	26662-A
12/20/40	Benny Goodman and his Orchestra	–	New York City	Columbia	35916	CO-29275-1
02/17/41	Dick Robertson and his Orchestra	V	New York City	Decca	3669	68716-A

Someday Sweetheart

Date	Performer	Vocal	Place	Label	Issue	Matrix
c 05/21	Alberta Hunter	V	New York City	Black Swan	2019	P-125-3
10/05/23	King Oliver and his Creole Jazz Band	–	Richmond, IN	Gennett	rejected	11637, -A-B-C
c 10/30/23	Jelly Roll Morton's Jazz Band	–	Chicago	OKeh	8105	8498-A
12/23	Jimmy Wade's Moulin Rouge Orchestra	–	Chicago	Paramount	20295	1620-1-2
02/25/24	Bucktown Five	–	Richmond, IN	Gennett	5405	11772
03/27/24	Georgians	V	New York City	Columbia	117-D	81655-2
07/23/26	King Oliver and his Dixie Syncopators	–	Chicago	Vocalion	rejected	E-3553
09/17/26	King Oliver and his Dixie Syncopators	–	Chicago	Vocalion	1059	C-657
c 12/13/26	Evelyn Thompson	V	New York City	Vocalion	1075	E-4224/5
12/16/26	Jelly Roll Morton's Red Hot Peppers	–	Chicago	Victor	20405	37254-2
12/16/26	Jelly Roll Morton's Red Hot Peppers	–	Chicago	BRS	1001	37254-3
01/04/27	Charleston Chasers	–	New York City	Columbia	rejected	143258-1-2-3
01/15/27	Original Black and Golds	–	New York City	Gennett	rejected	GEX-458, -A-B
01/21/27	Boyd Senter	–	New York City	OKeh	40819	80325-A
01/27/27	Charleston Chasers	–	New York City	Columbia	861-D	143258-5
c 03/03/27	John Williams' Synco Jazzers	–	Chicago	Gennett	rejected	12621, -A
04/27	Priscilla Stewart	V	Chicago	Paramount	12465	4354-2
05/21/27	John Williams' Band	–	New York City	Gennett	rejected	GEX-659, -A-B
08/12/27	California Ramblers	V	New York City	Banner	6050	7456-2
09/28/27	Original Indiana Five	V	New York City	Harmony	501-H	144805-2
10/14/27	Ethel Waters	V	New York City	Columbia	14264-D	144864-1-2
04/17/30	Ted Lewis and his Band	V	New York City	Columbia	2336-D	150479-4
10/22/31	Joe Venuti-Eddie Lang and their All-Star Orchestra	–	New York City	Vocalion	15858	E-37272-A
03/27/33	Henry Allen-Coleman Hawkins and their Orchestra	–	New York City	Pirate (Bruns)	MPC-513 (rej)	13183-A
08/08/34	Bing Crosby	V	Los Angeles	Decca	101	DLA-9-A
09/07/34	Louis Panico and his Orchestra	–	Chicago	Decca	159	C-9422-
07/13/35	Benny Goodman Trio	–	New York City	Victor	25181	92707-1
09/20/35	Mildred Bailey and her Swing Band	V	New York City	Vocalion	3057	18092-1
01/17/36	Georgia White	V	New York City	Decca	7166	60353-A
06/09/36	Harry Roy's Tiger-Ragamuffins	V	London	Parlophone	F-484	CE-7674-1
04/29/37	Artie Shaw and his New Music	–	New York City	Thesaurus	402	07888-1
05/18/37	Artie Shaw and his New Music	–	New York City	Thesaurus	389	07889-1
05/18/37	Artie Shaw and his New Music	–	New York City	Brunswick	7914	B-21170-1
11/09/37	Benny Goodman and his Orchestra	–	New York City	Columbia	ML-4591	–
12/01/37	Nat Gonella and his Georgians	–	London	Parlophone	F-978	CE-8769-1
11/05/38	St. Regis Jam Session	–	New York City	Jazz Panorama	LP-9	–
01/20/39	Hickory House Jam Session	–	New York City	Jazz Panorama	LP-9	–
05/25/39	Freddy Gardner and his Orchestra	–	London	Rex	9935	R-3618-2
07/07/39	Muggsy Spanier and his Ragtime Band	–	Chicago	Bluebird	B-10384	040261-2
08/11/39	Eddie Condon and his Chicagoans	–	New York City	Decca	18041	66075-A
08/15/39	Alberta Hunter	V	New York City	Decca	7727	66109-A

Date	Performer	Vocal	Place	Label	Issue	Matrix
11/07/39	Count Basie and his Orchestra	V	New York City	Columbia	35338	26283-A
03/17/42	Jimmy Dorsey and his Orchestra	V	New York City	Decca	18385	70526-A

Star Dust

Date	Performer	Vocal	Place	Label	Issue	Matrix
10/31/27	Hoagy Carmichael and his Pals	–	Richmond, IN	Gennett	6311	13190
c 05/02/28	Hoagy Carmichael	–	Richmond, IN	Gennett	rejected	13727, -A
10/13/28	Chocolate Dandies	–	New York City	OKeh	8668	401219-A
c 11/08/28	Mills Merry Makers	–	New York City	Pathe Actuelle	36903	108499
c 11/08/28	Mills Merry Makers	–	New York City	Cameo	9012	3455-A
c 09/20/29	Irving Mills and his Hotsy Totsy Gang	–	New York City	Brunswick	4587	E-30961
03/31	Fletcher Henderson and his Orchestra	–	New York City	Crown	3093	1231-3
05/01/31	Mills Blue Ribbon Boys	V	New York City	Banner	32066	10489-2-3
07/09/31	Washboard Rhythm Kings	V	Camden, NJ	Victor	23285	68265-2
10/12/31	Cab Calloway and his Orchestra	V	New York City	Banner	32295	10865-1-3
11/04/31	Louis Armstrong and his Orchestra	V	Chicago	OKeh	41530	405061-1
11/04/31	Louis Armstrong and his Orchestra	V	Chicago	OKeh	41530	405061-2
11/04/31	Louis Armstrong and his Orchestra	V	Chicago	OKeh	41530	405061-4
05/09/32	Hoagy Carmichael and his Orchestra [medley]	V	New York City	Victor	L-16009 (LP)	72557-1
12/06/33	Hoagy Carmichael	–	New York City	Victor	24484	78842-1
08/24/34	Art Tatum	–	New York City	Decca	306	38427-C
09/05/34	Jimmie Lunceford and his Orchestra	V	New York City	Decca	369	38544-A
09/27/34	Louis Prima and his New Orleans Gang	V	New York City	Brunswick	7335	B-16026-A
02/27/35	Nat Gonella and his Georgians	V	London	Parlophone	F-132	CE-6882-1
03/02/35	Coleman Hawkins	–	Paris	His Master's Voice	K-7527	OLA-349-1
06/06/35	[Benny Goodman] Rhythm Makers Orchestra	–	New York City	NBC Thesaurus	126	92220-1
06/27/35	Scott Wood and his Six Swingers	V	London	Regal Zonophone	MR-1771	CAR-3495-1
11/25/35	Garnet Clark	–	Paris	His Master's Voice	K-7645	OLA-731-1
01/17/36	Willie Lewis and his Orchestra (w/Benny Carter)	–	Paris	Pathe Actuelle	PA-817	CPT-2455-1
04/03/36	Tommy Dorsey and his Orchestra	V	New York City	Victor	rejected	99949-1-2-3-4
04/15/36	Tommy Dorsey and his Orchestra	V	New York City	Victor	25320	99949-5
04/23/36	Benny Goodman and his Orchestra	–	Chicago	Victor	25320	100379-2
06/18/36	Jimmy Gunn and his Orchestra	V	Charlotte, NC	Bluebird	B-6469	102688-1
c 01/37	Larry Adler	–	London	Rex	8959	F-2122
01/12/37	Phil Green	–	London	Parlophone	R-2335	CE-8038-1
03/03/37	Ballyhooligans [medley]	–	London	His Master's Voice	BD-5198	OEA-4836-1
05/10/37	Hudson-De Lange Orchestra	–	New York City	Mas	125	M-210-1
06/11/37	Fats Waller	–	New York City	Bluebird	B-10099	010653-1
08/18/37	Coleman Hawkins	–	Hilversum	Panachord	H-1045	AM-401-2
11/19/37	Benny Goodman and his Orchestra	–	New York City	Philips	PB-254	–
02/17/38	Edgar Hayes and his Orchestra	–	New York City	Decca	1882	63298-A
03/03/38	Joe Daniels and his Hot Shots	–	London	Parlophone	F-1077	CE-8984-1

Date	Performer	Vocal	Place	Label	Issue	Matrix
09/26/38	Ballyhooligans	–	London	His Master's Voice	BD-5436	OEA-6585-1
09/30/38	Les Brown and his Orchestra	V	New York City	Bluebird	B-7858	027431-1
11/11/38	Chu Berry and his "Little Jazz" Ensemble	–	New York City	Commodore	1502	23700-1
12/23/38	Artie Shaw and his Orchestra	–	New York City	Victor	LPT-6000 (LP)	–
03/15/39	Casa Loma Orchestra	V	New York City	Decca	2396	65180-A
09/28/39	Adrian Rollini Trio	–	Hollywood	Vocalion/OKeh	5376	WM-1085-A
10/02/39	Benny Goodman Sextet	–	New York City	Columbia	DJ-26134	WCO-26134-A
10/06/39	Benny Goodman Sextet	–	New York City	Polygon	6007	–
10/19/39	Jack Jenney and his Orchestra	–	New York City	Vocalion/OKeh	5304	26185-A
10/19/39	Jack Jenney and his Orchestra	–	New York City	Columbia	GL-100 (LP)	26185-B
02/02/40	Duke Derbigny's Orchestra	–	New Orleans	?	rejected	–
10/04/40	Eddy Howard	V	New York City	Columbia	35771	28795-1
10/07/40	Artie Shaw and his Orchestra	–	Hollywood	Victor	27230	055097-1
11/07/40	Duke Ellington and his Orchestra	–	Fargo, ND	Palm	30-11	–
11/11/40	Tommy Dorsey and his Orchestra	V	Hollywood	Victor	27233	055158-1
01/06/41	Will Bradley and his Orchestra	V	New York City	Columbia	35939	29414-1
01/21/41	Nat Gonella and his New Georgians	V	London	Columbia	FB-2571	CA-18294-1
05/11/42	Hoagy Carmichael	–	Los Angeles	Decca	18395	DLA-2982-A

Stompin' at the Savoy

Date	Performer	Vocal	Place	Label	Issue	Matrix
05/18/34	Chick Webb's Savoy Orchestra	–	New York City	Columbia	2926-D	152740-2
06/06/35	[Benny Goodman] Rhythm Makers Orchestra	–	New York City	NBC Thesaurus	127	92222-1
01/24/36	Benny Goodman and his Orchestra	–	Chicago	Victor	25247	96568-1
02/36	Chick Webb and his Orchestra	–	New York City	Polydor	423248	–
02/03/36	Isham Jones and his Orchestra	–	New York City	Decca	754	60432-A
04/06/36	Ozzie Nelson and his Orchestra	–	New York City	Brunswick	7659	B-18946
04/28/36	Willie Lewis and his Orchestra	–	Paris	Pathe Actuelle	PA-898	CPT-2630
05/11/36	Chicago Rhythm Kings	–	New York City	Bluebird	B-6412	101590-1
06/10/36	Gene Kardos and his Orchestra	–	New York City	American Record Corp.	6-09-03	19428-1
06/11/36	Milt Herth	–	Chicago	Decca	911	90766-A
06/12/36	Judy Garland [w/Bob Crosby and his Orchestra]	V	New York City	Decca	848	61165-A
07/27/36	Jimmy Dorsey and his Orchestra	–	Los Angeles	Decca	882	DLA-470-A
c 09/36	Tommy Kinsman's Fischer's Restaurant Dance Band	–	London	Octacros	1283	5899
12/02/36	Benny Goodman Quartet	–	New York City	Victor	25521	03514-1
12/02/36	Benny Goodman Quartet	–	New York City	Victor	25521	03514-2
01/16/38	Benny Goodman Quartet	–	New York City	Columbia	A-1049	–
01/39	Chick Webb and his Little Chicks	–	New York City	Jazz Archive	JA-33 (LP)	–
12/24/39	Benny Goodman Sextet	–	New York City	Vanguard	VRS-8524	–
01/21/41	Art Tatum and his Band	–	New York City	Decca	8536	68606-A

Date	Performer	Vocal	Place	Label	Issue	Matrix
03/12/41	Eddie South and his Orchestra	–	New York City	Columbia	36193	29928-2
07/12/41	Johnny Claes and his Clay Pigeons	V	London	Columbia	FB-2688	CA-18584-1

Sugar

Date	Performer	Vocal	Place	Label	Issue	Matrix
02/20/26	Ethel Waters	V	New York City	Columbia	14146-D	141707-1
05/27	Original Indiana Five	V	New York City	Banner	6008	7290-2
05/20/27	Fats Waller	–	Camden, NJ	Victor	21525	38044-1
05/20/27	Alberta Hunter [w/Fats Waller]	V	Camden, NJ	Victor	20771	38045-2
06/11/27	Bennie Moten's Kansas City Orchestra	–	Chicago	Victor	20855	38667-3
c 07/09/27	Blackbirds of Paradise	V	Birmingham, AL	Gennett	6211	GEX-719-B
09/27/27	Eddie Thomas' Collegians	V	New York City	Columbia	1154-D	144798-5
10/26/27	Red Nichols' Stompers	V	New York City	Victor	21056	40512-1
10/26/27	Frankie Trumbauer and his Orchestra	V	New York City	OKeh	40938	81575-B
12/08/27	McKenzie and Condon's Chicagoans	–	Chicago	OKeh	41011	82030-A
c 01/15/28	Fred Elizalde and his Music	–	London	Brunswick	150	473
02/28/28	Paul Whiteman and his Orchestra	–	New York City	Victor	25368	43118-1
02/28/28	Paul Whiteman and his Orchestra	–	New York City	Victor	21464	43118-2
04/02/28	Bessie Brown	V	Chicago	Vocalion	1182	C-1860-; E-7310
12/28	Beverly Syncopators	–	Chicago	Paramount	12747	21069-2
10/23/34	Adrian Rollini and his Orchestra	–	New York City	Decca	265	38875-A
12/27/37	Stephane Grappelly	–	Paris	Swing	69	OLA-2219-1
03/25/38	Benny Goodman Quartet	–	New York City	Victor	26240	021628-2
10/05/38	Vic Lewis and his American Jazzmen	–	New York City	Esquire	10-221	M-7-298
12/28/38	Ziggy Elman and his Orchestra	–	New York City	Bluebird	B-10096	030773-1
01/30/39	Teddy Wilson and his Orchestra	V	New York City	Brunswick	8319	B-24047-1
10/11/39	Jimmy McPartland and his Orchestra	–	Chicago	Decca	18043	91835-A
03/22/40	Andre Ekyan	–	Paris	Swing	98	OSW-115-1
07/10/40	Lee Wiley	V	New York City	Commodore	1507	R-3112
08/17/40	[Art Hodes] Chicago Rhythm Kings	–	New York City	Signature	105	1606

Sugar Blues

Date	Performer	Vocal	Place	Label	Issue	Matrix
08/11/22	Leona Williams and her Dixie Band	V	New York City	Columbia	A-3696	80517-2
c 10/17/22	Sara Martin	V	New York City	OKeh	8041	70935-D
c 01/23	Monette Moore	V	New York City	Paramount	12015	A-987-
01/23	Lillian Harris	V	New York City	Banner	1173	5052-1
01–02/23	Flo Johnson	V	New York City	Cameo	319	414-C
01/31/23	Sister Harris	V	New York City	Pathe Actuelle	020909	70043
02/13/23	Sister Harris	V	New York City	Bell	P-208	–
c 03/02/23	Ladd's Black Aces	V	New York City	Gennett	5075	8256
03/08/23	Edna Hicks	V	New York City	Victor	test	–
03/21/23	Edna Hicks	V	New York City	Victor	rejected	27666-1-2-3

Date	Performer	Vocal	Place	Label	Issue	Matrix
04/10/23	Edna Hicks	V	New York City	Victor	rejected	27666-4-5-6
04/11/23	Johnny Dunn's Original Jazz Band	–	New York City	Columbia	A-3878	80947-2
06/07/23	Tennessee Ten [medley]	–	New York City	Victor	19094	28057-1
02/18/31	King Oliver and his Orchestra	–	New York City	Brunswick	6065	E-36102-A
03/27/31	Blanche Calloway and her Joy Boys	V	Camden, NJ	Timely Tunes	C-1587	68940-1
03/27/31	Blanche Calloway and her Joy Boys	V	Camden, NJ	Victor	22661	68939-2
05/12/31	[Mills] Blue Ribbon Boys	V	New York City	Banner	32199	10625-2-3-4
09/11/34	Clarence Williams and his Orchestra	V	New York City	Vocalion	2805	15847-2
10/03/34	Alabama Jug Band	V	New York City	Decca	7042	38784-A
08/02/35	Fats Waller and his Rhythm	V	New York City	Victor	25194	92916-1
01/02/36	Mustang Band of Southern Methodist University	–	Los Angeles	Decca	rejected	DLA-295-
09/21/36	The Rhythm Wreckers	–	New York City	Vocalion	3341	19916
01/26/40	Ella Fitzgerald and her Orchestra	V	New York City	Decca	3078	67120-A
10/23/40	Benny Carter and his Orchestra	–	New York City	Decca	3588	68286-A
07/24/42	Count Basie and his All-American Rhythm Section	–	Hollywood	Columbia	36709	HCO-876-1

Sugar Foot Stomp (Dipper Mouth Blues)

Date	Performer	Vocal	Place	Label	Issue	Matrix
04/06/23	King Oliver's Creole Jazz Band	–	Richmond, IN	Gennett	5132	11389-B
06/23/23	King Oliver's Jazz Band	–	Chicago	OKeh	4918	8402-A
05/29/25	Fletcher Henderson and his Orchestra	–	New York City	Columbia	395-D	140639-2
11/14/25	Merritt Brunies and his Friars Inn Orchestra	–	Chicago	OKeh	40526	9491-A
12/17/25	Fred Hamm and his Orchestra	–	Chicago	Victor	20023	34039-3
12/17/25	Fred Hamm and his Orchestra	–	Chicago	Victor	20023	34039-4
05/29/26	King Oliver and his Dixie Syncopators	–	Chicago	Vocalion	1033	C-370
05/26/27	Devonshire Restaurant Dance Band	–	Hayes, Middlesex	Zonophone	2948	Yy-10760-1
04/25/28	Johnnie Miller's New Orleans Frolickers	–	New Orleans	Columbia	1546-D	146194-2
03/19/31	Fletcher Henderson and his Orchestra	–	New York City	Columbia	2513-D	151442-1
03/19/31	Fletcher Henderson and his Orchestra	–	New York City	Columbia	2513-D	151442-2
04/10/31	Fletcher Henderson and his Orchestra	–	New York City	Melotone	M-12239	E-36455-A
04/29/31	[Fletcher Henderson] Connie's Inn Orchestra	–	Camden, NJ	Victor	22721	53066-1
04/29/31	[Fletcher Henderson] Connie's Inn Orchestra	–	Camden, NJ	Victor	X EVA-2	53066-2
08/31	[Fletcher Henderson] Connie's Inn Orchestra	–	New York City	Crown	3194	1433-3
01/17/35	Dorsey Brothers Orchestra	–	New York City	Design	DLP-20	–
02/06/35	Dorsey Brothers Orchestra	–	New York City	Decca	561	38345-A
06/06/35	[Benny Goodman] Rhythm Makers Orchestra	–	New York City	NBC Thesaurus	295	92216-1
07/21/36	Milt Herth	–	Chicago	Decca	rejected	90801-
08/06/36	Artie Shaw and his Orchestra	–	New York City	Brunswick	7735	B-19669-2

Date	Performer	Vocal	Place	Label	Issue	Matrix
08/07/36	Louis Armstrong [w/Jimmy Dorsey and his Orchestra]	–	Los Angeles	Decca	906	DLA-542-A
03/04/37	Jay Freeman and his Orchestra	–	New York City	American Record Corp.	7-08-09	M-166-1
09/06/37	Benny Goodman and his Orchestra	–	Hollywood	Victor	25678	09689-1
09/06/37	Benny Goodman and his Orchestra	–	Hollywood	Jazum	7	09689-2
11/21/37	Benny Goodman and his Orchestra	–	New York City	Columbia	ML-4590	–
12/16/37	Harry Roy and his Orchestra	–	London	Parlophone	F-1109	CE-8814-1
05/23/38	Glenn Miller and his Orchestra	V	New York City	Brunswick	8173	B-22975-1
08/01/38	Larry Clinton and his Orchestra	–	New York City	Victor	26018	024428-1
10/21/38	Jan Savitt and his Top Hatters	–	New York City	Bluebird	B-10005	028140-1
01/09/39	Chick Webb and his Orchestra	–	New York City	Polydor	423248 (LP)	–
06/06/39	Pied Pipers	V	New York City	Victor	26320	037192-1
11/10/39	Muggsy Spanier and his Ragtime Band	–	New York City	Bluebird	B-10506	043377-1
03/40	Frankie Trumbauer and his Orchestra	–	New York City	Varsity	8256	US-1419-1
01/27/42	Bob Crosby and his Orchestra	–	Los Angeles	Decca	4390	DLA-2851-A

Sweet Georgia Brown

Date	Performer	Vocal	Place	Label	Issue	Matrix
04/18/22	Superior Jazz Band	–	New York City	Arto	rejected	20147-
05/02/22	Superior Jazz Band	–	New York City	Arto	9144	20147-5
03/19/25	Ben Bernie and his Hotel Roosevelt Orchestra	–	New York City	Vocalion	15002	575
04/28/25	Varsity Eight	–	New York City	Cameo	730	1435-B
c 04/30/25	Perley Breed's Orchestra	–	New York City	Gennett	rejected	9501
05/25	Jack Stillman's (Oriole) Orchestra	–	New York City	Bell	368	–
05/25	Jack Linx and his (Birmingham) Society Serenaders	–	Atlanta	OKeh	40365	9075-A
05/01/25	Oliver Naylor's Orchestra	–	Camden, NJ	Victor	19688	32565-3
c 05/01/25	Original Indiana Five	–	New York City	Gennett	3059	9505
c 05/05/25	Texas Ten	–	New York City	Banner	1540	6015
c 05/05/25	Texas Ten	–	New York City	Pathe Actuelle	036247	106007
05/13/25	Ethel Waters	V	New York City	Columbia	379-D	140597-1
05/14/25	California Ramblers	–	New York City	Columbia	380-D	140603-1
06/05/25	Isham Jones and his Orchestra	–	Chicago	Brunswick	2913	15936
c 03/05/26	Lillie Delk Christian	V	Chicago	OKeh	8317	9574-A
07/02/30	Red Nichols and his Five Pennies	–	New York City	Brunswick	4944	E-33305-A
05/21/31	Snooks and his Memphis Ramblers/Stompers	V	New York City	Victor	22779	69634-1
07/09/31	Cab Calloway and his Orchestra	V	New York City	Conqueror	7817	10727-2
09/31	Eubie Blake and his Orchestra	V	New York City	Crown	3197	1478-2
02/17/32	Champion Rhythm Kings	–	Richmond, IN	Champion	16387	18408
04/23/32	Bing Crosby	V	Chicago	Brunswick	6320	JC-8592-A
05/17/32	Pickens Sisters	V	New York City	Victor	24025	72594-1

Date	Performer	Vocal	Place	Label	Issue	Matrix
c 07/33	Freddy Johnson-Arthur Briggs and their All-Star Orchestra	V	Paris	Brunswick	A-500278	6461bkp
09/12/34	Earl Hines and his Orchestra	–	Chicago	Decca	182	C-9464-A
12/02/35	Albert Harris	–	London	Parlophone	rejected	CE-7323-1
01/15/36	Jimmy Noone and his New Orleans Band	–	Chicago	Parlophone	R-2281	90578-A
07/06/36	Harry Roy's Tiger Ragamuffins	V	London	Parlophone	F-522	CE-7723-1
10/20/36	The Swingtimers	V	London	Regal Zonophone	MR-2514	CAR-4238-1
10/20/36	Buck and Bubbles	V	London	Columbia	FB-1602	CA-15987-1
37	Avery "Kid" Howard's Band	–	New Orleans	Mono	MNLP-12 (LP)	–
09/29/37	Eddie South	–	Paris	Swing	8	OLA-2146-1
12/27/37	Django Reinhardt	–	Paris	Swing	35	OLA-2220-1
01/31/38	Quintette or the Hot Club of France	–	London	Decca	F-6675	DTB-3524-1
04/28/38	Coleman Hawkins and his All-Star Jam Band	–	Paris	His Master's Voice	K-8511	OLA-1745-1
10/12/38	Benny Goodman Quartet	–	Chicago	Victor	26091	025878-2
02/20/39	Harry James and his Orchestra	–	New York City	Brunswick	8327	B-24515-1
05/19/39	John Kirby and his Orchestra	–	New York City	Columbia	36001	24678-B
02/02/40	Duke Derbigny's Orchestra	V	New Orleans	Mono	MNLP-12 (LP)	–
06/10/40	Erskine Hawkins and his Orchestra	–	New York City	Bluebird	B-10854	051261-1
10/24/40	Gene Krupa and his Orchestra	–	New York City	OKeh	6070	28968-1
07/24/42	Teddy Powell and his Orchestra	–	New York City	Bluebird	rejected	075576-1

Sweet Sue

Date	Performer	Vocal	Place	Label	Issue	Matrix
04/06/28	Ben Pollack and his Californians	V	New York City	Victor	rejected	43541-1
04/26/28	Ben Pollack and his Californians	V	New York City	Victor	21437	43541-5
c 05/10/28	Sam Lanin's Troubadours	V	New York City	Pathe Actuelle	36802	108163-1
c 05/10/28	Sam Lanin's Troubadours	V	New York City	Cameo	8227	3111-A-B
05/15/28	Seger Ellis	V	New York City	OKeh	41061	400670-B
05/16/28	Jimmie Noone's Apex Club Orchestra	–	Chicago	Vocalion	1184	C-1938-C; E-7356
06/27/28	Ambrose and his Orchestra	–	Hayes, Middlesex	His Master's Voice	B-5508	Bb-13591-3
07/11/28	McKinney's Cotton Pickers	–	Chicago	Victor	rejected	46092-1-2
09/14/28	Wabash Dance Orchestra	V	New York City	Duophone	D-4009	E-28222-A
09/18/28	Paul Whiteman and his Orchestra	V	New York City	Columbia	50103-D	98584-1
10/02/28	Jack Payne and his BBC Dance Orchestra	V	London	Columbia	5074	WA-7922-2
01/20/30	Louisiana Rhythm Kings	–	New York City	Brunswick	4953	E-31946-
11/12/30	Joe Venuti's Blue Four	–	New York City	OKeh	41469	404550-C
02/18/32	Red Nichols and his Five Pennies	–	New York City	Brunswick	6266	B-11315-A
02/18/32	Red Nichols and his Five Pennies	–	New York City	American Record Corp.	F-152	B-11315-B
03/16/32	Ted Lewis and his Band	V	New York City	Columbia	2652-D	152140-4
04/26/33	Louis Armstrong and his Orchestra	V	Chicago	Victor	24321	75478-1

Date	Performer	Vocal	Place	Label	Issue	Matrix
05/18/33	Spike Hughes and his Negro Orchestra	–	New York City	Decca	F-3972	B-13356-A
05/15/34	Nat Gonella and his Trumpet	–	London	Decca	rejected	GB-6722-1-2
05/25/34	Nat Gonella and his Trumpet	–	London	Decca	rejected	GB-6722-3-4
08/31/34	Isham Jones and his Orchestra	–	New York City	Decca	443	38498-A-B
12/18/34	Scott Wood and his Six Swingers [medley]	–	London	Regal Zonophone	MR-1675	CAR-3125-1
03/35	Quintette of the Hot Club of France	V	Paris	Ultraphon	AP-1444	P-77241
06/24/35	Fats Waller and his Rhythm	V	Camden, NJ	Victor	25087	88998-1
06/24/35	Fats Waller and his Rhythm	V	Camden, NJ	Jazz Archives	7 (LP)	88998-2
06/28/35	Joe Daniels and his Hot Shots	–	London	Parlophone	F-211	CE-7069-1
09/24/35	Joe Paradise and his Music	–	London	Parlophone	F-327	CE-7168-1
11/01/35	Joe Daniels and his Hot Shots	–	London	Parlophone	F-211	CE-7069-3
11/30/35	Louis Prima and his New Orleans Gang	V	Los Angeles	Brunswick	7596	LA-1078-B
02/36	Sid Phillips and his Rhythm	–	London	Rex	8863	F-1730-2
02/15/36	Locke Brothers Rhythm Orchestra	V	Charlotte, NC	Bluebird	B-6332	99152-1
06/03/36	Ballyhooligans	–	London	His Master's Voice	BD-5074	OEA-2799-1
10/08/36	Ballyhooligans	–	London	His Master's Voice	rejected	OEA-3787-1
10/15/36	Willie Lewis and his Orchestra	–	Paris	Pathe Actuelle	PA-1030	CPT-2904-1
11/18/36	Benny Goodman Quartet	–	New York City	Victor	25473	03062-1
05/28/37	Don Redman and his Orchestra	–	New York City	Realm	52539 (LP)	M-510-1
05/28/37	Don Redman and his Orchestra	–	New York City	Vri	605	M-510-2
07/07/37	Dicky Wells and his Orchestra	–	Paris	Swing	16	OLA-1887-1
11/01/37	Chick Webb and his Orchestra	–	New York City	Decca	1759	62737-B
12/28/37	Michel Warlop	–	Paris	Swing	43	OLA-2312-1
03/08/38	Kenny Clarke's Kvintett	–	Stockholm	Odeon	A-255510	Sto-6320-1
04/08/38	Benny Goodman and his Orchestra	–	New York City	Victor	26089	022419-1
04/12/38	Jimmie Lunceford and his Orchestra	V	New York City	Decca	1927	63587-A
09/19/38	Siday-Simpson Quartet	–	London	Parlophone	rejected	CE-9329-1
10/31/38	Tommy Dorsey and his Orchestra	V	New York City	Victor	26105	028176-1
12/05/38	Danish Jam Session	–	Copenhagen	His Master's Voice	X-6212	OCS-1083-2
02/27/39	Gene Austin [w/Fats Waller group]	V	New York City	RFW	2	033993-1
08/07/39	Fats Waller and his Rhythm	V	New York City	Jazz Society	AA-535	–
10/26/39	Artie Shaw and his Orchestra	–	New York City	Victor	LPT-6000 (LP)	–
02/40	George Auld and his Orchestra	–	New York City	Varsity	8212	US-1381-1
04/06/40	Bechet-Spanier Big Four	–	New York City	Hot Record Society	2003	2804-2
12/13/40	Quintette of the Hot Club of France	–	Paris	Swing	118	OSW-154-1
02/28/41	Stephane Grappelly and his Musicians	–	London	Decca	F-7841	DR-5403-1

Tea for Two

Date	Performer	Vocal	Place	Label	Issue	Matrix
10/29/24	Varsity Eight	–	New York City	Cameo	617	1197-C
02/14/30	Red Nichols and his Five Pennies	–	New York City	Brunswick	4724	E-32041-A
06/30/32	Don Redman and his Orchestra	V	New York City	Brunswick	6354	B-12005-A
03/21/33	Art Tatum	–	New York City	Brunswick	6553	B-13162-A

Date	Performer	Vocal	Place	Label	Issue	Matrix
03/11/35	Fats Waller [medley]	–	New York City	Victor	LPT-6001	–
09/13/35	Scott Wood and his Six Swingers [medley]	–	London	Regal Zonophone	MR-1909	CAR-3589-2
07/02/36	Five Bright Sparks	–	London	Columbia	FB-1473	CA-15840-1
07/08/36	Ballyhooligans	–	London	His Master's Voice	BD-5086	OEA-3833-1
12/16/36	Teddy Wilson and his Orchestra	–	New York City	Brunswick	7816	B-20412-2
02/03/37	Benny Goodman Quartet	–	New York City	Victor	25529	04560-1
06/11/37	Fats Waller	–	New York City	Victor	25618	010655-1
06/23/37	Teddy Weatherford	–	Paris	Swing	5	OLA-1877-1-2
07/20/37	Benny Goodman Quartet	–	Los Angeles	MGM	E/X-3788	–
12/27/37	Michel Warlop	–	Paris	Swing	15	OLA-2216-1
12/27/37	Django Reinhardt	–	Paris	Swing	211	OLA-2221-1
03/03/38	Joe Daniels and his Hot Shots	–	London	Parlophone	F-1099	CE-8985-1
03/10/38	Bob Crosby and his Orchestra	–	New York City	Decca	1850	63390-A
12/06/38	Nat Gonella and his Georgians	–	London	Parlophone	F-1302	CE-9464-1
01/09/39	Chick Webb and his Orchestra	–	New York City	Polydor	423248 (LP)	–
02/39	Willie "the Lion" Smith	–	New York City	Commodore	518	B-541-3
02/15/39	Clarence Profit Trio	–	New York City	Brunswick	8341	B-24127-2
03/15/39	Tommy Dorsey and his Orchestra	–	Chicago	Victor	26321	034401-1
03/22/39	Quintette of the Hot Club of France	–	Paris	Decca	rejected	4972hpp, 4972 1/2hpp
04/12/39	Art Tatum and his Swingsters	–	Los Angeles	Decca	2456	DLA-1759-A
05/17/39	Quintette of the Hot Club of France	–	Paris	Decca	59006	5082hpp
08/07/39	Fats Waller	–	New York City	Victor	RD-7553	–
09/11/39	Sonny Burke and his Orchestra	–	Chicago	Vocalion/OKeh	5139	WC-2689-B
01/18/40	Bob Zurke and his Delta Rhythm Band	–	Chicago	Victor	26561	044634-1
01/26/40	Six Men and a Girl	–	New York City	Varsity	8193	US-1317-1
12/13/40	Bing Crosby	V	Los Angeles	Decca	3689	DLA-2271-A
01/21/41	[Will Bradley] Ray McKinley Quartet	–	New York City	Columbia	36101	29525-1
03/11/41	Maurice Rocco and his Rockin' Rhythm	–	Chicago	Decca	8574	93579-A
03/12/41	Eddie South and his Orchestra	–	New York City	Columbia	rejected	29929-
11/16/41	First English Public Jam Session [2 parts]	–	London	His Master's Voice	B-9249	OEA-9445-1; OEA-9446-1

That's a Plenty

Date	Performer	Vocal	Place	Label	Issue	Matrix
07/07/14	Prince's Band/Orchestra	–	New York City	Columbia	A-5582	36995-
03/12/23	New Orleans Rhythm Kings	–	Richmond, IN	Gennett	5105	11353
03/12/23	New Orleans Rhythm Kings	–	Richmond, IN	Gennett	5105	11353-A
03/12/23	New Orleans Rhythm Kings	–	Richmond, IN	Gennett	5105	11353-B
01/22/25	Anthony Parenti and his Famous Melody Boys	–	New Orleans	OKeh	40308	8895-A
04/15/27	New Orleans Owls	–	New Orleans	Columbia	1547-D	143981-1
01/10/28	Original Atlanta Footwarmers	–	Richmond, IN	Bell	585	13345

Date	Performer	Vocal	Place	Label	Issue	Matrix
03/31/28	Princeton Triangle Club Jazz Band	–	New York City	Columbia	115-P	170302-2
06/13/28	Benny Goodman	–	Chicago	Vocalion	15705	C-2006-A; E-7398
01/03/29	Ray Miller and his Orchestra	–	Chicago	Brunswick	4224	C-2743-
02/11/29	Slim Lamar and his Southerners	V	Camden, NJ	Victor	V-38044	49846-2
02/20/29	Louisiana Rhythm Kings	–	New York City	Vocalion	15784	E-29321-
04/19/29	Miff Mole's (Little) Molers	–	New York City	Odeon	279695	401816-A
04/19/29	Miff Mole's (Little) Molers	–	New York City	OKeh	41232	401816-B
04/19/29	Miff Mole's (Little) Molers	–	New York City	Odeon	A-189260	401816-C
08/27/29	Red Nichols and his Five Pennies	–	New York City	Radio Broadcast	33	XE-30718-A-B
10/25/29	Philip Lewis and his (Dance) Orchestra	–	London	Decca	F-1573	MB-595-3
07/32	Joel Shaw and his Orchestra	–	New York City	Crown	3352	1780-3
04/25/34	Lew Stone and his Band	–	London	Decca	F-5271	TB-1213-2
09/12/34	Earl Hines and his Orchestra	–	Chicago	Decca	182	C-9461-A
01/29/35	KXYZ Novelty Band	–	San Antonio	Bluebird	B-5852	87764-1
06/09/36	Tommy Dorsey and his Orchestra	–	New York City	Victor	25363	101264-1
06/09/36	Harry Roy's Tiger-Ragamuffins	–	London	Parlophone	F-484	CE-7673-1
c 07/20/36	Bunny Berigan and his Studio Orchestra [medley]	–	New York City	Thesaurus	298	102946-1
07/27/36	Joe Haymes and his Orchestra	–	New York City	Vocalion	3307	19621-1
02/08/37	Chick Webb and his Orchestra	–	New York City	Jazz Panorama	LP-2	–
07/02/37	Nat Gonella and his Georgians (medley)	V	London	Parlophone	F-832	CE-8457-1
09/14/37	Phil Napoleon and his Orchestra	–	New York City	Vri	669	M-629-1
10/01/37	Danny Polo and his Swing Stars	–	London	Decca	F-6550	DTB-3251-2
11/11/37	Milt Herth Trio	–	New York City	Decca	1553	62761-A
03/03/38	Joe Daniels and his Hot Shots	–	London	Parlophone	F-1099	CE-8985-1
07/22/38	Jan Savitt and his Top Hatters	–	New York City	Bluebird	B-7733	024071-1
08/30/38	Bluebird Military Band	–	New York City	Bluebird	B-3303	026682-1
10/19/38	Vic Lewis and his American Jazzmen	–	New York City	Esquire	10-231	M-7-303
06/01/39	Jan Savitt and his Top Hatters	–	New York City	Decca	2540	65717-A
04/06/40	Bechet-Spanier Big Four	–	New York City	Hot Record Society	Dividend	2802-2
04/06/40	Bechet-Spanier Big Four	–	New York City	Hot Record Society	2002	2802-3
06/10/41	Royal Air Force Dance Orchestra	–	London	Decca	F-8127	DR-5844-1
04/42	Lu Watters' Yerba Buena Jazz Band	–	San Francisco	Jazz Man	rejected	–

There'll Be Some Changes Made

Date	Performer	Vocal	Place	Label	Issue	Matrix
c 08/21	Ethel Waters	V	New York City	Black Swan	2021	P-147-1
05/29/23	Amanda Randolph	V	Richmond, IN	Gennett	Special	11484
06/06/24	Ted Lewis and his Band	–	New York City	Columbia	170-D	81811-3
10/24/24	Charlie Davis and his Orchestra	–	Richmond, IN	Gennett	rejected	12058
c 11/21/24	[Ben Selvin] Moulin Rouge Orchestra	–	New York City	Banner	1492	5745-1
c 12/24	Josie Miles	V	New York City	Ajax	17087	31749
03/06/25	Edith Wilson	V	New York City	Columbia	14066-D	140416-1

Date	Performer	Vocal	Place	Label	Issue	Matrix
06/21/27	Red McKenzie and his Music Box	V	New York City	OKeh	40893	81037-B
04/06/28	Chicago Rhythm Kings	V	Chicago	Brunswick	4001	C-1885-A
11/05/28	Eddie Lang	–	New York City	OKeh	8633	401293-B
10/24/29	Eddie and Sugar Lou's Hotel Tyler Orchestra	V	Dallas	Vocalion	1455	DAL-452-
03/21/32	Boswell Sisters	V	New York City	Brunswick	6291	B-11543-A
06/24/35	Fats Waller and his Rhythm	V	Camden, NJ	Bluebird	B-10332	88996-1
09/35	Arthur Briggs	–	Paris	Ultraphon	rejected	–
10/19/36	Benny Carter and his Swing Quintet	–	London	Vocalion	S-46	S-130-2
09/11/37	Ocie Stockard and the Wanderers	–	Dallas	Bluebird	B-7570	014025-1
08/31/38	Pee Wee Russell's Rhythmakers	–	New York City	Hot Record Society	1001	23392-1
02/15/39	Clarence Profit Trio	–	New York City	Brunswick	8341	B-24123-1
03/15/39	Bunny Berigan and his Orchestra	–	New York City	Victor	26244	035034-1
03/16/39	Mildred Bailey and her Oxford Greys	V	New York City	Vocalion	5268	24228-1
08/10/39	Benny Goodman and his Orchestra	V	Los Angeles	Columbia	35210	LA-1947-A
08/11/39	Eddie Condon and his Chicagoans	–	New York City	Decca	18041	66072-A
01/17/41	Gene Krupa and his Orchestra	V	Chicago	OKeh	6021	C-3528-2
02/12/41	Chick Bullock	V	New York City	OKeh	6100	29706-1
03/10/41	Una Mae Carlisle	V	New York City	Bluebird	B-11096	062749-1

Three Little Words

Date	Performer	Vocal	Place	Label	Issue	Matrix
11/14/29	Philip Lewis and his Orchestra	V	London	Decca	F-1600	MB-656-1
08/20/30	Duke Ellington and his Orchestra	V	Hollywood	Victor	rejected	61013-1-2
08/20/30	Duke Ellington and his Orchestra	V	Hollywood	Victor	rejected	61013-3
08/26/30	Duke Ellington and his Orchestra	V	Hollywood	Victor	22528	61013-5
10/30/30	Jimmy Noone and his Apex Club Orchestra	–	Chicago	Vocalion	1554	C-6466-
10/30/30	Duke Ellington and his Harlem Footwarmers	–	New York City	Odeon	ONY-36166	404520-C; 480028-C
11/13/30	Chick Bullock	V	New York City	Crown	81488	10232-
11/18/30	Ethel Waters	V	New York City	Columbia	rejected	150967-1-2-3
11/23/30	Seger Ellis	V	New York City	OKeh	41473	404562-B
11/28/30	Ethel Waters	V	New York City	Columbia	2346-D	150967-5
12/18/30	Jack Harris and his Orchestra	V	London	Decca	F-2174	GB-2424-2
02/08/31	Billy Milton	V	London	Decca	F-2234	GB-2678-1
05/25/32	Claude Hopkins and his Orchestra	–	New York City	Jazz Archive	4 (LP)	B-11893-A
11/28/32	Red Nichols and his Orchestra	V	Chicago	Brunswick	rejected	C-8824-
03/09/33	Claude Hopkins and his Orchestra	–	New York City	Jazz Archive	4 (LP)	B-13129-A
04/06/34	Claude Hopkins and his Orchestra	–	New York City	Brunswick	6864	B-15044-A
09/18/34	Red Nichols and his Orchestra	V	New York City	Brunswick	7460	B-15930-A
06/06/35	[Benny Goodman] Rhythm Makers Orchestra	–	New York City	NBC Thesaurus	295	92216-1
11/19/35	Gene Krupa and his Chicagoans	–	Chicago	Parlophone	R-2224	90462-A

Date	Performer	Vocal	Place	Label	Issue	Matrix
03/11/37	Seger Ellis and his Choirs of Brass Orchestra	V	Los Angeles	Decca	1275	DLA-749-B
12/14/37	Benny Goodman and his Orchestra	–	New York City	MGM	E/X-3788	–
06/14/38	Quintette of the Hot Club of France	–	Paris	Decca	F-6875	4212hpp
11/30/38	Bud Freeman Trio	–	New York City	Commodore	514	75957-A
11/02/39	Gene Krupa and his Orchestra	–	Chicago	Columbia	35336	WC-2826-A
01/08/41	Ella Fitzgerald and her Famous Orchestra	V	New York City	Decca	3608	68558-A
02/27/42	Hazel Scott	–	New York City	Decca	18341	70415-A

Tiger Rag

Date	Performer	Vocal	Place	Label	Issue	Matrix
08/17/17	Original Dixieland Jazz Band	–	New York City	Aeolian Vocalion	1206	–
03/25/18	Original Dixieland Jazz Band	–	New York City	Victor	18472	21701-3
05/19/19	Original Dixieland Jazz Band	–	London	Columbia	748	76468-3
c 07/19	Whiteway Jazz Band	–	New York City	Paramount	20014	801-2
12/19	Original Excentric Band	–	Berlin	Homochord	B-557	15984
01–02/20	Benny Peyton's Jazz Kings	–	London	Columbia	rejected	–
09/21	Southern Rag-A-Jazz Band	–	London	Edison Bell Winner	3607	6986-1
03/10/22	Husk O'Hare's Super Orchestra of Chicago	–	Richmond, IN	Gennett	4850	11066-A-B
06–07/22	Ethel Waters' Jazz Masters	V	Long Island City	Black Swan	2077	386-2
08/30/22	Friars Society Orchestra [New Orleans Rhythm Kings]	–	Richmond, IN	Gennett	4968	11183-C
01/05/23	Ted Lewis and his Band	–	Chicago	Columbia	A-3813	80765-2
c 04/20/23	Original Dixieland Jazz Band	–	New York City	OKeh	4841	71429-B
c 08/23	Jimmie's Joys	–	Los Angeles	Golden	B-1858	G-1858
01/21/24	Original Capitol Orchestra	–	Hayes, Middlesex	Zonophone	2447	Yy-4114-2
c 04/24	Jelly Roll Morton's Kings of Jazz	–	Chicago	Autograph	607	639
06/20/24	Wolverine Orchestra	–	Richmond, IN	Hot Record Society	24	11932
12/10/24	Mound City Blue Blowers	–	New York City	Brunswick	2804	14438
05/04/25	California Ramblers	–	New York City	Pathe Actuelle	036266	106005
11/25	[Wingy] Mannone's San Sue Strutters (sic)	–	Chicago	OKeh	rejected	9500-A
03/13/26	Jack Linx and his (Birmingham) Society Serenaders	–	Atlanta	OKeh	40619	9612-A
04/11/26	Paul Whiteman and his Orchestra	–	London	His Master's Voice	rejected	BR-262-1
c 05/26	Purple Pirates Orchestra	–	New York City	Paramount	none	2527-2
05/12/26	University Six	–	New York City	Harmony	224-H	142195-2-3
07/16/26	Ted Lewis and his Band	–	Chicago	Columbia	770-D	142444-2
c 12/26	Dixon's Jazz Maniacs	–	Chicago	Paramount	12405	2761-2
12/23/26	Phil Napoleon and his Orchestra	–	New York City	Edison Diamond Disc	51908	11395
12/28/26	Original Memphis Five	–	New York City	Victor	rejected	37190-1-2-3
01/15/27	Original Black and Golds	–	New York City	Gennett	rejected	GEX-459, -A-B
02/07/27	Phil Napoleon and his Orchestra	–	New York City	Victor	rejected	37744-1-2-3

Date	Performer	Vocal	Place	Label	Issue	Matrix
c 03/03/27	John Williams' Synco Jazzers	–	Chicago	Gennett	rejected	12620, -A
04/27/27	Charles Dornberger and his Orchestra	V	Camden, NJ	Victor	rejected	38011-1-2-3-4
05/10/27	Charles Dornberger and his Orchestra	–	Camden, NJ	Victor	20647	38011-7
05/21/27	John Williams' Band	–	New York City	Gennett	rejected	GEX-657, -A
06/03/27	Ernest Loomis' Orchestra	–	Butte, MT	Victor	rejected	PBVE-336-1-2
08/27	Fred Elizalde [medley]	–	London	Brunswick	20056	–
10/14/27	Curtis Mosby and his Dixieland Blue Blowers	–	Los Angeles	Columbia	1192-D	144764-1
12/27	Devine's Wisconsin Roof Orchestra	–	Chicago	Paramount	20582	20271-1-2
c 01/15/28	Fred Elizalde and his Hot Music	–	London	Brunswick	147	471
02/10/28	Lud Gluskin Ambassadonians	–	Paris	Pathe	X-6226	N-8406
05/21/28	Snoozer Quinn	–	San Antonio	Victor	rejected	42346-1-2-3
09/10/28	George C. Hill's Band	–	Richmond, IN	Gennett	rejected	14262, -A
11/28	[Meyer Davis] Home Towners	–	New York City	Duophone	D-4034	E-28680-A
11/10/28	Tommy Dorsey	–	New York City	OKeh	41178	401309-C
12/17?/28	Lud Gluskin Ambassadonians	–	Berlin	Tri-Ergon	TE-5463	MO-2188
01/08/29	Duke Ellington and his Orchestra [2 parts]	–	New York City	Brunswick	4238	E-28940-A-B; E-28941-A
01/16/29	Lud Gluskin Ambassadonians	–	Berlin	Homochord	4-3021	C-437-D
01/18/29	[Irving Mills] Hotsy Totsy Gang	–	New York City	Domino [?]	rejected	8476-1-2
01/28/29	Ray Miller and his Orchestra	–	Chicago	Sunny Meadows	F	XC-2883-
04/04/29	Paul Mills and his Merry Makers	–	New York City	Pathe Actuelle	37013	108864-3
04/04/29	Paul Mills and his Merry Makers	–	New York City	Banner	6355	8476-3
07/29	Maestro Sam Wooding y sus Chocolate Kiddies	V	Barcelona	Parlophone	B-25420	76520-2
09/11/29	Philip Lewis and his Dance Orchestra	–	London	Decca	F-1540	DJ-43-3
11/25/29	Reuben "River" Reeves and his River Boys	–	Chicago	Vocalion	rejected	C-4745-
11/25/29	Reuben "River" Reeves and his River Boys	–	Chicago	Vocalion	rejected	C-4747-
01/10/30	Jack Hylton and his Orchestra	–	London	His Master's Voice	B-5789	Bb-18541-2
01/15/30	Hotel Pennsylvania Music	V	New York City	Harmony	1092-H	149757-2
05/04/30	Louis Armstrong and his Orchestra	–	New York City	OKeh	8800	404002-B
07/15/30	Jimmy Dorsey and his Orchestra	–	London	Decca	F-1878	MB-1620-1
07/15/30	Jimmy Dorsey and his Orchestra	–	London	Decca	F-6142	MB-1620-2
07/25/30	Paul Whiteman and his Orchestra	–	New York City	Columbia	2277-D	150683-1
08/30	Phillips' Louisville Jug Band	–	Chicago	Brunswick	7194	C-5997-
10/21/30	Billy Cotton and his Band	–	London	Regal	MR-221	WAR-363-1
02/02/31	Red Devils	V	New York City	Columbia	14586-D	151261-1
03/31	Fletcher Henderson and his Orchestra	–	New York City	Crown	3107	1232-3
05/04/31	Paul Cornelius and his Orchestra	–	Richmond, IN	Gennett	rejected	17726
06/15/31	Whistler and his Jug Band	V	Louisville, KY	Victor	23305	69438-1
06/26/31	Mills Blue Rhythm Band	–	New York City	Victor	rejected	69979-1
11/10/31	Jack Teagarden and his Orchestra	–	New York City	Meritt	6 (LP)	10979-1
03/02/32	Louis Armstrong and his Orchestra	V	Chicago	OKeh	rejected	405155-A-B
03/11/32	Louis Armstrong and his Orchestra	V	Chicago	OKeh	41557	405155-C

Date	Performer	Vocal	Place	Label	Issue	Matrix
07/06/32	Washboard Rhythm Kings	V	Camden, NJ	Victor	24059	72694-1
c 08/32	Joel Shaw and his Orchestra	–	New York City	Crown	3383	1849-2
10/05/32	Jo Jo Brenner and his Starlane Dance Orchestra	–	New York City	Victor	rejected	73769-1
11/20/32	Spike Hughes and his Orchestra	–	London	Decca	F-3311	GB-5218-3
02/18/33	Billy Cotton and his Band	V	London	Regal Zonophone	MR-866	CAR-1772-1
02/20/33	Savoy Hotel Orpheans	–	London	Columbia	rejected	CA-13443-1-2
03/21/33	Art Tatum	–	New York City	Brunswick	6543	B-13164-A
04/21/33	Harry Roy and his Orchestra	–	London	Parlophone	R-1505	CE-6037-1
10/04/33	Ray Noble and his Orchestra	–	London	His Master's Voice	B-6425	OB-5119-1
12/07/33	Freddy Johnson and his Harlemites	–	Paris	Brunswick	A-500341	6646bkp
01/09/34	Lew Stone and the Monseigneur Band	–	London	Decca	F-3839	GB-6473-3
03/34	Jack Payne and his Band	–	London	Rex	8179	F-731-2
03/09/34	The Three Scamps	V	New York City	Victor	rejected	81866-1
07/11/34	Billy Cotton and his Band	–	Manchester	Regal Zonophone	MR-1413	CAR-2762-1
08/17/34	Georgia Washboard Stompers	–	New York City	Decca	7003	38342
08/31/34	Isham Jones and his Orchestra	–	New York City	Decca	262	38499
10/34	Louis Armstrong and his Orchestra	V	Paris	Brunswick	A-9683	14792wpp
11/20/34	Brian Lawrance and the Quaglino Quartet	V	London	Panachord	25661	GB-6769-3
12/34	Quintette of the Hot Club of France	–	Paris	Ultraphon	AP-1423	P-77162
01/28/35	The Wanderers	V	San Antonio	Bluebird	B-5887	87729-1
05/03/35	Nat Gonella and his Georgians	V	London	Parlophone	F-161	CE-6969-1
05/10/35	Ambrose and his Orchestra	V	London	Decca	F-5550	GB-7128-2
06/19/35	Rhythm Rascals	V	London	Crown	7	H-112-2
06/23/35	Ozzie Nelson and his Orchestra	–	New York City	Brunswick	7523	B-17726-1
08/06/35	Arthur Young and his Youngsters [medley]	–	London	Decca	F-5645	TB-1856-1
09/35	Art Tatum	–	Hollywood	Jazz Panorama	LP-15	–
09/35	Arthur Briggs	–	Paris	Ultraphon	rejected	–
09/06/35	Larry Adler	V	London	Regal Zonophone	MR-1842	CA-15220-1
12/30/35	Ballyhooligans	–	London	His Master's Voice	BD-5013	OEA-2658-1
01/02/36	Mustang Band of Southern Methodist University	–	Los Angeles	Decca	rejected	DLA-294-
02/27/36	Nat Gonella and his Georgians	–	London	Parlophone	R-2188	CE-7490-2
04/36	Coleman Hawkins	–	Zurich	Parlophone	B-35513	BB-1077-1
04/21/36	Milt Herth	–	Chicago	Decca	rejected	90696-
06/04/36	Bob Howard	–	London	Brunswick	02239	TB-2215-2
06/20/36	Benny Carter and his Swing Quartet	–	London	Vocalion	S-19	S-123-1
08/24/36	Jack Hylton and his Orchestra	–	London	His Master's Voice	BD-5128	OEA-4040-1
09/02/36	Nick Larocca and the ODJB	–	New York City	Victor	25403	0302-1
09/19/36	Billy Costello	V	London	Decca	F-6148	TB-2484-1
09/25/36	Original Dixieland Five	–	New York City	Victor	rejected	0497-1
09/28/36	Scott Wood and his Six Swingers	–	London	Columbia	FB-1520	CA-15945-1
10/08/36	Ballyhooligans [medley]	–	London	His Master's Voice	BD-5130	OEA-3785-1
11/10/36	Original Dixieland Five	–	New York City	Victor	25524	0497-2

Date	Performer	Vocal	Place	Label	Issue	Matrix
11/18/36	Benny Goodman Quartet	–	New York City	Victor	rejected	03064-1
12/02/36	Benny Goodman Trio	–	New York City	Victor	25481	03064-2
03/08/37	Cootie Williams and his Rug Cutters	–	New York City	Vri	rejected	M-189-1-2
03/12/37	Paul Ash and his Orchestra	–	New York City	Vri	505	M-225
07/07/37	Andre Ekyan	–	Paris	Swing	4	OLA-1891-1
07/14/37	Valaida	V	London	Parlophone	F-923	CE-8493-1-3
09/25/37	Larry Adler	–	London	Columbia	FB-1776	CA-16574-1
01/24/38	Eric Siday	–	London	Parlophone	R-2505	CE-8883-1
05/06/38	Joe Daniels and his Hot Shots	–	London	Parlophone	F-1148	CE-9099-1
05–07/38	Jelly Roll Morton	–	Washington, DC	Circle	1, 2	1641
c 08/38	Jelly Roll Morton	–	Baltimore	Swaggie	S-1213 (LP)	–
08/01/38	Teddy Wilson	–	New York City	Brunswick	rejected	P-23312-1
08/11/38	Teddy Wilson	–	New York City	Teddy Wilson School	none	P-23312-2-3
Summer/38	Roy Peyton	–	Oslo	Rex	EB-384	RP-03
10/19/38	Vic Lewis and his American Jazzmen	–	New York City	Esquire	10-251	M-7-299
10/19/38	Louis Armstrong and Fats Waller	–	New York City	Palm Club	10	
02/22/40	Art Tatum	–	Los Angeles	Decca	18051	DLA-1941-A
03/08/40	Gene Krupa and his Orchestra	–	New York City	Columbia	35454	27029-1
07/12/40	Felix Mendelssohn and his Hawaiian Serenaders	–	London	Columbia	FB-2494	CA-18067-1
10/21/40	Alix Combelle and his Swing Band	–	Paris	Swing	84	OSW-136-1
02/28/41	Stephane Grappelly and his Musicians	–	London	Decca	F-7787	DR-5404-2
c 05/41	Jack Teagarden and his Orchestra	–	Hollywood	[film: Birth of the Blues]	[promotional]	PP-302
05/26/41	Ted Lewis and his Band	–	Los Angeles	Decca	4272	DLA-2409-A
03/29/42	Lu Watters and his Yerba Buena Jazz Band	–	San Francisco	Jazz Masters	6	MLB-130

Tin Roof Blues

Date	Performer	Vocal	Place	Label	Issue	Matrix
03/13/23	New Orleans Rhythm Kings	–	Richmond, IN	Gennett	5105	11359
03/13/23	New Orleans Rhythm Kings	–	Richmond, IN	Gennett	5105	11359-A
03/13/23	New Orleans Rhythm Kings	–	Richmond, IN	Gennett	5105	11359-B
07/23/23	Tennessee Ten	–	New York City	Victor	rejected	28305-1-2-3-4
07/31/23	Nina Reeves	V	Richmond, IN	Gennett	Special	11562-C
08/18/23	Edna Hicks	V	New York City	Gennett	5234	8470-A
10/23	Young's Creole Jazz Band	–	Chicago	Paramount	20272	1535-1-2
10/04/23	Original Memphis Five	–	New York City	Victor	19170	28718-1
c 11/06/23	Original Indiana Five	–	New York City	Pathe Actuelle	036019	70397
c 02/12/24	New Orleans Jazz Band	–	New York City	Banner	1318	5422-1
04/02/24	California Ramblers	–	New York City	Bell	P-278	–
c 02/25	Johnnie Campbell's Orchestra	–	Chicago?	New Flexo	304	147
02/04/25	Ted Lewis and his Band	–	New York City	Columbia	rejected	140319-1-2
06/22/25	Ted Lewis and his Band	–	New York City	Columbia	439-D	140710-3
10/13/27	King Oliver and his Dixie Syncopators	–	New York City	Vocalion	rejected	E-6658/60

Date	Performer	Vocal	Place	Label	Issue	Matrix
11/18/27	King Oliver and his Dixie Syncopators	–	New York City	Vocalion	rejected	E-6808/9
02/25/28	King Oliver and his Dixie Syncopators	–	New York City	Vocalion	rejected	E-7172/3
06/11/28	King Oliver and his Dixie Syncopators	–	New York City	Vocalion	1189	E-7388-A; E-27684-A
08/28	Midnight Serenaders	–	Chicago	Paramount	20657	20789-1
08/28/30	[Wingy Manone] Barbeque Joe and his Hot Dogs	–	Richmond, IN	Champion	rejected	16949, -A-B
09/19/30	[Wingy Manone] Barbeque Joe and his Hot Dogs	–	Richmond, IN	Champion	16153	17059-E
09/12/34	New Orleans Rhythm Kings	–	New York City	Decca	161	38609-A
07/07/37	Louis Prima and his New Orleans Gang	–	Los Angeles	Vocalion	3657	LA-1379-A
07/15/38	Willie Farmer and his Orchestra	V	New York City	Bluebird	B-7724	024030-1
10/31/38	Tommy Dorsey and his Orchestra	–	New York City	Victor	26105	028175-1
01/20/39	Charlie Barnet and his Orchestra	–	New York City	Bluebird	B-10131	031538-1
11/27/39	Sherry Magee and his Dixielanders	–	New York City	Vocalion	5281	25692-1
c 05/40	Art Hodes' Blue Three	–	New York City	Signature	102	1602
c 03/14/41	George Hartman and his Orchestra	–	New Orleans	Keynote	K-601	GH-4-A
01/29/42	Bob Crosby and his Bob Cats	–	Los Angeles	Brunswick	04003	DLA-2870-A

12th Street Rag

Date	Performer	Vocal	Place	Label	Issue	Matrix
c 05/20	Six Brown Brothers	–	New York City	Emerson	10205	–
c 02/14/23	Eva Taylor	V	New York City	OKeh	4805	71260-A
04/19/23	Ted Lewis and his Band	–	New York City	Columbia	A-3972	80980-4
06/01/23	Richard M. Jones	–	Richmond, IN	Gennett	5174	11493
02/02/24	Euday L. Bowman	–	Richmond, IN	Gennett	rejected	11748
09/09/26	Abe Lyman and his Musicians	–	New York City	Brunswick	3316	E-20134/5
12/02/26	Johnny Marvin	–	New York City	Victor	20386	36991-3
c 04/20/27	Willard Robison and his Deep River Orchestra	–	New York City	Banner	6031	7201
05/11/27	Louis Armstrong and his Hot Seven	–	Chicago	Columbia	35663	80864-A
06/11/27	Bennie Moten's Kansas City Orchestra	–	Chicago	Victor	20946	38671-1
06/11/27	Bennie Moten's Kansas City Orchestra	–	Chicago	Victor	X LX-3025	38671-2
06/28/28	Three Jacks	–	Chicago	OKeh	rejected	400965-A-B
05/17/29	Mills's Musical Clowns	–	New York City	American Record Corp.	rejected	8762-(1-2-3?)
06/06/29	Mills' Merry Makers	V	New York City	Pathe Actuelle	37036	108931-6
06/06/29	Mills' Merry Makers	V	New York City	Banner	6441	8762-6
01/22/30	Georgia Cotton Pickers	–	New York City	Harmony	1090-H	149794-2
01/14/31	Duke Ellington and his Jungle Band	–	New York City	Brunswick	6038	E-35802-A
c 10/31	Fletcher Henderson and his Orchestra	–	New York City	Crown	3212	1503-2
05/02/32	Abe Lyman's California Orchestra	–	New York City	Brunswick	6314	B-11763-A
06/24/35	Fats Waller and his Rhythm	V	Camden, NJ	Victor	25087	88995-1
08/06/35	Arthur Young and his Youngsters [medley]	–	London	Decca	F-5645	TB-1857-1

Date	Performer	Vocal	Place	Label	Issue	Matrix
11/29/35	Joe Paradise and his Music	–	London	Parlophone	F-356	CE-7319-1
04/21/36	Milt Herth	–	Chicago	Decca	rejected	90694-
05/16/36	Billy Cotton and his Band	–	London	Regal Zonophone	MR-2185	CAR-4071-1
06/11/36	Milt Herth	–	Chicago	Brunswick	02294	90769-A
12/11/36	Milt Herth	–	Chicago	Decca	1344	91045-B
03/27/37	The Rhythm Wreckers	–	Los Angeles	Vocalion	3523	LA-1293-B
07/08/37	Joe Daniels and his Hot Shots	–	London	Parlophone	F-844	CE-8462-1
06/25/38	Leith Stevens and his Saturday Night Swing Club Orchestra	–	New York City	Vocalion	4350	23162-1
12/08/38	Euday L. Bowman	–	Dallas	American Record Corp.	rejected	DAL-759-1-2
04/05/39	Count Basie and his Orchestra	–	New York City	Vocalion	4886	24339-A
06/13/39	Lionel Hampton and his Orchestra	–	New York City	Victor	26362	037632-1
11/07/40	Andy Kirk and his Twelve Clouds of Joy	–	New York City	Decca	18123	68318-A
10/24/41	Sidney Bechet and his New Orleans Feetwarmers	–	New York City	Victor	20-3120	068112-1

Wabash Blues

Date	Performer	Vocal	Place	Label	Issue	Matrix
09/28/21	Benson Orchestra of Chicago	–	Camden, NJ	Victor	18820	25703-1
09/29/21	Benson Orchestra of Chicago	–	Camden, NJ	Victor	18820	25703-4
c 10/21	Lucille Hegamin	V	New York City	Arto	9105	–
c 10/29/21	Joseph Samuels' Jazz Band	–	New York City	OKeh/Apex	4474	70284-B
c 02/16/22	Mamie Smith and her Jazz Hounds	V	New York City	OKeh	4578	70481-B
c 07/22	Mitchell's Jazz Kings	–	Paris	Pathe	6566	6122
c 04/23	Abe Small's Rosemont Orchestra	–	New York City	Federal	5277	1-1924
04/02/25	Barbary Coast Orchestra	–	New York City	Columbia	72-P	170031-1
01/20/27	Boyd Senter and others	–	New York City	OKeh	40949	80313-B
02/25/27	Charleston Chasers	–	New York City	Columbia	909-D	143537-2
03/23/27	[Fletcher Henderson] Dixie Stompers	–	New York City	Harmony	407-H	143637-1
05/28/27	Tom Gates and his Orchestra	–	St. Paul	Gennett	6198	12825
10/07/27	Truett and George	–	San Francisco	Columbia	1182-D	144742-2
12/13/27	Coon-Sanders Orchestra	V	Kansas City	Victor	LPV-511	41371-3
03/14/28	Troy Floyd and his Plaza Hotel Orchestra	V	San Antonio	Parlophone	PMC-7082 (LP)	400509-B
10/23/28	Rhythm Makers	–	Los Angeles	Vocalion	15763	LAE-304
01/30/29	Boyd Senter and his Senterpedes	–	New York City	Victor	21864	49701-2
05/16/29	Campus Cut-Ups	–	New York City	Edison Diamond Disc	11049	N-899
05/16/29	Campus Cut-Ups	–	New York City	Edison Diamond Disc	52591	19195
08/21/29	Ted Lewis and his Band	–	New York City	Columbia	2029-D	148931-4
c 02/10/30	Louis Panico and his Orchestra	–	Chicago	Brunswick	4736	C-5379-C
05/23/31	Taylor's Dixie Orchestra	V	Charlotte, NC	Victor	23277	69343-1
09/07/34	Louis Panico and his Orchestra	–	Chicago	Decca	159	C-9421-

Date	Performer	Vocal	Place	Label	Issue	Matrix
11/07/34	Back Yard Follies	–	Chicago	American Record Corp.	rejected	C-802-A
06/07/35	Nat Gonella and his Georgians	–	London	Parlophone	F-179	CE-7015-1
08/06/35	Arthur Young and his Youngsters [medley]	–	London	Decca	F-5709	TB-1859-1
10/24/35	Mike Riley, Eddie Farley and their Onyx Club Boys	–	New York City	Decca	641	60107-D
07/06/36	Harry Roy's Tiger-Ragamuffins	–	London	Parlophone	F-522	CE-7724-1
09/21/36	Rhythm Wreckers	–	New York City	Vocalion	3390	19918-1
09/29/36	Claude Bampton and his Prince's Theatre Orchestra	–	London	Decca	F-6147	TB-2508-1
05/05/37	Joe Daniels and his Hot Shots	–	London	Parlophone	F-817	CE-8334-1
09/11/37	Ocie Stockard and the Wanderers	–	Dallas	Bluebird	B-8021	014035-1
01/03/38	Gerry Moore and his Band	–	London	Parlophone	F-1014	CE-8834-1
12/20/40	Sid Phillips Quintet	–	London	Decca	F-7758	DR-5187-1

The Wang Wang Blues

Date	Performer	Vocal	Place	Label	Issue	Matrix
08/09/20	Paul Whiteman and his Ambassador Orchestra	–	Camden, NJ	Victor	18694	24392-2
02/21	Cardinal Jazz Band	–	New York City	Cardinal	2033	650
c 02/19/21	Al Starita and his Society Orchestra	–	New York City	Grey Gull	L-1055	1178-B
03/21	Tim Brymn and his Black Devil Orchestra	–	New York City	OKeh/Apex	4310	7816-C
c 03/04/21	Lanin's Roseland Orchestra	–	New York City	Emerson	10355	41673-1
c 05/21	Lucille Hegamin	V	New York City	Arto	9068	18071-2
07/08/21	Jack Hylton's Jazz Band	–	Hayes, Middlesex	Zonophone	2167	Bb-351-2
07/18/21	Grace Brewer and her Jazz Orchestra	–	New York City	Victor	test	–
c 08/10/21	Sam Moore	–	New York City	OKeh/Apex	4423	70085-C
c 08/29/21	Seven Black Dots	–	New York City	Pathe Actuelle	020634	69349
c 09/05/21	Mamie Smith	V	New York City	OKeh	4445	70142-A
c 10/06/21	Georgia Jazz Band	–	New York City	Federal	5162	2-1192
09/17/26	King Oliver and his Dixie Syncopators	–	Chicago	Vocalion	1049	C-661
03/23/27	[Fletcher Henderson] Dixie Stompers	V	New York City	Harmony	407-H	143638-3
04/14/27	Goofus Five	–	New York City	OKeh	40817	80731-A
04/14/27	Goofus Five	–	New York City	OKeh	40817	80731-B
09/22/27	Paul Whiteman and his Orchestra	–	New York City	Victor	rejected	40231-1-2
01/22/29	Ben's [Pollack] Bad Boys	–	New York City	Victor	21971	49673-2
05/16/29	Fletcher Henderson and his Orchestra	–	New York City	Columbia	1913-D	148541-3
10/02/29	Mal Hallett and his Orchestra	–	New York City	Edison Diamond Disc	rejected	N-1170
10/27/30	Duke Ellington and his Orchestra	V	New York City	Brunswick	6003	E-35036-A
c 11/25/36	Les Brown and his Duke University Blue Devils	–	New York City	Thesaurus	335	03333-1
03/10/42	Benny Goodman Sextet	–	New York City	Columbia	36594	CO-32593-1

'Way Down Yonder in New Orleans

Date	Performer	Vocal	Place	Label	Issue	Matrix
10/22	Dixie Daisies	–	New York City	Cameo	284	312-A-B
c 12/08/22	Bailey's Lucky Seven	–	New York City	Gennett	5016	8141, -A
12/22/22	The Georgians	–	New York City	Columbia	A-3804	80744-2
01/23	Gene Fosdick's Hoosiers	–	New York City	Vocalion	14496	10636
c 02/23	Sammy Swift's Jazz Band	–	New York City	Black Swan	2117	–
c 02/09/23	The Cotton Pickers	–	New York City	Brunswick	2404	9870
02/21/23	Paul Whiteman and his Orchestra	–	New York City	Victor	19030	27611-4
c 07/23	Orchestre Syncopated Six	V	Paris	Pathe	6611	6934
05/13/27	Frankie Trumbauer and his Orchestra	–	New York City	OKeh	40843	81084-B
08/27	Fred Elizalde	–	London	Brunswick	115	R-267
06/19/30	Boyd Senter and his Senterpedes	–	Hollywood	Victor	rejected	54843-1-2-3
09/11/34	Red McKenzie with the Spirits of Rhythm	V	New York City	Decca	186	38633-A
05/10/35	Ray Noble and his Orchestra	–	Camden, NJ	Victor	rejected	88965-1-2
06/10/35	Ray Noble and his Orchestra	–	New York City	Victor	25802	88965-4
01/15/36	Jimmie Noone and his New Orleans Band	–	Chicago	Parlophone	R-2281	90576-A
06/23/36	Dick McDonough and his Orchestra	V	New York City	American Record Corp.	6-09-08	19469-1
07/03/36	Scott Wood and his Six Swingers	V	London	Columbia	FB-1472	CA-15841-1
07/06/36	Nat Gonella and his Georgians	V	London	Parlophone	F-504	CE-7703-1
10/28/36	Brian Lawrence and his Lansdowne House Sextet	V	London	Decca	F-6171	TB-2591-1
04/21/37	Harry Roy's Tiger-Ragamuffins	–	London	Parlophone	F-837	CE-8287-1
11/30/37	Max Abrams and his Rhythm Makers	–	London	Parlophone	R-2474	CE-8767-1
06/14/38	Coleman Hawkins Trio	–	Hilversum	Panachord	H-1046	AM-490-1
09/08/38	Kansas City Six	–	New York City	Tax	8000 (LP)	23421-1
09/08/38	Kansas City Six	–	New York City	Commodore	512	23421-2
09/28/38	Bill Coleman et son Orchestre	–	Paris	Swing	214	OSW-43-1
04/25/39	Van Alexander and his Orchestra	–	New York City	Bluebird	B-10278	036528-1
12/24/39	Kansas City Six	–	New York City	Vanguard	VRS-8523	–
11/07/40	Duke Ellington and his Orchestra	V	Fargo, ND	Palm	30-11	–
06/10/41	Royal Air Force Dance Orchestra	–	London	Decca	F-8127	DR-5845-1
02/04/42	Henry Levine and his Strictly from Dixie Jazz Band	V	New York City	Victor	27830	071767-1
02/05/42	Bob Crosby and his Orchestra	V	Los Angeles	Decca	4403	DLA-2885-A

The Weary Blues

Date	Performer	Vocal	Place	Label	Issue	Matrix
12/19	Louisiana Five	–	New York City	Emerson	10116	4738-1-2
05/10/20	Windy City Trio	–	New York City	Victor	test	–
02/21	Cardinal Jazz Band	–	New York City	Cardinal	2033	651
03/12/23	New Orleans Rhythm Kings	–	Richmond, IN	Gennett	5102	11355-B

Date	Performer	Vocal	Place	Label	Issue	Matrix
05/23	Clarence Williams	–	New York City	OKeh	4893	71528-D
05/07/24	Vic Meyers and his Orchestra	–	Los Angeles	Brunswick	2664	A-20/22
c 09/24	Jelly-Roll Morton's Kings of Jazz	–	Chicago	Autograph	607	638
04/12/26	Parenti's Liberty Syncopators	–	New Orleans	Columbia	1264-D	142003-1
11/27/26	Barbary Coast Orchestra	–	New York City	Columbia	94-P	170259-1
04/27/27	Johnny Dodds' Black Bottom Stompers	–	Chicago	Vocalion	15632	C-792
05/11/27	Louis Armstrong and his Hot Seven	–	Chicago	OKeh	8519	80863-A
08/04/27	Red Snodgrass's Alabamians	–	Bristol, TN	Victor	rejected	39769-1-2-3
08–10/27	The Jazz Kings	–	Berlin	Tri-Ergon	TE-5055	MO-806
10/02/27	Ray Miller and his Hotel Gibson Orchestra	–	Chicago	Brunswick	3677	C-1153
08/22/29	Smizer's Dixie Serenaders	–	Chicago	Brunswick	rejected	C-4157-
09/19/30	[Wingy Manone] Barbeque Joe and his Hot Dogs	V	Richmond, IN	Gennett	7320	17060
05/12/33	Abe Lyman and his California Orchestra	–	New York City	Brunswick	6637	B-13327-A
01/29/34	Sam Wooding and his Orchestra	–	New York City	Columbia	test	176356-1
01/17/35	Dorsey Brothers Orchestra	–	New York City	Design	DLP-20	–
02/01/35	Dorsey Brothers Orchestra	–	New York City	Design	DLP-20	–
02/06/35	Dorsey Brothers Orchestra	–	New York City	Decca	469	39340-A
02/06/35	Dorsey Brothers Orchestra	–	New York City	Decca	15013	39341-A
09/26/35	Tommy Dorsey and his Orchestra	–	New York City	Victor	25159	95142-1
09/12/38	Erskine Hawkins and his Orchestra	–	New York City	Bluebird	B-7839	026859-1
11/28/38	Tommy Ladnier and his Orchestra	–	New York City	Bluebird	B-10086	030321-1
12/23/38	New Orleans Feetwarmers	–	New York City	Vanguard	8523 (LP)	–
08/21/40	Henry "Kid" Rena's Jazz Band	–	New Orleans	Delta	806	806

You Rascal You

Date	Performer	Vocal	Place	Label	Issue	Matrix
06/18/30	Clarence Williams	V	New York City	OKeh	8806	404219-B-C
07/15/30	[Andy Kirk] Seven Little Clouds of Joy	V	Chicago	Brunswick	rejected	C-6018-
07/29/30	Jimmie Noone's Apex Club Orchestra	V	Chicago	Vocalion	1584	C-5950-A
08/30	Tampa Red and his Hokum Jug Band	V	Chicago	Vocalion	1540	C-5998-A
10/09/30	Andy Kirk and his Twelve Clouds of Joy	V	Chicago	Brunswick	7180	C-6435-
04/28/31	Louis Armstrong and his Orchestra	V	Chicago	OKeh	41504	404871-A
05/26/31	Red Nichols and his Five Pennies	V	New York City	Brunswick	6133	E-36831-A
06/04/31	[Washboard] Rhythm Kings	V	Camden, NJ	Victor	23279	68218-1
06/30/31	Mound City Blue Blowers	V	New York City	OKeh	41526	404995-A
07/17/31	[Fletcher Henderson] Connie's Inn Orchestra	V	New York City	Melotone	M-12216	E-36928-A
08/31	[Fletcher Henderson] Connie's Inn Orchestra	V	New York City	Crown	3180	1431-2-3
08/21/31	Chick Bullock	V	New York City	Banner	32252	10769-2-3
08/28/31	Luis Russell and his Orchestra	V	New York City	Victor	22793	70195-1

Date	Performer	Vocal	Place	Label	Issue	Matrix
09/23/31	Cab Calloway and his Orchestra	V	New York City	Brunswick	6196	E-37221-A
10/14/31	Jack Teagarden and his Orchestra	V	New York City	Columbia	2588-D	151839-1
01/19/32	Bob Howard	V	New York City	Columbia	14650-D	152082-1; 405124
02/03/32	Ray Starita and his Ambassadors	V	London	Sterno	900	S-2202
02/04/32	Roy Fox and his Band	V	London	Decca	F-2805	GB-3924-2
02/13/32	Billy Cotton and his Band	V	London	Regal	MR-541	CAR-1064-1
c 03/25/32	The Blue Mountaineers	V	London	Broadcast	3176	A-1082-1
12/21/32	Louis Armstrong and his Orchestra	V	Camden, NJ	Victor	36084	74878-2
c 12/33	Garland Wilson	–	Paris	Brunswick	A-500359	5750bdp
09/35	Andre Ekyan and his Orchestra	–	Paris	Ultraphon	AP-1545	77527
09/13/35	Scott Wood and his Six Swingers [medley]	–	London	Regal Zonophone	MR-1909	CAR-3588-1
01/29/36	Nat Gonella and his Georgians	V	London	Parlophone	F-393	CE-7424-2
12/27/37	Django Reinhardt	–	Paris	Swing	35	OLA-2215-1
11/16/41	Louis Armstrong and his Orchestra	V	Chicago	Decca	4140	93790-A